EASTER MONDAY & TUESDA

Gallery, 6d. Particulars, see Small Bill

¡VIVA LA CONFEDERACION ARGENTINA!
MUERAN LOS SALVAGES UNITARIOS!

TEATRO ARGENTINO.
Gran Funcion Estraordinaria, á Beneficio del Sr.
Robert y su Esposa.
El Jueves 3 de noviembre   dé 1842.

PARTE 3.ª

Ocupará la escéna la Sra. Robert y desempeñará otras dificiles y raras pruebas, entre éllas los juegos de Malabar, y el nuevo juego de los—

PLATOS DE LOZA,
que agradará mucho á los espectadores. Despues se introducirá el manejo de los seis Puñales orientales, el de los ocho aros de bronce, un hermoso vuelo amplificado, y varias suertes que no se espresan. El baile de la

TRANGA
con fuegos artificiales en cada estremidad. El gracioso equilibrio de los dos PERROS, vestidos de Marqueza y Marquez. El de los cinco fusiles de municion, cuyo peso será apoyado en una sola bayoneta puesta sobre un diente. Finalizará el todo de la funcion por el estraordinario equilibrio de la—

Bandera Nacional
con un jóven en el estremo del palo.

NOTA.—Los Beneficiados teniendo en consideracion los muchos gastos que han impendido para la presente funcion, y recabado el permiso del Sr. Gefe de Policía, han hecho la variacion siguiente en los precios de las apuestadurias y entradas—á saber.—PALCOS de primer órden 20 ps.—id bajos 25 LUNETAS 6 ps. id. de CAZUELA 1.ª línea 7 id. de 2.ª 5.—ENTRADA—cuatro pesos.

A LAS 8.
Imprenta de la LIBERTAD—Buenos Ayres.

GREATEST WONDER
UNDER THE PATRONA
HER MOST GRACIOUS MAJES

CANTE
PATENT
HYDRO-INC
OR EGG-HATCHING
AS SHOWN BY COMMAND AT
CHICK

SPELTERINI,
A REAL
ASS,
a Ladder,
time holding
a
Pound Weight.

A Feat never attempted by any one, except hi

56

he Summer Seafon.

, and three horfes, ftand-
ly one, of her fex, that

orfes on full speed, with-
and abilities.

ay, or any other rigging,
feats of activity, fuch as
s to infert.

were performed by any
y are on full speed, and
high: also leaps back-
he horfe is on full speed;

EXTRAORDINARY EXHIBITIONS

Extraordinary Exhibitions

THE WONDERFUL REMAINS
OF AN ENORMOUS HEAD,
THE WHIMSIPHUSICON
& DEATH TO THE
SAVAGE UNITARIANS

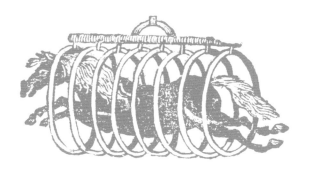

BROADSIDES FROM THE COLLECTION OF

RICKY JAY

THE QUANTUCK LANE PRESS

New York

For Susan Green, Larry Vigon and Patrick Reagh, with gratitude
And for Michael Zinman, who giveth and who taketh away...

This book has been published in conjunction with the show
Extraordinary Exhibitions: Broadsides from the Collection of Ricky Jay,
curated by Renny Pritikin, and presented at Yerba Buena Center for the Arts
from January 23 through April 3, 2005.

 YERBA BUENA **CENTER FOR THE ARTS**

701 Mission Street, San Francisco, CA 94103-3138
415.978.2700 — www.YBCA.org

The text of this book is composed in Bembo
With the display type in Weiss
Book design and composition by Larry Vigon, Vigon/Ellis
Manufacturing by Mondadori Printing, Verona

ISBN: 1-59372-012-2

The Quantuck Lane Press, New York
www.quantucklanepress.com
Distributed by: W.W. Norton & Company, 500 Fifth Avenue, New York, NY 10110
www.wwnorton.com
W.W. Norton & Company Ltd., Castle House, 75/76 Wells Street, London, WIT 3QT

1 2 3 4 5 6 7 8 9 0

ALSO BY RICKY JAY

* *
*

Cards As Weapons

Learned Pigs & Fireproof Women

Many Mysteries Unraveled:
Conjuring Literature in America 1786–1874

The Magic Magic Book

Jay's Journal of Anomalies

Dice: Deception, Fate & Rotten Luck
with photographs by Rosamund Purcell

CONTENTS

Charles Dickens, on a house-hunting trip to London, saw "an old warehouse which rotting paste and rotting paper had brought down to the condition of an old cheese. It would have been impossible to say, on the most conscientious survey, how much of its front was brick and mortar, and how much decaying and decayed plaster. It was so thickly encrusted with fragments of bills, that no ship's keel after a long voyage could be half so foul. All traces of the broken windows were billed out, the doors were billed across, the water-spout was billed over. The building was shored up to prevent its tumbling into the street; and the very beams erected against it were less wood than paste and paper, they had been so continually posted and reposted. The forlorn dregs of old posters so encumbered this wreck, that there was no hold for new posters, and the stickers had abandoned the place in despair, except one enterprising man who had hoisted the last masquerade to a clear spot near the level of the stack of chimneys, where it waved and drooped like a shattered flag. Below the rusty cellar-grating, crumpled remnants of old bills torn down rotted away in wasting heaps of fallen leaves. Here and there, some of the thick rind of the house had peeled off in strips, and fluttered heavily down, littering the street; but still, below these rents and gashes, layers of decomposing posters showed themselves, as if they were interminable. I thought the building could never even be pulled down, but in one adhesive heap of rottenness and poster. As to getting in—I don't believe that if the Sleeping Beauty and her Court had been so billed up, the young Prince could have done it."

"Bill-Sticking," *Household Words*, March 2, 1851

SHOWBILLS ARE THE BLACK SHEEP of theatrical memorabilia. They have never enjoyed the respectability of souvenir prints or programs, let alone the forum of big museum shows devoted to their favored sibling, the full-color lithographic poster. But posters have attracted critical attention relatively recently, and it is possible that ephemeral bills like the ones shown here will soon bask in the limelight. That is of little concern to me. I love these sheets, which often provide the only surviving data on singular performers. These bills and broadsides are their legacy, and I pursue these documents less as a collector of rare ephemera than as a celebrant of their accomplishments. This volume and the associated exhibition have afforded me the chance to re-examine many of the subjects I have spoken of and written about over the last twenty-five years. My enthusiasm for the genre is unabated, and my chief interest remains the extraordinary characters who are the subjects of these broadsides.

PROF. A. A. STARR, OF NEW YORK CITY, WILL GIVE
AN EXHIBITION OF THE HYDRO-OXYGEN MICROSCOPE
AND VENTRILOQUISM. (1878)

To place all the showmen who inhabit these pages between two covers requires a capacious corral. They exhibited in a daunting variety of venues. In the seventeenth or eighteenth century you might see fairground performers barking for attention over myriad other attractions; or in a "commodious large room" of an assembly hall; or commanding the ring of a nascent circus, billed beneath the star horse. A barely illuminated catacomb might provide the atmosphere for the projection of ghosts known as phantasmagoria. By the end of the eighteenth century, a conjurer might command a stage for a full theatrical evening.

Fifty years later, a tavern performance was still feasible—as was the chance to entertain at the White House. The "gift show" was created as an attempt to fill a town hall by giving away prizes, and audiences attended perhaps more for the hams, hats, and turkeys than for the display of variety skills. Lecture rooms bustled with exhibitions of spiritualism, while magicians proffered exposés of so-called otherworldly phenomena. The repertoire of the scientific demonstrator might be viewed in a hall or museum. Eventually the burgeoning field of vaudeville offered opportunities for a grand array of specialty acts. By the end of the nineteenth century, full-evening shows might be presented by mystery-workers who were lauded with the same gusto as the stars of theater, dance, and opera.

The size and style of the early handbills, letterpress affairs usually no larger than six by eight inches, seem modest by today's standards (our full-color "one-sheet" posters are about twenty-eight by forty inches). These early examples of the genre were typically unillustrated, and the printer's skill was exemplified principally in the choice of type: usually classic roman faces, almost subdued in contrast to the flamboyant display type that became conventional by the mid-nineteenth century. A decorative border or a crest denoting permission to perform might create visual interest; an occasional woodcut greatly enhanced the overall appeal. The major strategy, however, was always verbal: hyperbolic, florid, orotund language evoking provocative or unique attributes of astonishing acts.

I especially love the language of these playbills—the rodomontade and encomia of "professors of natural philosophy," or "celebrated posture masters and buffos," or "jugglers to the king"; the lure of untranslatable neologisms (the whimsiphusicon, the eidopolyphoscopia, or the enchanted sciatoricon); the grandiloquent attempts of performers trying to stake a claim of originality in a vast expanse of competition.

I have often been dazzled by collections of automata, hand-carved ventriloquist dummies, and fine-turned boxwood magical apparatus, but I am not, as a rule, particularly engaged by these *objects d'art*. I am fascinated by the artifacts of showmen, and, I confess, I would dearly love to own the original speaking machine of Prof. Faber, or Phillipstahl's magic lantern, or Tom Thumb's pants. But, oh, that paper. I love the look, the feel, and the texture of paper. I find beauty in the irregularity of the deckled edge, the watermarks, and even the effects of natural attrition—small holes left by vermin, corners broken from years of handling, the discoloration of foxing. The Thai menus of yesteryear, these sheets were handed out to passersby, or placed under doors to be perused, then dismissed and discarded. I admire them as survivors that have endured the handling of unsympathetic, clumsy, or soiled hands, outlasted the ravages of time, and escaped the wrath of the elements.[1]

Early showbills were often produced on rich, creamy sheets of paper and set with metal type. I love type. I love the elegant roman faces of the eighteenth century and the ornate display types of the Victorian era. And I love the woodcuts that sometimes embellish these placards. Such illustrations were often primitive attempts to render animals or apparatus, or the performers themselves, but they are wonderfully evocative of time and place. Occasionally, as in the image that graces the dust jacket of this volume, copper engravings were created by fine craftsmen.

A digression into terminology may be appropriate. A broadside is a single sheet of paper usually printed on one side only, while a playbill might be defined as a broadside announcing a theatrical production, sometimes including its cast. The examples I present in this book are perhaps best considered broadside showbills that feature exhibitions and performances that are not conventional dramas. The variations on this theme are significant, but rarely addressed. One pleasant exception is David Robert Gowen's doctoral dissertation, completed in 1998, "Studies in the History and Function of the British Theatre Playbill and Programme." Among the many categories enumerated in this important history are big-bills, bills-of-the-day, broadsides, daybills, dodges, double-bills, hand-bills, placards, posters, streamers, throw-aways, and window bills.

Perhaps it would be helpful to define our showbills by content as well. In a lecture on early magic broadsides, Volker Huber specified ten items that they should incorporate in order to be considered "fully developed." Starting in the seventeenth century one would likely find: permission (from the king, magistrate, or local authority sanctioning the show); date of performance; place of performance; name of performer; the artist's self-recommendation in presenting his show; an enumeration of the highlights of the show; additional attractions that might share the stage; special efforts taken by the performer for the comfort of the spectators; additional services offered by the performer (private engagements were frequently arranged in the houses of wealthy patrons, or wares might be offered for sale); and the range of seating and prices. While some historians have proposed that the first example of a magic broadside appeared in the 1790s, a bill of the conjurer known as the Great Hollander was printed a century earlier, as Huber notes; and if the criteria are loosened a bit, the yet earlier announcements of entertainers who spouted color-changing streams of water might be included.[2] I might suggest broadening the criteria still further to allow for a showman who presented a learned horse performing card tricks. The first broadside displayed here features such a sagacious steed, c. 1618 (see p. 19).

By the very early eighteenth century, playbills began to promote "benefit nights." Such performances singled out a particular person who was to receive revenue for this occasion in addition to his weekly salary (the number of benefit nights per season was often a point for negotiation). The artist featured would often solicit spectacular stunts or their most famous friends in the attempt to fill the hall and increase the profit. A number of benefit bills are included in this volume (see, for instance, Simpson at Vauxhall Gardens, p. 98, Nelson the Clown, p. 108, and Mr. Robert, p. 112).

A poster is usually distinguished from a playbill as advertising an attraction not limited to a specific date or engagement. Posters are primarily visual, while a bill is more likely to emphasize text. Showbills are typically printed letterpress and, if they are illustrated, most often employ woodblocks or wood engravings. Color, if incorporated at all, is used sparingly. Posters are generally reproduced by lithography, a technique invented in the last decade of the eighteenth century but not widely employed in the theatrical trade for nearly fifty more years. This volume could be viewed as a look at broadside showbills that I have assembled—except that a few are printed on both sides of the sheet, and a few on more than one sheet, and a few advertise a general rather than a specific appearance, and a few no appearance at all. And while most of the items displayed here were evanescent, I have decided to include some that received more careful treatment and were meant to be saved rather than discarded. But these exceptions are presented sparingly, and only when their inclusion seems justified by, well, me…

JUST FINISH'D AND TO BE SEEN. THE PRESENT COURT OF ENGLAND IN WAX…MADE BY THE MOST DESERVEDLY FAMOUS MRS. MILLS. PERSONS MAY HAVE THEIR EFFIGIES MADE OF THEIR DECEAS'D FRIENDS ON MODERATE TERMS. (EARLY EIGHTEENTH CENTURY)

My collection parallels my interest in two major areas: the broad field of deception (and the subgenres of illusion, cheating, fraud, and swindling); and the exploits and accomplishments of unusual entertainers. My interest in these fields began in childhood and has never waned.

The happiest times of my youth were spent under the tutelage of my grandfather, a talented amateur magician, and I spent the largest part of each day in the practice of sleight of hand. I was naturally drawn to the milieu of conjuring, but as my grandfather numbered among his friends not only great illusionists but also puppeteers, jugglers, and ventriloquists, I soon became intrigued by those arts as well. I began to delve into the history of all these pursuits.

It was a longtime friend, the statistician and sleight-of-hand expert Persi Diaconis, who was the catalyst for my transition from an interested reader to an enthusiastic researcher and collector. When barely out of my teens, I became intrigued by nineteenth-century fraudulent mediums who duped the public by appropriating and repackaging magic effects. I started reading the classic books in the field. Excitedly, I asked Persi if he was knowledgeable in this area. "Not particularly," he said, "I suppose I've read the standard hundred texts, but it's never become a passion." I had read seven. His response was delivered without pretense, but it was an eye-opening appraisal I have never forgotten.

As I began to amass my own library I was often struck by the wonderful iconography of the subjects that interested me, and I began, on those rare occasions when I could afford it, to supplement my diet of books with an occasional helping of visual ephemera: especially prints, posters, and playbills. I remember Milbourne Christopher's delightful *Panorama of Magic* as an early catalyst of my curiosity. As a kid I would turn to it again and again to stare at the wonderful posters and playbills he reproduced.

MONS. MARTINE WILL INTRODUCE HIS HIGHLY ADMIRED AND ASTONISHING CORPUSCULAR FLEXIBILITY. HE WILL PARTICULARLY DISPLAY THE FOLLOWING ASTONISHING FEATS, HITHERTO CONSIDERED INCOMPATIBLE WITH THE ORGANIZATION OF THE HUMAN FRAME. (1841)

A decade or two performing on the road afforded me the opportunity to scour libraries, bookshops, and print dealers and my holdings grew. What I had envisioned as a research resource was becoming a repository of rare titles and images as well. I began to use my collection to write and illustrate books. *Learned Pigs & Fireproof Women* (1986) was my first tome on unusual entertainment, and it was embellished with reproductions of numerous pieces that I had assembled. My pursuit of these materials at times seemed borderline obsessive, and my performing then took a back seat to my quest for historical material.

In 1985, I became the curator of one of the great collections of material in my field, the Mulholland Library of Conjuring and the Allied Arts. I spent five years in this position—the only straight job I have held in my adult life (if you consider cataloging books, traveling around the world to purchase rarities, and organizing conferences on magic history, straight). Perhaps because of the surfeit of riches and rarities under my care, I became more and more intrigued by the peripheral and offbeat items that crossed my path, and my writing evolved in the same direction. I had always preferred to chronicle the exploits of curious and little-known performers rather than the major ones. I preferred the Houdini imitators—Howdini, Oudini, and Martini-Szeny—to the famous "Handcuff King & Jail Breaker" himself. Of all the ephemera that passed through my hands, nothing appealed to me more than the broadsides and playbills of peculiar performers.

My interest continued to expand. It was an easy segue from conjuring to automata, the marvelous mechanical devices often exhibited by magicians. Then another small leap brought me to scientific attractions like speaking machines, orrerys, or magic lanterns, and then to inventions claiming to have conquered the unconquerable mystery of perpetual motion. Which takes us back to deception and fraud; which calls to mind broadsides for the exhibition of tools used by pickpockets and burglars, displayed in a detective museum; which leads to museums themselves—which often exhibited physical anomalies that seemed related to exotic ethnological attractions, which spawned an interest in unusual animals and menageries, which relates to the circus, which in its early years often featured magicians…And thus, the course of my collecting took me from the magicians I had admired in childhood to a vast sphere of performance and entertainment—and back to magicians again. My appetite for these materials, no matter how far afield it seemed to go, added up to a weirdly variable but also comprehensive mosaic of the history of entertainment. (Richard Altick's marvelous work *The Shows of London*, if it did not define my areas of interest, certainly reaffirmed them, and I consulted no book more frequently in the preparation of this volume.)

TO BE SEEN ALIVE A MOST EXTRAORDINARY MARINE ANIMAL HITHERTO UNDESCRIBED BY NATURALISTS, AND WHICH WAS DRIVEN ASHORE DURING THE LATER SEVERE GALES IN THE ISLE OF THANET. IT IS FOUR FEET LONG, AND HAS SO MANY HEADS THAT THEY ARE COMPLETELY INCALCULABLE, BUT PROBABLY AMOUNTING TO SEVERAL THOUSANDS. (1818)

The playbills I had amassed were interconnected in revealing ways: Daniel Wildman was noted for his remarkable control over swarming bees while simultaneously riding on horseback—but a perhaps more intriguing discovery was that his best pupil was the wife of the proprietor of Astley's circus. The broadside of George Washington's alleged nursemaid, Joice Heth, was interesting in its own right but particularly significant as a record of the first attraction presented by P. T. Barnum. His exhibition of a mermaid leads us in turn to an earlier and obviously fabricated mermaid of 1789 (see p. 52). The broadside for a pig-faced lady of 1815 (see p. 70) was obviously a hoax, but clean-shaven bears donning gloves, gowns, and hats were passed off as pig-faced humans to a credulous fairgoing public later in the century.

These bills also partook of the broader controversies of cultural history. The jingoistic wars of rope-dancers mirrored the conflicts of nation-states; the origins of the human species, considerably before Darwin, were plumbed in demonstrations where monkeys acted like men (and men acted like monkeys); magical illusions inspired heated reaction as interpreters struggled with competing conventions of veracity.

Ramo Samee the Original Indian Performer from Madras to Commence with the Erection of His Superb Chinese Pagoda on His Lip. (1842)

Among the attractions that reveal most about the cultural preoccupations of the public are those ethnological exhibitions of curious folk who hailed from the remote corners of the globe (see, for instance, the accounts of the Hottentot Venus, p. 68, or the Chinese Lady with "Lotus Feet," p. 128). Occasionally such exotics were welcomed even if they were not displayed. Such was the case of the king and queen of the Sandwich Islands, who were greeted with much fanfare and received into society in London in 1824. On May 31 a playbill announced that they would attend the Theatre Royal, Covent Garden, to witness Sheridan's *Pizarro*. King George IV, the bill announced, would welcome the Islanders into his private box for the occasion. I was especially delighted to secure a broadside for that performance because it contained the following holograph annotation:

The playbill for their above Majesties, were, as is usual on royal visits, printed on white satin. The Queen being ignorant of its meaning, very cordially used it to wipe her nose with on several occasions, until it fell over into the pit, where a violent scuffle ensued, as to who should bear away so delicate and precious a relic.

A Melange by Signor Meyer, in the Costume of a Parrot. (1841)

The printer of bills, the poster of bills, the reader of bills—all were once a vital part of metropolitan life. The printer would create the document, the bill poster would affix it to a wall, and the playbill reader, whether king or commoner, would learn about the exhibition and consider parting with specie to marvel in person.

Bill posting, a task of considerable concern even for today's theatrical promoters, was accomplished by a workforce that was not always held in the highest regard. W. J. L. Millar, some forty years after the fact, mused on the distribution of his playbills for the magician Bosco (p. 132): "I then went to the head printer, Mr. Avery…and contracted for printing and got hold of the billposters. In those days most billposters were to be found at the public house or in bed sleeping off the effect of a recent 'boose,' but now, I am pleased to say, they are a most respectable and trustworthy body of men."[3] Charles Dickens' exegesis on bill posting is excerpted in the epigraph to this introduction.

The relationship between the printer and performer is intricate, indeed crucial. In addition to producing the bill itself, the printer often secured the halls, alerted prominent families to the exhibition, served as bill stickers for some pieces, ran various errands, and even sold tickets. His advice was solicited about the best halls to hire and the best times to perform, and how much to charge.

I am fortunate to be able to offer examples from the correspondence between various showmen and the venerable printing firm of J. Procter in Hartlepool, England. Here is an undated midcentury letter, in full, from the conjurer Powis Royle:

Dear Sir

Be kind enough to arrange for Wednesday and Thursday if the Town Hall is not engaged for Thursday, if it is, for Wednesday only. I herewith enclose a copy of bill. The posters and block you will get on Saturday Morning from Stockton. So get the bills ready for the block so that they can be posted and distributed on Saturday afternoon, the time will be short enough to give publicity to the affair—enclose bills in envelopes to all the principal families and let the bill sticker deliver them on Monday at the latest. The posters must be posted with a day bill on each side of them, and as many may be posted singly as convenient. should you require tickets before I arrive—you can write them, signing your own name to them, let me know per return of the posters respecting Wednesday evening—your attention will oblige

Yours obtly [obediently]

Powis Royle

Another showman asks Procter "to oblige me by calling at the Druggist Shop—I don't know the name—it is a little higher up the street on the opposite side to you…Please purchase six lb. of Chlorate of Pottash & send off to me first train—and I will remit you the amount." (My relationship with my favorite printer, the formidable Patrick Reagh, is a bit different, but no less important.) Occasionally one printer would warn another about a deadbeat. John Jordan wrote to his friend Procter about the non-payment "cock-and-bull story" of the magician Shaw, and recommended that he be on his guard, as the conjurer was again in the territory.[4]

THE RUSSIAN GAMBLING DOG, WHO PLAYS AT ALL-FOURS AND PUT, RESOLVES ARITHMETICAL QUESTIONS, AND WHAT IS STILL MORE SURPRISING, WILL PLAY A GAME AT DOMINOS WITH ANY GENTLEMAN PRESENT. (1816)

Broadsides and deception were linked from the earliest times. As Richard Altick has splendidly stated, "of all the classes of documents that historians may be called on to deal with, few are more engagingly disingenuous or downright mendacious than show business publicity, where honesty possesses neither virtue nor advantage." Most often the subterfuge was in the prevaricating claims of the showmen, who offered attractions that were either much exaggerated from reality or simply did not exist.

The oldest English playbill extant announced a performance of a grand spectacle at the Swan Theatre in 1602. Called "England's Joy" (an epithet for Queen Elizabeth), it suggested intricate staging, a series of elaborate vignettes, and a large and supple cast ending with this finale, as vividly set forth by Arthur Freeman in *Elizabethan Misfits*: "To wind up the festivities, 'a great triumph is made with fighting of twelve gentleman at barriers, and sundry rewards sent from the throne of England,' which as the Nine Worthies and various seraphim re-crown the Queen, and she in her throne is pulled up into heaven, where she reappears surrounded by 'blessed souls,' and under the stage, a piece of elegant theatrical craft dating back to the mystery cycles, 'set forth with strange fire-words, divers black and damned souls,' wonderfully described in their several torments."[5] Those who with anticipation plunked down their coin saw not the extravaganza promised but rather the back of the promoter, one Richard Vennard, who escaped with the receipts, not on horseback, but up the Thames in a small boat. The ensuing destruction of the theater by the outraged audience provides an apt link to the "Bottle Conjurer" hoax of 1749

(see p. 34). Vennard, who was early described as a "grand coneycatcher," the Elizabethan term for a con man, is dubbed by Freeman, in a slightly different register, one of the earliest "theatrical dadaists."

Other deceptive techniques concerned the names or the identities of the performers listed on the bills. Minor infractions might involve featuring a famous act such as the Davenport Brothers in prominent display type (an instance that Wood notes), revealing only in very small print that the performance would instead duplicate the stunts of the Davenports, expose the illusions of the Davenports, or feature the appearance of a relative whose brother's sister knew one of the Davenports. Far more egregious was the appropriation of a performer's character (it would appear that identity theft is not just a modern form of fraud). There are also playbills for inconsequential performers who try to capitalize on the fame of others by, for instance, claiming to be the son of the prominent prestidigitator Bartolomeo Bosco, the wife of Bosco—or even the original Bosco himself.

Perhaps the most notorious of these usurpers was Harry Graham, an East-End Londoner who pretended to be the most famous conjurers of the day by turns, John Henry Anderson, Robert-Houdin, Robin, and Philippe (see pp. 126 and 136). He specialized in foreign magicians who, as they achieved success in London, initiated Graham's impersonation in the provinces. Said to be most comical was Graham's attempt to mimic accents. He tried to speak in foreign-flavored broken English but, according to one contemporary observer, in each of his speeches "a practiced ear could have detected a strong sprinkling of the vocabulary of Petticoat Lane."[6]

THE COLLECTION OF ANATOMICAL AND NATURAL PREPARATIONS COMPRISE OVER 20,000 OBJECTS OF WONDER. THE ATTENTION OF VISITORS TO THIS POPULAR INSTITUTION IS PARTICULARLY DIRECTED TO THE FOLLOWING FEATURES: THE GREAT CAESARIAN AND CIRCUMCISION OPERATIONS; THE HORNED MAN; THE WORLD RENOWNED VENUS—THE NE PLUS ULTRA OF FEMININE BEAUTY; AND SPLENDID DISSECTIONS OF THE LUNGS OF A BULL-FROG. (C. 1870)

What criteria, you may ask, does one use in adding to a collection? How far is one willing to stretch when the irresistible urge to own another item arises? Some years ago I purchased a sheet entitled "To The Curious. The Word Scissars Appears Capable Of More Variations In The Spelling Than Any Other." Printed in the 1830s, it enumerated 480 ways to spell that one word. My acquisition was based not on a latent interest in orthography but rather on the description provided by the bookseller, Martin Hamlyn, who distinguished it as "possibly the most sublimely fatuous broadside known." It was indeed cosmically absurd. I have since misplaced it, but rather than searching for it, I am content with the thought that it will give me pleasure when it is found. (I have a very silly photograph of a conjurer calling himself "Famous George Ross, Master Magician." No illusionist I have shown it to has ever heard of him. He wears a sequined dinner jacket and corduroy pants and stands behind a child who is suspended on a board covered with a gaudy cloth. Famous George stands on another piece of the same fabric. The expression on the face of the elevated youngster is inscrutable. I periodically hide the photo, shuffling it in among a stack of papers that will be filed in the garage, so that at some later date I may experience the joy of rediscovery.)

Once one is attuned to the subterranean but inevitable presence of broadsides and playbills, they may appear in the most unexpected places. When I visited Michael Wilson in London, he showed me a great print from his marvelous photography collection. It was of Nelson's monument, taken by the legendary William Henry Fox Talbot. What really excited me, however, was a hitherto unrecorded playbill of the great Viennese magician Leopold Ludwig Doebler, visible at the bottom of the photo.

I am fascinated by the itinerant trajectories of ephemera, the way that a piece moves from place to place, from owner to owner. You may notice the mark of a rusted paper clip on the upper edge of some of the broadsides here displayed. This identifies the piece as having a significant and extended provenance: from the famous Gardner collection on the topography of London, to the circus aficionado Fred Martin, to Lord Sidney Bernstein, who later auctioned it at Sotheby's. Years later I managed to obtain the three pieces with this provenance that are shown in this group (see The Mermaid, Moritz's Troupe, and Astley's Ampitheatre, pp. 52, 64, 60) from three different dealers on two continents.

Every new generation of collectors, after viewing the distinguished repositories in their field, think it unlikely that they will be able to garner significant acquisitions of their own. Bob Lund, the late proprietor of the American Museum of Magic, told me how he was inspired but also discouraged by the great collections that preceded his, and how skeptical his contemporaries were of his wish to seek the treasures of magic, but he eventually put together a remarkable assemblage.

How, I often wonder, was I fortunate enough to find playbills of the greatest conjurer of the early eighteenth century, Isaac Fawkes, when none were thought to exist? How did I become the grateful guardian of broadsides of the lauded but elusive practitioners of the eighteenth-century magic world: Buchinger, Breslaw, Philadelphia, Lane, Gyngell, Palatine, Boaz, Jonas, Rea, and Pinetti? How did I propitiously acquire bills for Price, Sampson, Wildman, Hughes, Astley, and Zucker, equestrians and impresarios of the primitive circus in the 1760s and 1770s?

I am one of those people who wakes on alternate days thinking I am the luckiest, or the unluckiest, man in the world. In spite of my profound and perhaps hereditary fondness for complaining, it is clear that I have been a fortunate fellow. Aided by dealers in antiquities who are surprisingly accommodating to both my needs and my financial vicissitudes, and the munificence of friends and colleagues, I have managed to secure a sizeable cache of material, which in the end is more or less aptly designated by that extremely loaded term, a collection.

Merely locating a desirable piece does not guarantee its acquisition. In 1983 I attended a sale in London of the marvelous collection of materials on physical anomalies assembled by the famous Broadway writer-director Burt Shevelove. I was able to secure just a fraction of what I had hoped to attain. Over the next twenty years, however, almost all the pieces I coveted made their way, often circuitously, or even mysteriously, to my home. A number of them are featured in this volume (for example, Joice Heth, Chang & Eng, pp. 102 and 146).

Collecting is societally sanctioned greed, perhaps the only form in which this deadly sin may be respectably pursued. Rarely have I encountered collectors with a true generosity of spirit, perhaps because that disposition is at cross-purposes with the concept of owning (and, more darkly, hoarding) material. Coping with one's own coveting, and the coveting of others, may be the most trying obstacles to good behavior. And yet I have known a few who balanced these opposing impulses splendidly, those who respected both the individuals they encountered and the materials they desired.

SEE HOLTUM CATCH WITH HIS NAKED HANDS A SOLID IRON 21 LB. BALL, FIRED FROM A REAL CANNON BY POWDER ONLY....THE CONCUSSION OF THE EXPLOSION WOULD PARALYZE ANY ORDINARY MAN.(C. 1870)

Nothing gives me more pleasure than appearing on stage, although seeing a book come off the press is a close second. Perhaps I am ultimately drawn to this material because it is a record of a live performance, a unique event that creates a bond between the artist and his audience.

They share an experience, on a given occasion, that cannot be duplicated. Marian Hannah Winter has written, "Mountains of ephemera were created to induce the 'wish to see' and meet the 'desire to remember.' "[7] If the desire to remember is commemorated in the broadsides in this volume, the wish to see may be reflected in the following preposterous notice from 1824.

EXHIBITION EXTRAORDINARY.--There is now exhibiting, at the Lye-say-hum in the Strand, a FEMALE HOTTENTOT INFANT, four months and five days old, without hands or arms, the Greatest Wonder in the World!!! She plays on the Piano Forte, at sight, the most difficult sonatas with her feet, and executes the most rapid passages with an exactness and precision in timing and expression, far exceeding the ability of the ablest Performers. She gives lessons on the Double Bass, and plays Concertos on the Trumpet, speaks seven different languages fluently, teaches the use of the Small Sword, beats the Double Drum, while she sings Il Penseroso, and dances a Scots Reel! As a Ventriloquist, she excels the notorious LE SUG, holding three distinct and different conversations at one and the same time, in English, French, and Arabic! She gives Imitations of all the most celebrated English, French, and Italian Actors, and concludes her Performances with an Ascent á la Richer from the Stage to the Gallery!!! Tickets of admission 15s. each, to be had at the Office, of HERCULES HYPERBOLE, ESQ.

1. Although I here emphasize their embattled survival, when I served as guest curator for the "Imagery of Illusion" exhibition at the Harvard Theatre Collection, I learned that they held some five million playbills. Few of these, however, fall within the historical purview of this study.

2. Blaise Manfre's bill for this feat is reproduced in Theodor Hampe, *Die fahrenden Leute* (Leipzig, 1902).

3. [W.J.L. Millar], *How an American Brought the Great Italian Wizard before H.M. Queen Victoria* (London, 1899).

4. Letters quoted are from the author's collection, through the good graces of Allen Berlinski. For more on the relationship of show printers to performers, see Robert Wood's *Victorian Delights* (London, 1967), which reproduced the Royle letter; and his *Entertainments, 1800-1900* (London, 1971). Wood's correspondence with Berlinski is also illuminating. Wood suggests that the specific demands issued to printers by performers in midcentury already constituted a change in the way shows were arranged and presented: "the intimate and friendly atmosphere of the old troupers disappeared." An image that always haunts me is the picture of Wood gazing for the first time at thousands of filth-encrusted broadsides and letters preserved on spike files five feet high. For important information on Wood, see Berlinski's charming *Purvis: The Newcastle Conjuror* (Northville, Mich., 1981).

5. Arthur Freeman, *Elizabethan Misfits: Brief Lives of English Eccentrics, Exploiters, Rogues, and Failures, 1580–1660* (London, 1983).

6. David Prince Miller, *Life of a Showman* (London, 1851).

7. Marian Hannah Winter, *The Theatre of Marvels* (New York, 1964). Her marvelous theatrical ephemera reposes in the Harvard Theatre Collection.

EXTRAORDINARY EXHIBITIONS

THE LEARNED HORSE

C. 1618

WANDERING IN THE PIAZZA DEI MERCANTI in the center of Milan early in the seventeenth century, one would have been mightily engaged by the virtuosity of a learned horse. The horse had been trained from the age of two months by its owner "with every devotion, discipline, and patience," and it was now matriculated through five years. The playbill proclaims that this marvelous animal "comes from far," and brings with him the notices of royal patronage. Perhaps these travels had enabled him to master English, French, and Italian, all of which he was said to understand. He told the time in those languages, performed card tricks, and pretended to be dead, lying on the ground until cued to rise. The horse collected money and fetched wine, and drank to the health of the audience.

Was this the equine star Marocco, who had garnered more than sixty allusions from a veritable "Who's Who" of the London literary scene? Ben Jonson, Dekker, Nashe, Middleton, Markham, Webster, and Shakespeare himself had all acknowledged the accomplishments of William Banks and his talented quadruped, whose repertoire was similar to that described on this broadside. But despite these features in common, it is improbable that this accomplished animal was Marocco, who had also appeared in Paris and whose last performance was thought to have been in 1606,
when he would already have reached the advanced age of sixteen.

Perhaps more athletic than Marocco, this accomplished animal would jump through four, six, or eight hoops. The broadside was printed in Milan by Giacomo Angelo Nava, who was active there from 1618 to 1625, a particularly early example of a sheet used to advertise a specific performance. It features a floriated border and a lovely woodcut of the horse jumping through eight balloons, as these hoops were sometimes called. Similar iconography, perhaps inspired by this early image, was often used to advertise equine skills (a cut very much like this one is featured in a playbill of "Mr. Zucker's Learned Horse," who appeared in London in 1761).

Our star attraction was not only athletic but also a model of decorum and docility. He did his master's bidding as a servant, fetching and returning objects and carrying a bucket of water to a particular spectator. He then politely proffered that person a towel. It was said that he was particularly respectful and solicitous of the ladies present. "Lastly," it was stated, "he turns to the spectators with a deep bow to thank them for being so kind." Sadly, we are unable to acknowledge this gesture properly, as the names of both horse and tutor have been lost to posterity.

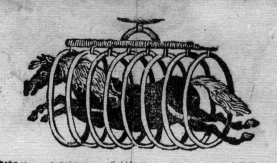

OPERAZIONE MERAVIGLIOSA
D'UN CAVALLO

SI dà avviso come è arivato in questa Nobilissima Città il N. per divertire questo Pubblico con un Cavallo venuto da lontani Paesi, di cui forse simile giamai sarà stato veduto per le sue virtuose Operazioni, le quali altrove già sono state ammirate, e approvate; Principalmente da Sua M. C. C., e da non pochi altri Principi, e Dame di diversi Paesi, perciò regalato il Padrone con preziosi doni, e favorito di passaporti, e raccomandazioni, per lo che benignamente hà avuto l'approvazione di Sua Eccellenza il Sig. Conte Governatore.

Si vedrà la bellezza, e virtù di questo Cavallo, quale da due mesi sino alli cinque anni è stato dal Padrone con ogni ritiratezza, diligenza, e pazienza ammaestrato, essendo di lui professione di ammaestrare tal sorte di Cavalli in esercizj, che non sono ordinarj, e tutto singolari a tal sorta di Animali. Primieramente egli intende le Lingue Inglese, Francese, Itagliane. 2. Riceve gli Spettatori con una riverenza. 3. Sarà posto alla sentinella, e darà segno al tempo della sua muta, serve al suo Maestro come un servidore. 4. Se il Maestro lascia cascare qualche cosa sia un guanto, o fazoletto, lo prende, e porta al Padrone. 5. Egli si sede alla maniera de Cani. 6. Prende un secchio, e reca acqua per lavar le mani a qualch' uno. 7. Porge una servietta per asciugare. 8. Dà segno quanto vale ciascuna carta nel givoco. 9. Prende una bussola per raccogliere un poco di danaro per comprare del vino. 10. Và alla porta, e bussa, acciò gli si dia del vino, e lo riceve. 11. Beve alla salute delli Spettatori. 12. Dà segno, che moneta si presenta. 13. E' assai ammirabile, e notabile, che nel suo esercizio si dimostra molto cortese, ed usa rispetto verso le Dame. 14. Vvota lambendo un bichiero pieno di acqua, o vino come un Cane. 15. Si finge malato, quando il Padrone dice, và a bere, ponendosi in terra come volesse morire, ma quando il Padrone dice di levarsi, e lo intimorisce con chiamare il Scorticatore, subito si leva, e guarda all'intorno se quello viene. 16. Salta 4. 6., e 8. Serchj un piede distante l'uno dall'altro. 17. Guarda all'Orologio quante ore sono, e fà ancora altre Operazioni, quasi qui non si spiegano, ma sono assai ridicole, e maravigliose agli Aspettatori. Per ultimo si volge verso gli Spettatori con una profonda riverenza, come a ringraziarli della loro benignità.

Si darà principio alle prove alli 27. del corrente mese di Febbrajo, con avvertenza, che sarà alle ore 22. sino alle 24., durando un'ora per volta l'esercizio, & questo si vedrà alla Piazza de Mercanti.

Li Curiosi non manchino, mentre la dimora sarà per poco tempo. Di più si fà sapere, che vi si trovaranno siti commodi secondo la qualità delle persone, fra gli altri uno tapezzato per le Dame, e Cavaglieri. Avvertendo, che per gli luoghi tapezzati vi saranno viglietti particolari, da pagarsi distintamente

IN MILANO per il Nava.

PIETRO STADELMANN
ARMLESS DULCIMER PLAYER
C. 1620

THE MOST POPULAR NON-SECULAR SUBJECT addressed in early modern broadsides may well have been monsters. The etymological ancestor of the word, *monstre*, meant "to warn," and physical anomalies were typically trumpeted as divine portents, omens of some untoward occurrence. Conjoined geese, limbless humans, and otherworldly combinations of human and animal forms often elicited symbolic or sanctimonious commentary. By the mid-seventeenth century, a different consensus had emerged, at least among learned Italians, as Daston and Park note in their *Wonders and the Order of Nature*: "marvels should evoke neither horror nor wonder, only distaste," was the prevailing view. "No longer portents of impending doom or ornaments of God's creation, monsters became rather problems in theodicy."

The anomalies themselves often expressed a different sentiment. Thomas Schweicker, born without arms or hands in Swabia in 1541, was celebrated for his accomplishments. A famous print pictures him writing with his feet, in excellent calligraphy and in Latin, the exclamation "God is Wonderful in his Works!" The personal stories of those who gratefully accepted their condition, however limited, and praised God in spite of it were clearly thought inspirational.

Such was the case with Pietro Stadelmann, the armless dulcimer player. The title of his broadside, "Admirable God in his own Work," introduces an account of his accomplishments and his faith. He was born on September 4, 1598, in Lucerne, Switzerland, to parents of limited means. Though without hands or arms, he "nonetheless attended to all his needs with his feet, as you see here below, in the most stupefying manner." Although handicapped, he was not discouraged: "But instead…I bore my cross with patience: because my Savior Jesus Christ enriched me with such grace that I could do with my feet various things"—including playing instruments, throwing a knife with precision, and, more prosaically, eating, drinking, writing, and sewing. He also mentions his prowess at casting dice and playing cards, which, if not traditional arenas of moral accomplishment, were also part of the repertoires of later armless prodigies such as Johann Valerius and Mathew Buchinger (see no. 24).

This broadside was probably produced in the early seventeenth century but bears no date or printer's mark. The striking woodcut shows Stadelmann surrounded by objects from his demonstration while manipulating the dulcimer with picks on his toes—again reminiscent of Buchinger, about whom it was proclaimed:

> His Dulcimer he next attacks
> With nimble and melodious Thwacks,
> The Strings, like Birds with warbling Throats,
> Send forth ten Thousand blended Notes,
> Though great the Numbers, all agree
> In well concerted Harmony.

Perhaps Stadelmann was more widely acknowledged for his faith than his skill. Unlike a legion of armless artists whose formidable exploits were well documented, Stadelmann's achievements are apparently unrecognized and unrecorded, apart from the witness of this broadside.

MIRABILIS DEVS IN OPERIBVS SVIS.

Breue informatione d'vn Giouinetto, che nell'Anno 1598. à quattro di Settembre nel paese de' Suizzeri, sotto il
Dominio di Lucernesi à Dobelschrand in Entlebuech, nacque di due persone chiamate, l'vna Andrea
Stadelmanno, l'altra Cattarina Krumenacherin, venuto al mondo senza braccia, e mani:
Con tutto ciò prouede assai bene à tutti i suoi bisogni co i piedi, come quì
à basso segue, in modo, che è stupore, e merauiglia.

Breue informatione del Giouinetto.

IO son chiamato Pietro Stadelmanno
Nato di bassa stirpe in vna Villa
D'Eluetia à Lucernesi sottoposta
Detta Entlebuech nell'Anno del Signore,
Che à nouerar fà mille cinquecento,
E nonant'otto, à quattro di Settembre,
Come i miei genitori ne san fede:
Se ben per mala mia sorte, ò ventura
Nacqui infelice, senza braccia, e mani,
Con tutto ciò non mi v'uò perder d'animo:
Ma portar la mia Croce in patienza;
Poi che il mio Saluatore Giesù Christo
M'hà dotato altamente di tal gratia,
Che posso far con piedi varie cose;
Come suonar di più sorti instromenti,
Mangiare, bere, scriuere, e cucire;
Sò girare vn tagliero gentilmente,
Giocare à Dadi, e a Carte per ragione,
Contar danari, e ritenerli saldi:
Molte altre cose appresso, che non posso
Così distesamente annouerar quì.
Chi n'hauesse per sorte qualche dubbio,
In fatti il tutto, come quì stà scritto.
All'hor potraisi di sicuro credere,
Poiche visto s'haurà con gli occhi proprii
Ben si comprende in me, quanto è sia gráde
La diuina bontà con simil dono.
Voi hauete hor quì breuemente inteso
La mia nascita, nome, età, lignaggio,
E quai sorti di gratie Iddio m'hà dato;
E con ciò vi desio la vita eterna.

Oratione di questo putto à Dio.

ECco ò mio degno Creatore, e Dio,
Che hai fatto Cielo, Terra, Sole, e Luna,
Stelle, e quanto comprende il Firmamento.
Gl'Augelli in Aria, i pesciolin nell'Onde,
Diuerse herbe, e radici, vaghi fiori,
Tutti conforme la lor spetie, e sorte;
Poscia per tua bontà, che non hà fine,
Creasti l'huomo à tua sembianza, primo
De' quai fù Adamo, e della costa sua
Eua: mà per hauer nel Paradiso
Essi mangiato del vietato pomo
Vna pena, ò castigo con ragione
Signore à l'human genere imponesti:
Ciò fù, che nel sudor de' nostri volti
Guadagnassimo il pan, non altramente.
Chi m'ama, dice Christo istesso, pigli
La sua Croce, e mi segua: perciò occorre
Vna cosa à costui, à quello vn'altra;
Ne huomo è alcun, che sia contento in tutto.
Quindi, essendo piacciuto à te ò Signore,
Ch'io sfortunato in questo mondo sia
Venuto senza braccia, e senza mani,
Quantonque la cagion non mi sia nota,
Pur ti prego, ò Signor, quanto più posso,
Che mi concedi gratia di portare
In patienza tutti i giorni miei,
Tal Croce, e peso, e mi dij tale aiuto,
Che conforme la tua santa Dottrina,
A prieghi ancor de la tua Santa Madre
Immacolata Vergine Maria
Io sia alleuato nel timor tuo Santo.
Accioche quando? sarà gionta l'hora,
Riceui lo mio spirto, e l'Alma accogli
Nella Celestiale tua regal sala.
Così Signor ti prego hora, e per sempre.

JACOB HALL

ROPE DANCER

C. 1670

THIS SIMPLE PIECE OF PRINTING from the 1670s is a remarkable survival. Until it surfaced in recent years, we knew of it only as cited by the notorious scholar and forger John Payne Collier in 1859, and his compromised credibility called its very existence into question. It now seems likely that this copy was once owned by Collier.

With only ten lines of type set beneath an impressive royal crest, it is both an announcement and a challenge. It is an official notice of the collaborative efforts of two troupes of rope dancers, one directed by Richard Lancashire and the other by Jacob Hall, "Sworn Servant to his Majestie." In addition to perambulations on the rope, this placard offered a "Variety of Rare Feats of Activity and Agility of Body upon the Stage," with acrobatics, somersaults, vaulting over drawn swords, and diving through hoops. Even a clown offering "Witty Conceits" was promised. The enterprising performers concluded their advertisement with a "Challenge [to] all Others whatsoever, whether *English-men*, or *Strangers*, to do the like with them for Twenty Pounds, or what more They please."

Balancing and cavorting on a suspended rope was one of the most popular amusements of the day. The variety of technique was surprising: one could mount low or high ropes, slack ropes or diagonally mounted vaulting lines to make ascents or descents between the tops of buildings and the pavement below. In this period numerous equilibrists of myriad nationalities paraded before the public, but Hall was the most famous. He is mentioned by Samuel Pepys, who lauded him in two diary entries of the 1660s, and subsequently by other important literary figures including Dryden, Shadwell, and Pope. Hall's notoriety seems to have been based on private as much as public performance, both of which took advantage of his grace and pleasing physiognomy. According to one contemporary account, women found him "a due composition of Hercules and Adonis." He was a lover of Lady Castlemaine, the influential Duchess of Cleveland, who made him the recipient of many favors.

Hall was among the English performers who also plied their trade at the St. Germain Fair in Paris, where he was identified with the Charles Allard and Maurice Vondrebeck troupe, and he appears to have taken a French wife, Suzanne Roy. The next generation continued in the trade. A playbill, c. 1700, mentions their progeny at Bartholemew Fair among six performing troupes headlined by the rope dancers Barnes and Finley: "the late *Jacob Hall's* Son and his *Company*, perform to Great Satisfaction."

No notice of his death appears in the standard sources. In a scrapbook of materials on Bartholomew Fair, I have a handwritten account citing the *Protestant Mercury* of February 18, 1682: "Jacob Hall, the noted Funambulo and rope dancer was accidentally killed at Paris, for a quarrel happening and he running to part the combatants one of them ran him through."

C   R

THese are to give Notice to all *Gentlemen* and *Others*, That there is Joyned together
Two of the Best *Companies* in *England*, viz. Mr. *Jacob Hall* (Sworn Servant to his
Majestie) and Mr. *Richard Lancashire*, with several Others of their Companies; by Whom
will be performed Excellent Dancing and Vaulting on the Ropes; with Variety of Rare
Feats of Activity and Agility of Body upon the Stage; as doing of Somersets, and Flip-
flaps, Flying over Thirty Rapiers, and **over several Mens** heads; and also flying through
severall Hoops: Together with severall other Rare Feats of Activity that will be there
Presented : With the Witty Conceits of Merry *WILL*: In the performing of all which,
They Challenge all Others whatsoever, whether *English-men*, or *Strangers*, to do the like
with them for Twenty Pounds, or what more They please.

MATHEW BUCHINGER
"THE GREATEST GERMAN LIVING"

1726

MY PASSION FOR "The Little Man of Nuremberg" remains unabated, despite decades collecting material, distilling data, and chronicling his life. Born in Anspach, near Nuremberg, in 1674, Buchinger eventually moved to the British Isles and gave exhibitions of conjuring, swordplay, bowling, and dancing, and played more than half a dozen musical instruments—all without hands or legs. He never grew to more than twenty-nine inches in height but married four times and fathered fourteen children. He died in Ireland in 1739.

Of all his accomplishments, perhaps the most enduring are his intricate family trees, crests of nobility, and marriage "pictures," customized *ketubahs* of his own devising. He was the master of a wide variety of calligraphic styles, and he often created micrographic specimens of exquisite penmanship, visible to the human eye only with the aid of magnification. He made these pieces by manipulating a pen between his two flipperlike excrescences. In contrast to the bombast typical of playbills, an example in the British Library recounts his marvelous skills with understatement, noting that he "writes several hands as quick and as well as any writing master, and will write with any for a wager; he draws faces to the life, and coats of armes, pictures, flowers …with a pen very curiously." To this day, samples of his work grace many important museum collections.

This poetic broadside, one example of myriad literary tributes, gives some idea of the esteem in which Buchinger was held. The most famous of these verse encomia was a lament for the Little Man, eloquent but as a eulogy premature, as it was issued long before his death. It has been attributed (most likely erroneously) to Jonathan Swift. The tenor of this paean, which poked fun at his size and condition, may be judged by this excerpt:

> Nor wou'd thy Fame have been so great
> Had Nature form'd thee quite compleat.

Our broadside features a theatrical cut. Buchinger appears seated on his customary cushion between the gathered curtains of a stage. An oboe and a trumpet, two instruments among several that he played, are close at hand. This crude figure also appears on a playbill for an appearance in Scotland in my collection. I reproduce this piece, however, because it offers much more insight into what Buchinger actually did in his performances.

Although this broadside is not listed in Foxon, it was featured in the famous collection of John Elliot Hodgkin. It was listed for sale in a Lucille magic catalog of the 1930s. It is possible that the piece shown here is the same one described in both of these sources. The broadsides and playbills announcing Buchinger's appearance are less frequent survivals than the drawings that he made and the prints on which he was featured, as these are far more likely to have been saved by devoted fans.

P O E M

ON

MATHEW   BUCKINGER,

The greateſt G E R M A N living.

SEE Gallants, wonder and behold
This German, of imperfect Mold,
No Feet, no Leggs, no Thighs, no Hands,
Yet all that Art can do commands.
Firſt Thing he does, he makes a Pen,
Is that a Wonder! Well what then ?
Why then he writes, and ſtrikes a Letter,
No *Elziverian* Type is better.
Fix'd in his Stumps, directs the Quill
With wondrous Gravity and Skill ;
Upward, downward, backward, forward,
Eaſtward, Weſtward, Southward, Northward.
In Short to every Compaſs point,
Tho' ſhortned at the Elbow Joint.
The Foliage round it he diſplays
Does more our Admoration raiſe,
For Hair Stroaks to the Eye they paſs,
And yet they're Letters thro' a Glaſs.
Thus he with double Art can write,
At once to pleaſe and cheat the Sight.
When with his Wife at Cards he plays,
The Trumps already play'd conveys
Into his Stumps ; the Standers by
Confeſs them quicker then their Eye :
His Wife exclaims, but all in vain,
He plays them o'er and o'er again,
Nay what is more when all is done
They own the Game is fairly won.
He throws the Dice as careleſs down
As any Gameſter in the Town.
And tho' the Number caſt be three
Two Sixes you ſhall ever ſee :
Thus raffling with his Wife he wins,
And every pleas'd Spectator grins ;
All croſs Legg'd whilſt he is at play,
A Compliment he can't repay.
His Dulcimer he next attacks
With nimble and melodious Thwacks ;
The Strings, like Birds with warbling Throats,
Send forth ten Thouſand blended Notes,
Though great the Numbers, all agree

In well concerted Harmony:
No Sound can pleaſe the Ear ſo much,
No Hand can have ſo ſweet a Touch ;
And yet you'd think 'twou'd more beccme
His Stumps to thump a Kettle Drum.
The Tricks he plays at Cups and Balls,
'Tis wrong in any Man, who calls
Them Slight of Hand, as he gives out,
Their Slight of Stumps, and are no Doubt.
The Nine-Pins quite ſurpaſs my Muſe,
In vain his Art ſhe there purſues,
The wond'rous Wiſdom of his Bow,
For ſurely it muſt have a Soul,
When one Direction makes it go
To this, to that, and too and fro,
Trips up theſe Pins, and lets thoſe ſtand,
Obſerving *BUCKINGERS* Command.
Thus *Homer* made his Jav'lins fly,
And choſe the Men that were to die.
Great Sir, of three Foot high to raiſe
To thee a Monement of Praiſe,
Requires a lofty *German* Strain,
A noble and exalted Vein.
No, ſhe's not worthy, my poor Muſe,
I cannot ſay to wipe your Shooes ;
But had you Shooes to wipe, I Swear
It ſhou'd be thine great *BUCKINGER*.
Great Trunk of Man be not aſham'd,
That Nature has thy Body maim'd, ;
In thee juſt Emblem, ſhe wou'd try
The mighty Force of Induſtry ;
What Gifts are to thy Mind deny'd,
By Art and Care may be ſupply'd.
Obſerve the Moon, the Stars, the Sun,
How conſtant thro' their Work they run ;
Among them all we cannot ſpy
A Hand, or Foot, a Leg, or Thigh.
The Oak could not the Thropy bear
Till that the Branches cropped were,
Nor wou'd thy Fame have been ſo great,
Had Nature form'd thee quite compleat.

Printed in the Year 1726.

ISAAC FAWKES
"DEXTERITY OF HAND"
C. 1729

ISAAC FAWKES was THE MOST FAMOUS magician of the early decades of the eighteenth century. I was tempted to say, most recognizable, but that honor must fall to the armless and legless twenty-nine-inch tall Mathew Buchinger, featured elsewhere in this narrative (see no. 24), whose startling physique was widely promulgated. Fawkes, whose conjuring repertoire certainly exceeded that of Buchinger, left behind fewer traces of his exploits on the stage. This playbill of 1729, along with two others that came to light only a few years ago and miraculously made their way to my home, are the only known broadsides advertising his performances.

Fawkes' prominence rested not on his own promotional material but rather on the amount of attention that he garnered in contemporary newspapers and books. He attained the status of celebrity. His show, which was a major attraction at both Bartholomew and Southwark Fairs in London, consisted of sleight of hand with cards, coins, ribbons, birds, and magical automata. Here is a contemporary description of his signature illusion: "He takes an empty Bag, lays it on the Table, and turns it several Times inside out, then commands 100 Eggs out of it, and several Showers of Real Gold and Silver; then the Bag beginning to swell, several sorts of wild Fowls run out of it." At various times Fawkes also presented in his booth puppeteers, contortionists, acrobats, mechanical views, and even a horned woman.

The clockwork machine that he here entitles "Arts Masterpiece" is likely the same device referred to a short time later as "The Artificial View of the World." "In this curious Piece," says *Fogg's Journal*, "is seen the Firmament spangled with a multitude of Stars: the Moon's Increase and Decrease; the Dawn of Day; the Sun diffusing his Light at his Rising, the beautiful Redness of the Horizon at his Setting, as in a fine Summer's Evening. The Ocean is also represented with Ships under Sail, as tho' at several Miles Distance, others so near that their Shadow is seen in the Water; and as they pass by any Fort, Castle, or fortified Town, they salute each other with their Guns, the Report and Eccho of which is as plainly heard as tho' from the real Places they appear to be." The prospects of Venice, Gibraltar, and Windsor Castle were shown, but in subsequent weeks views of Cairo and Algiers appeared instead.

A replacement for the five-year-old contortionist was Anthony Le Blain, the "French Scaramouch, a balance master from Paris," who would become the subject of some controversy in the press. Fawkes said that his stunts were so impressive that "no Person in these Kingdoms does the same but himself." Both the fame of Fawkes and the jingoistic resentment of the newspaper correspondent are revealed in this newspaper excerpt: "Such a fellow as this [Le Blain] is beneath the Resentment of the Publick, and deserves to be treated only with Contempt. He may, perhaps, divert the Mob for some Time with his Monkey Tricks; but Men of Sense will laugh at Him and Despise Him. I am only sorry that the celebrated Mr. *Fawks* (who really is a great Artist in his Way) should be so far imposed upon by this *vain Braggadocio*, as to suffer Him to perform in his Theatre and bring such a Scandal upon the *brightest Genius'* of his native Country."

FAWKES   At his   Theatre,

In *James-street*, **G**   **R**   near the

Hay-   *Market*;

Performs the following Entertainments.

First, **H**IS Surprizing and Incomparable DEXTERITY of HAND, in which he will perform several intirely new Curiosities. that far surpasseth any thing of that kind ever seen before. *Second,* a curious MUSICAL CLOCK, that he lately purchas'd of Mr. *Pinchbeck,* Clock-Maker in *Fleet-street,* that plays several fine Tunes on most Instruments of Musick. and imitates the Melodious Notes of various kinds of Birds, as real Life : Also Ships sailing. with a number of curious and humorous Figures, representing divers Motions as tho' Alive *Third,* another fine CLOCK or MACHINE, call'd Arts Masterpiece, or the *Venetian* Lady's Invention, which she Employ'd Workmen to make, that were Seventeen Years contriving ; the like of which was never yet Made or Shewn, in any other part of the World, for variety of moving Pictures, and other Curiosities. Th re is also the said Lady's Picture very finely Painted on the Machine that moves by Clock-work, like Life.

Besides his inimitable *Posture-Master,* who is vastly Improv'd in his Performances, he has a little CHILD of five Years of Age, who shews such wonderful *Turns of Body,* that it is impossible to beli ve without seeing.

N. B. During our short stay, we shall begin every Evening precisely at 7 o' Clock. This is the last Week of Performing here.

MILLS' SINISTER DECEPTIONS

C. 1740

THIS SMALL, STRAIGHTFORWARD mid-eighteenth-century handbill, emblazoned with the engraved arms of King George III, announces the performance of a conjurer called Mr. Mills. It is a piece tantalizing in its brevity. For everything that Mills reveals we would like to know more. We are given a list of his noble clientele, but we are not told when or what he performed for them. He was apparently an Englishman returned from exhibiting abroad, but we do not know the details of his itinerary. We read that he performs "more Curiosities upon Cards than any other Person whatever," but not a single effect is specified. We are told that he "eats Fire faster than a Person can eat Bread," a provocative claim to be sure, but speed has never been thought an essential attribute of pyrotechnic ingestion. The conjurer is clever enough to court the women in his audience by promising to predict, for young ladies, "when they are to be Married," but again, no further details are forthcoming.

"What makes his Performance still greater," the bill avers, "is that he does all these feats of Dexterity and Deception with his Left Hand, having lost his Right Hand in an Engagement." But other than the name of his commanding officer at the time of the injury, there is nothing to enlighten us about these circumstances. We are left to wonder, was he an entertainer before he lost his arm, or did he take up magic in recuperation?

Conjuring with one hand is not unprecedented. Mills returned to England in 1744, just five years after the death of the nearly armless Mathew Buchinger (see no. 24). A contemporary of Buchinger was Johannes Grigg, who had no legs and no left hand. He used his right hand to advantage in displaying his skills with various illusions, including the classic "Cups and Balls."

It is likely that my interest in Mr. Mills was piqued because one of the best sleight-of-hand artists I have ever seen is the one-armed Argentinean magician René Lavand. He manages to orchestrate drama of amazing range from his table-top theater, basing his pieces on the works of Borges and Lorca, of George Bernard Shaw and Li Po. His technique is so accomplished that he executes with one hand what most of his colleagues are unable to perform with two. A first-time viewer may not even realize that he uses only his left arm; those who do will be rewarded with many lovely touches, such as the opening of a pocket knife or the perfect knotting of his bow-tie. He embodies the definition of legerdemain as sleight of hand.

G. III.   R.

Mr. MILLS,

Lately arrived from Abroad, who has been in Foreign
Parts ever since the Year 1744,
Who tells Young Ladies   when they are to be Married.

Where he exhibits this and every Evening;

HAS lately had the high Honour of performing before their present
Majesties and several of the Royal Family, at Kew, as well as various
others of the principal Noblemen and Gentry, at their own Houses,
viz. the Dukes of Marlborough, Ancaster, Beaufort, Richmond, Montague,
Newcastle, and St. Albans; General Conway, Sir Watkins William Wynn,
Bart. with the utmost Degree of Applause, as likewise to numerous Gentlemen
and Ladies too tedious to mention; in particular, he performs Dexterity of
Hand surprizingly astonishing to the Spectators, and more Curiosities upon Cards
than any other Person whatever. He causes Birds, Fruit &c. to appear upon
the Table, to the great Surprize of every Beholder. He also eats Fire faster than
any Person can eat Bread. He engages to perform with any Man for 100l.

What makes his Performance still greater is, that he does all these Feats of
Dexterity and Deception with his Left Hand, having lost his Right Hand in an
Engagement, under the Command of Admiral Sir Edward Hawke, K. B. in
the last War.

He is ready to perform at any Gentleman's House, at what Hour they shall
please to appoint.

Doors at his own Appartments to be opened at 6 and to begin at 7 o'Clock.
Front Seat 1s.—Second Seat 6d.—Back Seat 3d.

6⁹⁄₁₆ x 7½

The Famous African Hermaphrodite

c. 1750

HERMAPHRODITES ARE RARELY the subject of polite conversation, but as both medical curiosities and exhibited marvels they have attracted considerable scrutiny. Sometime after 1740 a "Famous African" returned to London from unspecified travel abroad and was exhibited near Ludgate Hill. A twenty-seven-year-old from Angola, this anomaly possessed the physical characteristics of both sexes, and a demeanor said to be perfectly manly while its smile was perfectly feminine. From the waist up the body was "Robust, Brawny and wholly Masculine...the Arms and Hands slender; the Thighs and Legs a perfect Model of Female Symetry." The anatomical description, which in the original is given in a sort of "Wayne's World" Latin, continues: "In place of a clitoris, the male penis extends to four fingers at a minimum, when, as is often the case, it is experiencing an erection."

This celebration of anomaly, with its combined appeal to prurience and scientific discovery, was in practice democratizing, providing one of the few forums where the classes mingled. Richard Altick has characterized the audience for these exhibits:

A common curiosity erased social distinctions: the quality and the rabble, the cultivated and the ignorant mingled to see the latest marvel. Although most came because their innate relish for the sensational, the mysterious, and the grotesque was titillated by stridently announced new importations, some—the educated minority—came out of genuinely scientific motives, to amplify and verify the descriptions they had read in learned treatises.

Our subject is almost certainly the same one referred to in a bill in the British Library advertising a hermaphrodite, "lately brought over from Angola." Like our example, this playbill describes the general features of the exhibit in English but reserves Latin for the anatomical details. The citing of medical sources and the descriptions in Latin added prestige to what might otherwise have been considered a sordid show. It was clearly the prurient, however, that sustained the exhibition of hermaphrodites as a mainstay of the twentieth-century carnival sideshow. Almost every carnival talker pronounced the word as "morphodite," and almost every attraction was spurious. Among the better-known acts were those called George/Georgina or Robert/Roberta.

When as a youngster I first worked as an outside talker and carnival magician, the "blow off" of the "five-and-one" (five attractions in the same show) consisted of paying an extra fee to see the "hermaphrodite" reveal itself in the back of the tent. "Adam and Eve, boy and girl, brother and sister—all in one. It will expose itself, not to be rude or vulgar, but to show you one of mother nature's curious mistakes." As I reached the denouement of my most impressive card mystery, from behind the curtains at each performance I would faintly hear the unforgettable refrain, "and this is my male sex, but as you can see it is useless..."

Just arriv'd from ABROAD,

To be seen a few Doors from **Ludgate-Hill**, *in the* Old-Bailey, *on the* Left-Hand, *opposite to the* Blue-Bell,

From Ten in the Morning to Nine at Night;

The Famous AFRICAN,

Mention'd by WILLIAM CHESELDEN, Efq; *in Page* 314 of his ANATOMY, where he gives an engraved Figure, and a Defcription of the Parts; and by Doctor *PARSONS* in his Treatife of *Hermaphrodites*; though erroneoufly defcrib'd by this latter AUTHOR.

BEING a Native of *Angola*, about 27 Years old; of Mafculine Features, which feem perfectly Feminine in the Circumftance of Smiling or Joy; the Parts of the Body upwards Robuft, Brawny and wholy Mafculine; the Mufcles above the Elbow very ftrong, the Arms and Hands neat and flender; the Thighs and Legs a perfect Model of Female Symetry.

For a particular Defcription of the Parts which diftinguifh the Sexes, we refer to the fhort Account of *Latin* following.

Scroti *quippe vice funguntur* Vulvæ Labia, Tefticulos *binos largos & mobiles involventia.* Clitoridis *loco* Penis Virilis *ad quatuor minimum prominet digitos, ubi (quod fœpius fit) erigitur;* imperforatus quidem, fed ex Corporibus cavernofis, Glande, Urethra, Præputio & Frænulo vere conflatus. *Adfunt præterea, plane ac in Mulieribus,* Meatus urinarius & Vagina *fatis ampla, huc ufque tamen nulla huic* ANDROGYNÆ *effluxerunt Catamænia.*

Thofe who faw this Curiofity, in *London*, in 1740, are all unanimous, that it was then but a Wonder in minature in refpect to what it now is; Nature having fo far improved the Wonder in this unparallel'd Curiofity fince that time; that feveral Paintings and Drawings which were then taken of it, fcarce carry any Refemblance of it in its prefent State, which has render'd new ones abfolutely neceffary. Not only the Parts by, which the Sexes are ordinarily diftinguifh'd, but alfo the whole Body from Head to Foot is a moft wonderful Mixture of Male and Female.

N.B. *When we were laft in Town, in* 1740, *we were honour'd by Numbers of Ladies of undoubted and unqueftionable Reputation; there is now good Conveniency, and the Ladies will be attended by a prudent Gentlewoman, with the utmoft Decency.*

Note, A new engraved Figure of the Parts in their prefent State, fold at 6d each Figure. Good lights in the Evening, and Attendance given Abroad, if defired.—The Price, while in the CITY, only One Shilling each.

MR. WILLIAMS
CONJURER FROM BARBADOS

C. 1750

THIS MID-EIGHTEENTH-CENTURY PLAYBILL describes the repertoire of an elusive conjurer known only as Williams. He has arrived in England from Barbados and implies that he is a native of the West Indies, certainly an exotic pedigree for an itinerant performer of that era. He has set up shop in St. Martin's Lane, an area that today is in the heart of the London theatrical district.

Williams serves as a transitional figure between the acclaimed magicians of the mid-eighteenth century, Fawkes (see p. 26) and Buchinger (see p. 24), and the fairground conjurers who were popular fifty years later: Lane (see p. 46), Palatine (see p. 38), Rea, and Gyngell. He performs with common objects and seems partial to eggs. He turns eggs into birds, or birds into eggs. He swallows a handkerchief and then produces it from an egg. He borrows a watch that he divides and restores. He boasts his command of fifty tricks with cards, but he is infuriatingly unspecific about them. He only promises "a great Variety of delightful and surprizing Performances, exhibited by this celebrated Artist, which are too numerous to be inserted in this Bill, and are not to be credited without seeing."

The wonderful crude woodcut pictured here reveals that, like Fawkes and Buchinger, he featured the Cups and Balls illusion. Fruit, birds, and mice were apparently produced from the cups as a finale to this classic effect. In contrast, Hyman Saunders, who was performing in the West Indies in 1775, was dissociating himself from what he considered a dated repertoire. According to his advertisement in the *Jamaica Gazette*, "Mr. Saunders has been honoured with the greatest applause by his Majesty and all the Nobility that have seen his great performances, in Europe, America and the West Indies; and is allowed to be the most astonishing proficient in the art of clear conveyance, that ever attempted an exhibition of the kind, without descending to the low tricks of cups and balls, ribbands, etc." Saunders does exemplify the change in style of the next generation of conjurers. Although not original in his own choices, he did offer a series of effects likely unknown to Williams or Fawkes. He pulled off his shirt while still wearing his vest and coat, he placed a borrowed ring on a sword even though the ends were firmly held by two spectators, he fried German pancakes in a gentleman's hat, and, in perhaps his most novel mystery, he promised "some very astonishing performances with walnuts."

Mr. Williams, perhaps more restrained, sits in a chair holding a magician's wand in his left hand and seems to scale cards with his right. As I am closely associated with the skill of card throwing, I would like to fantasize that it is pictured at this early date. It is much more likely, however, that Williams is performing an impressive mystery of his day, in which cards chosen by spectators are made to fall from the ceiling upon command.

This is to acquaint the Nobility, Gentry and Others,

That   the   F A M O U S

Mr. WILLIAMS

(From the Island of *Barbadoes*, in the *West-Indies*)

Will exhibit, this prefent Evening,

His whole Art of Dexterity of Hand.

HE has had the Honour to perform before moft of the Nobility and Gentry, to their entire Satisfaction. He performs feveral furprizing Tricks by Money, Rings, Handkerchiefs, Ribbands, Laces, Eggs, Balls, Fruit, Birds, Mice, &c. and upwards of fifty curious Things with Cards. He will caufe Fruit to appear on the Table at the Word of Command. He turns Eggs into Birds, or Birds into Eggs, as the Spectators fhall chufe. He fwallows a Handkerchief, and produces it out of an Egg. He alfo borrows any Gentleman's Watch, divides it into feveral Parts; and, in one Minute, is entirely whole, as received from the Gentleman. With a great Variety of delightful and furprizing Performances, exhibited by this celebrated Artift, which are too numerous to be inferted in this Bill, and are not to be credited without feeing.

To begin at   o'Clock.   *Vivat Rex.*

⁎ He is to be heard of at Mr. *Morrifon's*, in *Cecil-Court*, near St. *Martin's-Lane*; and will perform at any Lady's or Gentleman's Houfe, if defir'd, on giving two Hours Notice.

6 7/16 x 9 9/16

DUNCAN MACDONALD
"THE SCOTTISH EQUILIBRIST"

1753

THIS HANDSOME BROADSIDE, engraved from a drawing by Boitard, features one of the more remarkable illustrations of an entertainer ever recorded. Originally published by Fenwick Bull in London in 1753, it now graces the dust jacket for this volume. The letterpress text tells the tale of Duncan MacDonald, an extremely accomplished slack-wire walker who, like a number of his compatriot Scotsmen, was compelled to leave England for safe haven in France. There was once considerable speculation that this broadside was a piece of anti-Jacobean propaganda describing a nonexistent performer. No doubt the credibility-straining stunt pictured here precipitated such rumors.

According to the text, MacDonald cavorted on the wire wearing a pair of large and cumbersome boots to which quart bottles were affixed, neck downward. He balanced a wheel on his right toe, on top of which was a spike on which rested a pewter plate on edge that in turn supported a rack with sixteen wine glasses—on top of which was a globe on which was balanced a piece of straw. With his left index finger he lifted a chair on which a small dog perched, and from which two hundred-pound weights were suspended. With his nose he balanced a sword, point downward, on whose pummel rested a pipe with two eggs delicately set against the bowl. He simultaneously played two distinct tunes on a trumpet and a French horn. Beneath him, instead of a safety net, were sword blades pointing upward like a bed of iron spikes.

It is thought that the famous description of a wire walker in Tobias Smollett's novel *Humphrey Clinker* was inspired by this engraving. The character Winifred Jenkins reports: "I saw such tumbling and dancing on the ropes and wires that I was frightened and ready to go into a fit. I tho't it was all enchantment, and believing myself bewitched, began to cry. You knows as how the witches in Wales fly on broom-sticks; but here was flying without any broomstick or thing in the varsal world, and firing of pistols in the air and blowing of trumpets and singing, and rolling of wheelbarrows on a wire (God bless us!) no thicker than a sewing thread; that to be sure they must deal with the Devil."

In Willson Disher's *Pleasures of London* there is an unusual overprinting that appears at the very top of the engraving of MacDonald on this bill. A line of text is added: "Now where's your Bottle Conjurer." This apparently enigmatic phrase refers to a famous hoax of January 1749, in which a conjurer announced that at a public performance he would offer for examination, and then physically enter, a common quart wine bottle. On the highly publicized occasion the theater was filled to capacity at a very stiff ticket price. When after a long delay no one took the stage, a wag suggested that for double the admission the conjurer would insert himself into a pint bottle. The audience realized that they had been duped; they rioted and destroyed the Haymarket Theatre. The event was for more than a century cited as evidence of the gullibility of the English public.

Of course, whoever thought that MacDonald's performance was a hyperbolic hoax was also likely duped. As Disher suggests, the image of the funambulist probably depicted a composite repertoire: "Several distinct feats, performed separately, are made to appear as one astonishing ensemble by the designer of this poster-engraving." A 1752 notice for MacDonald's performance at Bartholomew Fair is more measured: "There will be two Youths from the Highlands of Scotland (the MacDonalds) that do several new and curious Performances on the slack Wire, scarcely perceptible; the eldest of which will at the Conclusion perform a Highland Dance, and balance a Straw on his Nose all the Time."

It may be difficult for modern readers to grasp the popularity of such acts or the jingoist partisanship they elicited. Jacques Bonnet, in his *Histoire générale de la danse* (Paris, 1723), reports that another very accomplished equilibrist, a Turk, who performed in France at the end of the seventeenth century, lost his life at the fair of Troyes: "One of his companions, an Englishman, also a famous dancer, greased the oblique rope upon which the Turk had to descend backwards preserving an upright attitude. Of course the fall was at once fatal."

DUNCAN MACDONALD,

of the *Shire* of Caithneſs *Gent.* the Celebrated Scotiſh Equilibriſt.

Engrav'd from the Original Drawing by F. Boitard, & *Publiſh'd according to Act of Parliam.* June 1753, *by* Fenwick Bull, *Map & Printſeller at y.* White Horſe *on* Ludgate Hill.

Price. 6ᵈ.

THIS *Gentleman* (who performs on the ſlack Wire what neither *Caratha the Turk,* or any other would preſume to attempt in that ſurpriſing Art) being unhappily involved in the late *Rebellion* was obliged, with ſeveral of his Countrymen, to fly to *France* as a Place of Refuge, and as he danced perfectly well, flattered himſelf that Talent would ſubſiſt him as he was then deſtitute, but found there to his great Diſappointment few Perſons in that Claſs who even got a Comfortable Subſiſtance, the *French* being more inclined to re-eſtabliſh their Marine, than encourage a Set of *uſeleſs Caperers,* and *England* the only happy Climate for thoſe Volatile Geniuſſes, where they wallowed in Luxury. Neceſſity then prompted him to turn *Equilibriſt* being kindly aſiſted by Nature with an extraordinary Gift of Agility, the Succeſs of which this Print exhibits, whereby he is rendered capable of gaining a genteel Subſiſtance, and enabled to remit proper Sums to his diſtant Wiſe and ſix Children. *Imprimis,* With a Pair of *French Poſt Boots,* under the Soles of which are faſtened *quart Bottles* with the Necks downwards, He exhibits ſeveral Feats of Activity on the ſlack Wire, after which he Poizes a Wheel on his Right Toe, on the Summit of which is plac'd a Spike whereon is ballance'd by the Edge a Pewter Plate, on that a Board with ſixteen Wine-Glaſſes, at the Top, a Glaſs Globe with a Wheaten Straw erect on the ſame, He then fixes a ſharp-pointed Sword on the Tip of his Noſe, on the Pummel of which he Ballances a Tobacco Pipe, and on the Bowl two Eggs erect ; with his Left Fore-finger he ſuſtains a Chair with a Dog ſitting in it, and two Feathers kept erect, on the Nobs, and to ſhew the Strength of his Wriſt there are two Weights of 100 each, faſtened to the Feet of the Chair, after which a *French Horn* and Trumpet are brought him, both which he Sounds diſtinctly at the ſame Inſtant two different Tunes, the one being the Banks of the *Tweed,* the other not proper to mention, as a Proof of his Certainty of not Falling he places on the Stage, under the Wire, ſeveral Swordblades with the Points upwards.

II x 16³⁄₁₆

AUTOMATON FLAUTISTS

C. 1760

"ON AN AFTERNOON LATE IN April, 1738, the members of the Paris Académie Royale des Sciences listened intently as twelve airs were played for them upon a German flute. Those whose ears were keen noted the exceptional clarity with which the flautist rendered the fastest passages, and some listeners found the tasteful treatment of dynamics, tempos and ornamentation particularly striking. Most of the Academicians, however, fixed their attention far more closely on the performer than the performance, for…the flautist was a musical automaton." Thus Linda Strauss engagingly sets the scene for the exhibition of one of the most famous and impressive of all mechanical marvels, the flute player of Jacques de Vaucanson.

Constructed from wood, it stood five and one-half feet tall, and was patterned after the sculpture of a marble faun by Coysevaux. It was taken to represent either Apollo or Pan, both known for musical prowess. The figure's impressive repertoire consisted of a dozen different tunes.

Vaucanson initially met with skepticism, largely because an earlier "automaton" harpsichord player had housed a five-year-old human director, in the manner of the so-called Automaton Chess Player (see no. 96). Held up to the rigorous scrutiny of the Academy, furthermore, Vaucanson's flute player was more than an entertaining exhibition: it provided fodder for an ongoing philosophic debate about the nature of man and machine. As it duplicated the embouchure of a wind player, and actually fingered the instrument, its ability to imitate human attributes was debated almost as earnestly as its musical production. Its ability to "breathe" was especially important, as it produced musical sounds much as a human being would. Voltaire, among the many notables who praised him, hailed Vaucanson as the new Prometheus.

More scientist than showman, Vaucanson was heralded as a major figure in the world of mechanics and soon took up a government post, leaving others to exhibit his automata throughout Europe. In the aftermath of his success, not surprisingly, rivals offered copycat attractions.

Automata historians Alfred Chapuis and Edmund Droz cite at least ten derivatives; some of these only simulated playing, while others were based on the detailed account given by Vaucanson in his own memoir.

Vaucanson's figure was exhibited in Britain in 1741 and, shortly after midcentury, Londoners could delight to duets from an impressive pair of automaton flautists, "A Shepherd and Shepherdess, as big as life in an Opera Dress as the above print represents them." The couple, exhibited in conjunction with a remarkable walnut bureau, reposed in Jerom Johnson's Cut-Glass Warehouse in Piccadilly. A Mr. Hildebrand billed himself as the "Proprietor and Maker of the most Magnificent Cabinet in the World."

To rebut that claim, this broadside (in form, style, and illustration almost identical to one that featured Hildebrand) was issued to announce that "Mr. Wilcke, (lately arrived from Berlin)…is the Real Maker of this amazing Cabinet and Figures." Even this attribution, however, is unconfirmed. The surprising piece of furniture featured a series of more than one hundred changing drawers and even provided a magic effect: one compartment "will make disappear, and appear again, any thing that is put into it, as often as one pleases."

The flute players were constructed to provide pleasure not only by their music but also by their interaction. They sympathetically glanced at each other as they played. Doubting spectators were challenged to test the automata by putting bits of paper under the fingers of the musicians or by stopping up their mouths, both of which would render them incapable of playing and thereby attest to their mechanical construction.

The provenance of even such celebrated attractions is often difficult to trace. This pair was probably the couple advertised in a broadside for "Microcosms, Exhibition of Mechanical Wonders at No. 90 King-Street, Ramsgate." The proprietor is described only as "a native of Germany." The ultimate fate of these figures, as well as those made by Vaucanson, is unknown.

This is to give NOTICE,

That Mr. *Wilcke*, (lately arrived from BERLIN) who is the Real Maker
of this amazing Cabinet and Figures.

Is Removed to Mr. *Jerom Johnson*'s, Cut-Glafs Warehoufe, oppofite the *Black-Bear*, *Piccadilly*, in which
is a Light-Room, extremely proper for viewing the moft Minute Parts of this Matchlefs Performance,
and will there exhibit to public View.

Two moft wonderful and unparalleled PIECES OF ART:

1. Two AUTOMATONS, viz.

A SHEPHERD and SHEPHERDESS,

As big as Life in an Opera-Drefs, as the above Print reprefents them.

THESE two Figures play very naturally on two German Flutes, the Firft and Second, as completely
as living Men can do, to the utmoft Surprize of thofe that fee and hear them. It is well known
that the German Flute is one of the moft difficult Inftruments for Man to learn to play upon,
and therefore inconceivable how inanimated Figures fhould move their Fingers according to fo
many different Notes, and blow the wind out of their Mouths in fuch various Degrees.

The SHEPHERDESS begins with fome Preludes, by way of Trial, then cafts her Eyes upon
the SHEPHERD, as if fhe would give him Notice to be careful in exactly feconding of her; the
SHEPHERD looking at her, feconds her fo perfectly, that no Player on the German Flute, merely by
hearing, and without Notes, will be able to play after them.

Firft they play a March, then a Minuet, and after this a Polonefe; then a Prelude again in another
Key, which is followed by three fucceffive Minuets played by them together; towards the End of the laft
of which, the SHEPHERD continues feconding, while the SHEPHERDESS make the moft
charming Variations.

At laft they play an exceeding fine Air, of a pathetic Compofition, in a mafterly Manner.

Some will perhaps imagine that there is an Organ in thefe Figures; but the putting a Bit of Paper under
the Fingers of the Images will caufe the Tone to be falfe; and the ftopping of their Mouths prevent the
Flutes playing: which are Proofs whereby every one will be convinced of the contrary.

2. A moft celebrated *Royal* CABINET.

THIS incomparable Piece ftrikes its Beholders with Admiration. The Outfide reprefents a Bureau of
an half oval Form of Walnut-tree, adorned with gilt Borders and other Ornaments, inlaid with different
Sorts of Metal, Mother of Pearl, Ivory, and Wood of various Colours, in a Manner which furpaffes the Imagination, representing whole Hunting-matches, Men, Animals, Flowers, Perfpectives, Profpects, &c. fo
like and lively as Nature itfelf. It does not yield to the beft Painting; many of the Colours of the Wood
far exceed Oil-colours, and the Relief is fo delicate that the Eye can hardly believe the Levelnefs the Hand feels.

The whole Difpofition is a Compound of Art.

1. In the Middle there is a fmall Porch, with a Door; when this is opened, there appears a little Com-
mode with fix Drawers; the Door being fhut and opened again, there is to be feen a little Jewel-box, with
eighteen Drawers; immediately after this, a Profpect of twenty-fix Drawers; and at laft, after fhutting and
opening the Door, the Looking-glafs of a Lady's Toilet fhews itfelf.

2. Another very little Door being opened, there appears a minute Drawer, the pufhing in and pulling
out of which, will make difappear, and appear again, any thing that is put into it, as often as one pleafes.

3. Is a wonderfull Addition made to the Cabinet fince its laft Exhibition; the Extraordinary Effects of
which is too hard to defcribe, and if not feen wou'd exceed Belief.

4. One hundred and fix Drawers of different Sizes prefent themfelves at once in the whole CABINET.
The outfide Drawers come out as if it were by playing on a Harpfichord; for by touching one of the Keys a
Drawer comes out; and in this Manner they may all be made to come out.

5. At laft there appears a Table, of which no body could have the leaft Idea from whence it fhould come;
it makes of the CABINET a comodious Writing-Defk.

What has been faid is but a flight Sketch of this wonderful Work; for an ample Defcription of it would
require a whole Volume.

Mr. *Wilcke*, entreats the Nobility, Gentry, &c. not to delay examining this very extraordinary Curiofity, as his Stay in *England* will be but fhort; and begs Leave to affure them that he defires no further
favour than his Merit deferves.

☞ ADMITTANCE from Ten in the Morning till Eight in the Evening, at *One Shilling* each Perfon.

7¼ x 13¼

HIGHMAN PALATINE'S
"HUNDRED SURPRISING THINGS"
C. 1763

THIS STRAIGHTFORWARD BUT well-designed playbill is distinguished by an engaging woodcut of the German conjurer Highman Palatine. Glass in hand, he seems to beckon the audience to join him in a celebration of his mysteries. A single playing card on the ground may be a representation of the first effect he advertised: "If a Gentleman pitches on any Card, he will make the Card follow him three Yards; and where the Gentleman goes in the Room the Card will follow him."

For this engagement in Derby, Palatine offered various deceptions featuring rings and clothing: "If a gentleman has a ruffled Shirt, and any Person cuts a Piece of it, in less than five Minutes he will put it on as well as before. Any Gentleman in Company may take his Ring off his Finger and throw it out the Window, and he will tell the Gentleman that shall have the Ring in his Pocket." He began one especially elaborate and improbable effect by asking for any person to send for a half dozen eggs that he would then break in front of the company. In the first he would find a card previously selected and burned, from a second he produced hundreds of iron nails, and from the third a child's bed linen with a ruffled shirt. In other venues he would follow this startling presentation by performing with pigeons, wigs, oranges, and potatoes, and swallowing an assortment of knives, forks, punch ladles, and candle snuffers. He claimed to perform entirely "a-la-mode Italiano, and does not exhibit by the Help of Confederacy." His greatest effect here may have been a composite one, to be accomplished with astonishing speed: "150 surprizing

Tricks, and the Company will not be detain'd longer than an Hour and a half."

Highman Palatine was performing in France as early as 1753 and again in 1771. He went to England in 1763, probably shortly after the Peace of Paris, and Great Britain seems to have become his base of operations. On this playbill he offered a reward of ten pounds for any conjurer who could match his skill. Perhaps a misplaced confidence in his own ability tempted him later to raise the offer to a hundred guineas (like the conjurer Lane only a few years earlier; see no. 46).

In 1788, Palatine acquired a competitor in a man named Monsieur Boulevard, who had earlier performed at Bartholomew Fair with his "New Deceptions and Philosophical Experiments." He displayed effects with dice, doves, and pistols, and featured an illusion in which "Several Ladies and Gentlemen may put their Rings into a Glass on the Table, then cover the Glass with a Plate, and the same Rings shall dance in the Glass for several Minutes, and shall likewise answer any questions; after which the Rings shall be drawn out of the Glass by the Company." He concluded his show by highlighting the talents of the "Original Musical Infant," a four-year-old who played multiple selections on the pianoforte.

Boulevard challenged Palatine on slightly modified terms, and took him on for the evening's receipts at the Bush Tavern in Bristol. Boulevard, according to Milbourne Christopher, won the duel and ingratiated himself with the locals by donating the money to the Marine Society.

By Permission of the MAYOR of *DERBY*.

This is to give NOTICE, that

HIGHMAN PALATINE, a *High-German*,

Who does such Performances as never were done before, and will pay Ten Guineas to any Man who can do the like.

Will Perform at the *Old Assembly-Room* in *Irongate*, four Times in a Week, viz. *Monday*, *Tuesday*, *Wednesday*, and *Thursday*.

IF a Gentleman pitches on any Card, he will make the Card follow him three Yards; and where the Gentleman goes in the Room the Card will follow him. If a Gentleman has a ruffled Shirt, and any Person cuts a Piece of it, in less than five Minutes he will put it on as well as before.—Any Gentleman in Company may take his Ring off his Finger and throw it out of the Window, and he will tell the Gentleman that shall have the Ring in his Pocket.——Any Gentleman thinking of a Card may have the *Liberty* of burning the same after drawing it: Any Person sending for half a Dozen of Eggs, and after drawing either of them, may break the same in Presence of the Company when he will find, first, the Card he had before burn'd; second, one Hundred of Iron Shoe-Nails; third, a complete Parcel of Child-bed Things, made of Silk and Linnen, together with a Ruffle Shirt.—He mentions these four Things in particular. Likewise he will perform a Hundred surprizing Things one after another.

The whole Performance will consist of above 150 surprizing Tricks, and the Company will not be detain'd longer than an Hour and a half.

The Doors will be open'd at 7 o'Clock, and the Performances will begin exactly at half an Hour past Seven.

Prices, the first Seat 1 s. 6 d. the second 1 s. and Gallery 6 d.

6½ x 8⅛

PRICE'S FEATS OF HORSEMANSHIP

C. 1767

THE HARVARD THEATRE COLLECTION preserves a handsome engraving of Thomas Price on horseback surrounded by eight vignettes of his equestrian demonstration. While it is not surprising that one would cherish such an elaborate piece, the survival of the broadside featured here seems miraculous by comparison. Who kept this scrap of paper in lovely condition for almost two hundred and fifty years? About the size of an index card, it is an incunable of the circus.

In the years before Philip Astley assembled the elements that comprise the modern circus, a number of equestrians had already demonstrated remarkable riding skills. One of these was Thomas Price, a horseman of distinction, whose performance in Bristol in 1763 was advertised with these verses:

> Upright he stands, and swift as rapid Tides,
> With Ease at once—upon three horses rides:
> Now on a single Steed he scours the Plain,
> Flying dismounts—without the Dread of Pain
> And now as quick as Lightning mounts again.
> Between two horses now with wond'rous Speed;
> (His Feet in either Stirrup of each Steed)
> Lo! with impetuous Force he skims along,
> Admir'd by a numerous brilliant Throng.
> And now the wond'ring Spectators to please,
> He on the Horse's Backs lies down with Ease;
> Up in a moment, now on one foot stands,
> Holding the Bridle careless in his Hands:
> Now on his Head—he fill each Breast with Fire,
> And all pronounce him Matthews on the Wire.

In 1766 Price was in Islington, the section of London that was then the hotbed of equestrian activity. He performed in a field next to the famous Three Hats, a venue that earlier had featured a similar show by the horseman Thomas Johnson, "The Irish Tartar." Soon after, as shown on this bill, Price was at the equally renowned Dobney's Bowling Green, where Thomas Wildman would later direct swarms of bees while on horseback (see no. 42).

Citing royal patronage, Price offered "Original Feats of Horsemanship." He offered a series of springing maneuvers and flying leaps, and rode three horses simultaneously. For the finale, Price capped his performance by "riding a single Horse on full Gallop, standing on his Head on the Saddle, his Feet up-right in the Air, and discharging a Brace of Pistols at the same time." Price was also one of the first equestrian jugglers, spinning plates on the tops of walking sticks while riding around the ring.

Price and Sampson, a contemporary rival of great skill, were involved in an encounter of revenge and high drama. Price felt himself jilted by a horsewoman who subsequently married Sampson, and she was soon billed as the "first equestrienne" of the nascent circus. The couple proved a strong attraction and worthy competitors. Feigning friendship, Price lured Sampson, via drink and another woman, into a compromising situation. The woman blackmailed the foolish rider and ruined Sampson's reputation irreparably, while Price apparently retired with a fortune of £14,000.

Mr. PRICE's
Original Feats of HORSEMANSHIP,
(Which he exhibited before their MAJESTIES,)

Will be performed exactly at Six o'Clock, and continue every Evening during the Summer Season, (if the Weather permits) at the Prospect-House, known by the Name of Dobney's Bowling Green, Islington, Admittance One Shilling each.

I. HE makes his Horse go through several extraordinary as well as entertaining Performances

II. He rides on full Gallop, standing with one Foot on the Saddle.

III. He then rides full speed, takes up any thing from the Ground, or will ride for a considerable time, both his Hands sweeping the Ground all the while.

IV. Whilst the Horse is on full speed, he leaps from his Saddle, and springs over his Horse backward and forward several different times, discharging his Pistols at the same Instant.

V. He Gallops his Horse on three Leggs as he sits on the Saddle, holding the right Foot in his right Hand.

VI. He rides two Horses, one Foot in each Horse's inside Stirrup; likewise standing upright on the Saddles, or lying across them, his Head on one Horse and his Feet on the other; and in any of those positions he will take a flying leap over any height they are capable of clearing.

VII. Likewise several other agreeable performances on 2 or 3 Horses, too tedious to mention.

Lastly, He concludes his Performances with riding a single Horse on full Gallop, standing on his Head on the Saddle, his Feet upright in the Air, and discharging a Brace of Pistols at the same time. *N. B. Removed from the Three Hatts.* The doors to be open'd at Five, and Mr. *Price* mounts exactly at Six o'Clock.

DANIEL WILDMAN
EQUESTRIAN APIARIST

C. 1770

MAGICIANS TRADITIONALLY HAVE HAD a difficult time distinguishing themselves from their competitors. If a fellow suspends a woman in midair and successfully supervises her descent to terra firma, it is difficult for the public to appreciate the innovations or intricacies distinguishing that presentation from a similar form of levitation performed by another conjurer. It seems to me that this presents a challenge no other entertainer faces. We enjoy talented singers without expecting them to write their own material; we see production after production of the same operas and symphonies; but when more than one illusionist presents the same effect, it is harder to appreciate the magic of the performance. If a magician is a person with special powers, the very notion of magic is diminished as the number of persons with those powers increases.

Perhaps that is why Daniel Wildman, who advertised his "Dexterity and Deceptions" and performed some standard conjuring effects, like the decapitation of a hen, felt it necessary to vary his repertoire. In doing so he became one of the more innovative performers of the 1770s. Already accomplished as a horseman, he added his skills as a bee trainer to become the first and foremost equestrian apiarist.

In the early days of the modern circus, Wildman rode around the ring standing, with one foot in the saddle and the other on the neck of his mount while as many as five swarms of bees covered his face. Upon his command the "bee blindfold" parted and he was able to drink a salute from a glass of wine while still riding. He also showed his domination over the creatures by ordering them to alight on specific locations, such as the swords, canes, or hats of designated spectators.

The management of the bees was based on a "secret." Known as "caging the queen," the technique relied on isolating the queen bee and controlling her movements to direct the entire swarm. This method is explained in magic chapbooks well into the nineteenth century.

I have not been able to discover how Wildman learned his trade as a conjurer; his uncle Thomas was a well-known beekeeper and demonstrator and the author of a classic work on the subject. Daniel set up shop in London and sold his own brand of hive, which he claimed would yield three times the normal amount of honey. In Fraser's history of the subject he was called the "the first English professional beekeeping appliance maker."

The woodcut of the bees and hive shown here, and an identical cut on a different broadside issued shortly before he performed his act in France, are the only illustrations associated with Wildman that I have ever seen. Although not the first to control bees, Wildman was almost certainly the first to do so on horseback. He was so popular that he spawned imitators, including a German performer who took his name without permission.

In 1772, Wildman rode with Astley's Circus (see p. 60). His most famous disciple was Mrs. Astley. On the title page of the Dublin edition of *The Compleat Guide for the Management of Bees* (1774) is the imprint "Also, sold by Mrs. Astley, so well known for her great Command over the Bees." According to a contemporary description, she circled the ring on horseback with the insects covering her arms like a muff. Wildman's training and harvesting techniques were unchallenged, however, as this verse encomium attests:

> He with uncommon art and matchless skill
> Commands those insects who obey his will;
> With bees others cruel means employ,
> They take their honey and bees destroy;
> Wildman, humanely with ingenious ease
> He takes the honey but preserves the bees.

At WILDMAN's Exhibition Room,

Oppofite Southampton-ftreet, in the Strand,

By Defire of feveral of the Nobility and Gentry,

Mr. WILDMAN
WILL EXHIBIT,

This and every Day, at Twelve o'Clock in the Forenoon, precifely;

And as his Stay in London will be fhort, he will perform at Seven every Evening, as ufual.

At each Time he will difplay

All his amazing Performances and different Changes with the BEES.

To which will be added, his new invented and extraordinary

DEXTERITY and DECEPTIONS,

In a moft aftonifhing Manner,

Such as were never performed before by any other Perfon in this Kingdom.

Many different amazing Deceptions each Time.

The Room is warm and commodious, and will be illuminated with Wax Lights in the Evening.

FRONT SEATS Two Shillings, BACK SEATS One Shilling.

Places to be taken and Tickets to be had at the Exhibition Room.

A PRIVATE EXHIBITION may be had if defired.

N.B. *Fine Virgin Honey to be fold either in the Combs or out; alfo his new invented Hives, either for the Chamber or Garden, and any Quantity of Bees, from one Stock to one Hundred*

6³⁄₁₆ x 8⅝

CHARLES HUGHES
ASTLEY'S RIVAL

1772

CHARLES HUGHES, THE GREAT RIVAL of Philip Astley (see p. 60), once demonstrated trick riding in his employ. In 1772 he left to set up a new establishment in direct competition with his former boss. Hughes was a great rider, strong enough to carry an ox upon his back, extremely handsome, very ambitious, and possessed of a volatile temperament. In 1782, in partnership with the equally irascible Charles Dibdin, he launched a scheme to unite the ring and the stage and created "The Royal Circus and Philharmonic Academy," the first establishment to use the word circus in its modern sense. Hughes, quite independently of his partnership with the composer Dibdin, suffered various tribulations, and as his productions were frequently short-lived, advertisements and documents of his shows survive with much less frequency than those of Astley. This broadside, a seminal document of the nascent circus, is apparently unrecorded. It is distinguished by a number of attributes: its formidable size, in contrast to typical playbills of the day; its handsome overall design; charming woodcuts, in surprising quantity (twenty!); and the arresting application of red ink, not merely for rubrication or emphasis, but for the entire document.

In 1772, when this broadside was issued, Hughes published *The Compleat Horseman; or, the Art of Riding Made Easy, Illustrated by Rules Drawn From Nature and Confirmed by Experience with Directions to the Ladies to Sit Gracefully and Ride with Safety*. Nine of the smaller illustrations shown on the bill appear in this volume, of which only a few copies survive. The text, a rather dry affair, was taken from Jackson's

and Thompson's earlier equestrian works, without credit. Astley published a plagiarized version of *The Compleat Horseman*, which he called *The Modern Riding Master*, in 1775. The same year, Astley claimed authorship of a book called *Natural Magic*, which he lifted shamelessly from *The Conjurer Unmasked*, by Decremps. Both Astley and Hughes presented magic demonstrations in their spectaculars (the famous illusionist Breslaw performed with Hughes this very year), and their actions reveal that the usurpation of uncredited material, which was to blacken the name of the conjuring arts, also prevailed in the circus.

Another link between magic and the circus was the performance of the "Horse of Knowledge," advertised on this bill. In addition to his more cerebral accomplishments, we are told in a contemporary newspaper advertisement, the horse would "fetch and carry," fire a cannon, and deliver a whip from the ground to Mr. Hughes as he stood upright on his steed.

In addition to his own performance, Hughes featured the riding of his sister, Sobeiska Clementina; the equestrian team Mr. and Miss Huntley, an eight-year-old girl prodigy (who in addition to her own prowess rode while balanced on Hughes' head as he circled the ring at full gallop); and a version of the most important comic sketch of the early circus, "The Tailor's Ride to Brentford." The bill concludes with a dare, a reward of two hundred guineas for any rider who equaled Hughes' horsemanship. Apparently he was at the height of his powers, as he had previously offered only a hundred guineas in the same challenge.

The celebrated Sobiefka Clementina rides one, two, and three horfes, ftanding upright on the faddles full fpeed: fhe is the only one, of her fex, that ever exhibited on one, or three horfes.

A young Lady, only eight years old, rides two horfes on full fpeed, without any other affiftance than her own amazing courage and abilities.

An Englifh Tar exhibits without bridle, faddle, fore-ftay, or any other rigging.

Mr. and Mifs Huntley perform feveral furprizing feats of activity, fuch as throwing a fomerfet over two horfes, &c. too numerous to infert.

Hughes rides in fifty different attitudes that never were performed by any other horfeman; fuch as leaping over three horfes as they are on full fpeed, and leaping over two horfes as they leap a bar, three feet high: alfo leaps backwards and forwards fifty times over a fingle horfe, as the horfe is on full fpeed: rides with one foot on each fide the horfe's tail, and his back to the horfe's head, with forty other feats that never were performed but by himfelf.

Sobiefka Clementina takes leaps in different attitudes, ftanding in the ftirrups, like an ancient pretender to horfemanfhip.

Hughes exhibits his horfe of knowledge as ufual, being the only one in this metropolis that will fetch and carry, walk lame when ordered, &c. &c.

By particular defire, this evening, Hughes will exhibit and rehearfe that unparalleled piece, *The Englifh Warrior* on his road to France; with the Maccarony Taylor going to Paris for new modes and fafhions; alfo the Taylor and his Deputy to Brentford, in drefs and character.

Doors open at five, the diverfions of the Riding-School begins at fix, and Hughes's Horfemanfhip at half paft fix o'clock.

*** A commodious room for the Nobility, eighty feet long.

N.B. Any horfeman who can equal Hughes, or only one of his capital feats, let him make his appearance any evening this feafon, at Hughes's Riding-School, Black-Friars Bridge, and perform them, or any one of them, and he fhall receive a premium of 100 Guineas.

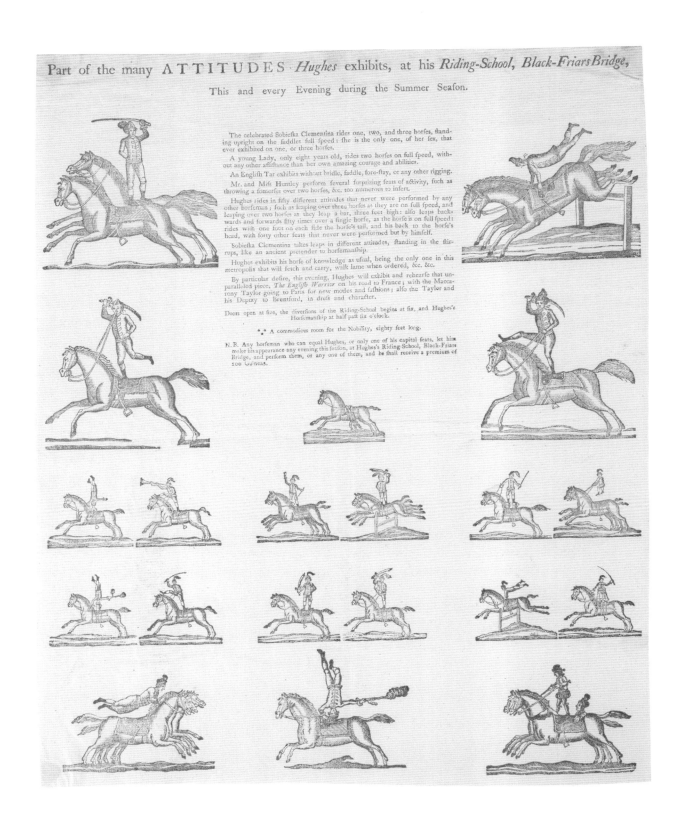

MR. LANE
FAIRGROUND SHOWMAN

C. 1786

THIS BROADSIDE FOR THE MAGICIAN Lane was produced for his appearance at Bartholomew Fair. Although the copy was frequently altered in the half dozen or so advertisements I have seen for his shows, the illustration never varied. He is always depicted in his fashionable feathered head-dress, surrounded by the tools of his trade: playing cards, coins, a pocket watch, two boxes containing numbered blocks for an experiment he called "Unparalleled Sympathetic Figures," and a live bird, presumably hatched from an egg in an experiment called "Palingenesia, or Regeneration" (see p. 124).

Lane was a popular entertainer at British fairs in the last two decades of the eighteenth century. He called himself "His Majesty's Conjurer" or "First Conjurer to the King"— not, as can well be imagined, an exclusive billing. This broadside, probably distributed in 1786, lists five major effects. He also challenges anyone to duplicate his show for a hundred guineas, and offers to perform at a private showing on an hour's notice.

My favorite title for a Lane illusion is "The Enchanted Communicative Tabulum." This was an early experiment in what we would now call telepathy. One person from the audience was asked to fix his thoughts on a number that another spectator "will conceive in his own mind without a single word being spoken by Mr. Lane, or either of the parties to each other." In 1794 Lane presented his "Sagacious Swan, the only one in England for forty years; the last was shewn at Exeter Change, London; this little inanimate bird is seen a-float on the basin of water; a card is drawn or an hour thought on, when this beautiful Swan will seem to hesitate for a minute, and then she will swim to tell the card or discover the thoughts to the great surprise of all present."

Lane was a droll fellow, and he offered for a show at Peckham Fair to "drive about forty twelve-penny nails into any gentleman's breech, place him in a loadstone chair, and draw them out without the least pain! He is in short, the most wonderful of all the wonderful creatures the world ever wondered at." This hyperbole alludes to a famous parody of a magic performance attributed to Jonathan Swift, or to his friend Dr. Sheridan, entitled, "Wonder of all the Wonders that ever the World Wondered At." He also offered a poetic broadside with multiple verses, each capped by the refrain: "Oh rare Lane, Cockalorum for Lane, well done Lane, you are the man." This is the last stanza:

> There's a lady in London, this is very true,
> Would give fifty pounds Lane's performance to view
> If you want for to know where the lady to find
> She lives in St. Giles, and she is stone-blind.

In later years Lane, who performed until at least 1794, combined his entertainments with the feats of the famous slack-wire artist Mr. Wilkinson. Miss Lane, presumably our subject's daughter, performed on the tight rope. A few years later a Mr. Gregory presented "Dexterity of Hand" and "The Wonderful Dog of Knowledge," billing himself as "Successor to the Late Mr. Lane, The Real King's Conjurer."

Grand Exhibition, by Mr. LANE firſt Performer to the KING*

In the Great Room, at No. 10, on the Pavement, Weſt-Smithfield, during the Fair.

To begin each Day at Twelve o'Clock. ——Firſt Seats 6d. Back Seats 3d.

Mr. LANE will give one hundred Guineas to any one that will perform the like, as he confeſſedly ſtands as a performer unrivalled by any other either Native or Foreigner.—The Cut repreſents ſome of the Performances. READ therefore and JUDGE.

I.   His enchanted Sciatoricon.

BEING the only one in the known world. This wonderful machine (by means of an inviſible agent,) will diſcover to the company the exact time of the day or night, by any propoſed watch, though the watch may be in a gentleman's pocket, or five miles diſtant if required ; it alſo points out the colour of any lady or gentleman's clothes, by the wearer only touching it with his finger : and is further poſſeſſed of ſuch occult qualities as to diſcover the thoughts of one perſon to another, even at an unlimited diſtance.

II.   The operation Palingeneſia, or Regeneration.

Any perſon in the company ſending for a couple of eggs, may take the choice of them, and the egg being broke, produces a living bird of the ſpecies deſired, which in half a minute receives its full plumage, takes wings and flies away. The other egg being put into a gentleman's hat, will, at the requeſt of the company, leap from thence into any other perſon's that is preſent, and will continue to leap from one hat to another, to the number of twenty different ones, if required.

III.   His unparallelled Sympathetical Figures.

Whereby the great force and power of ſympathy is diſplayed by an operation with two boxes, containing an equal number of figures, which are capable of being varied 24 different ways. The two boxes of figures being put on a table, any perſon may take one of them into another room, or wherever he pleaſes, and range the figures therein in what manner he thinks proper ; the figures in the other box, without any perſon touching them, will immediately form themſelves into ſuch order as exactly to correſpond with the others ; this they will do, though altered a hundred different times, to the aſtoniſhment of every beholder.

IV.   His Magical   Tea Caddie.

This of all other curioſities is well worthy the attention of the curious, being the firſt that has appeared in public. Any perſon in company may take a pack of cards, and take a card out ever ſo privately, and put it in the cheſt in the ſight of thoſe preſent, and lock the caddie, and when opened again, to their great ſurpriſe, the card that was put in will be gone to another part of the room ; the card is then put into the pack again, and any perſon may hold the cards that pleaſes, when the performer will command the card back into the cadie without touching the card or the cheſt all the time.

V   His Magical Card Deceptions.

Which are too numerous to attempt a deſcription of, ſuffice it to ſay, that moſt of them are the product of his own invention, and never attempted by any but himſelf. He mentions theſe five articles in particular, but will perform above one hundred others, therefore it is deſired that what is here ſaid of his performance may not paſs for an account of the whole, but only what is thought neceſſary for the readers to form ſome idea thereof.

⁎   A Private Performance may be had at one hour's Notice.

THE MONSTROUS CRAWS

1787

THIS BROADSIDE ANNOUNCES the arrival of two women and a man, extraordinary human specimens, who have made their way to London from an unnamed location in South America. They were distinguished physically by their small stature (they were under four feet tall) and by the unusual excrescences extending from their chins. These goiters gave rise to their billing as "The Monstrous Craws."

They were exhibited at Mr. Beckett's shop in the Haymarket. Beckett, a trunk maker, was apparently quite fond of anomalous attractions, as he also featured, on various occasions, a learned goose and a woman, Margery Gasson, who was said to have been pregnant for six and one-half years. I have been unable to account for his interest in such exhibitions, or for that matter, the similar preoccupation of Mr. Hatch, another trunk maker, who exhibited attractions such as a stone-eating man (see p. 50). The promoters of the Craws supplied tempting exotica: that the trio hailed from an uncharted part of South America, and that they were an unknown species. Their skin, dark olive at the time of their discovery, changed, in a transformation like that of a modern pop star, "astonishingly, by degrees...to the colour of that of Europeans."

They were exhibited to the nobility, including a showing at Windsor Castle, and adopted for a caricature in 1787 by James Gillray, who most unflatteringly pictured King George III with his wife and son as "The Monstrous Craws, at the New Coalition Feast." A later caricature, by Thomas Rowlandson, depicted only a single Craw.

This bill features a prudent but appealing selection of roman types and a lovely woodcut in which the gentleman sports an umbrella. I have another playbill that extols the virtues of the Craws with language almost identical to the claims of this piece. There the dramatis personae are two men and a woman, and that same configuration appeared in the Royal Circus under the patronage of Charles Hughes in 1787 (see p. 40).

In a newspaper account of October 20, Hughes indignantly reported the trio's abduction: "the craws having early this morning made their escape from the set of villains, who had forcibly taken them from their apartments at the Circus, during the night of the 16th they are again returned to him to implore his protection from the wretches, who not content with realizing immense sums by them, in a free country, wished to treat and confine rational Human Beings like mere brute beasts, as they had before done with impunity, and in defiance of the law." Hughes proudly announced their reinstatement at the circus and promised that "the Female Craw, particularly, will perform several feats on one, two and three Horses." This poem appeared shortly after the kidnapping.

THE MONSTROUS CRAW ON HORSEBACK
AT THE ROYAL CIRCUS, ST. GEORGE'S FIELDS

As novelty pleases the great and the small,
A new exhibition attention must call;
The Monstrous Craw will the matter decide
At the Circus each night she on horseback will ride.

She will gallop and trot as the Horse keeps its pace,
And ride like a Craw with a monstrous gate;
To please every fancy, if one will not do,
She will mount up again, and will ride upon two.

To say any more wou'd be vain and absurd;
If you see, you'll believe, and will then take my word;
To see and believe is a very old law,
And this will be prov'd by the Monstrous Craw.

To the Nobility, Gentry, and the Curious for inspecting most
Extraordinary Human Beings, of the wild Species born.

Just Arrived from Abroad,

And to be Seen at Mr. Becket's, *Trunk Maker*, No. 31,
HAY-MARKET,

From Ten o'Clock in the Morning, till Nine in the Evening,

Three Wonderful Phœnomena,

Wild Born, of the Human Species:

THESE are Two Females and a Male, of a very SMALL STATURE,
being little less or more than *Four Feet High*;

Each with a Monstrous C R A W

under the Throat, containing within, some Three, some Four, some Five
BALLS or **GLANDS**, more or less big than an Egg each of them, and which
play upwards and downwards, and all ways in their *Craws*, according as incited
and forced, either by their Speaking, or Laughing. These Three

Most wonderful wild born Human Beings,

whose Country, Language, and Native Customs are yet unknown to all Mankind, it is supposed started in some Canoes from their Native Place (believed
to be some still unknown remote Land of South America) and being after
Wrecked, were picked up by a Spanish Vessel, which in a violent Storm,
was also lost off Trieste, in Italy, when these Three People, and another of the
same kind, since Dead, were providentially saved from perishing; though, it
is imagined, there were more on board of their Species.—At that period they
were of a dark Olive Complexion, but which has astonishingly, by degrees,
changed to the colour of that of Europeans.

These Three *truly-surprising* Beings, have attracted to themselves the most
minute Attention, and great Admiration of all the Princes, celebrated Ana-
tomists, and Naturalists, to whom they have been presented in Europe, for
their Rare, and yet Unknown Species; and not less indeed, for their most
apparent and surprising Happiness, and Content among themselves; most
endearing Tractableness and respectful demeanour towards all Strangers, as
well for their unparallel'd and natural, chearful, lively, and merry Disposition,
Singing and Dancing (in their most extraordinary Way,) at the will and
pleasure of the Company.

Admittance, Two Shillings Each:—Children Half price.

THE STONE EATER

1788

FAME IS UNPREDICTABLE AS WELL as fleeting. Even the most impassioned fans of unusual entertainment would be hard pressed to comprehend the singular notoriety of an attraction devoted to the digestion of pebbles. As this neatly executed, modest bill printed by J. Denew in London in 1788 attests, the Stone Eater was not identified by name. Nevertheless, he achieved genuine celebrity from his diet of stones and flints, which, as this broadside promises, he "Gnaws, Crunches and Reduces…to the smallest Pieces, at the same time, by striking him on the Stomach, the STONES, resound as in a Sack." Here you have it all—there was no variation on the weekends, no grand finale. At every meal, at every performance, he ate stones.

The amount of press he generated is substantial and surprising. At its most pretentious it portrayed the Stone Eater as one whose very existence overturned the laws of nature and reason. What prompts exegesis, of course, is not so much that he ate stones, but that he ate *only* stones.

As I chronicled in my *Learned Pigs & Fireproof Women*, this Stone Eater's widening popularity elicited accounts of his precursors' feats in the press, and copycat successors appeared on the stage. I have recently uncovered the description of a seventeenth-century Londoner who was also distinguished for this diet, identified only as a "Dwarfish Corn-Cutter." He roamed the street in search of troubled feet but would at any time, upon receipt of his fee—sixpence and a pot of ale—swallow twenty pebbles. A contemporary, Thomas Gobsill, provided the only rationale with which I am familiar for consuming such a diet. Tortured with wind, Gobsill was advised to swallow round white pebbles. According to the well-known physician Sir Charles Hall, he followed this regimen to the point of extreme discomfort for most of his life. The procedure, it should be acknowledged, did improve his flatulence.

In the eleventh century a fellow digested three pounds of stones, with no ill effect, in Prague. But the most famous forerunner of our subject is Francis Battalia. He was interviewed by the physician John Bulwer, who saw him swallow a spoonful of pebbles followed by a beer chaser. Bulwer recorded in his *Anthropometamorphosis: Man Transform'd; or the Artificiall Changling* (1653) that Batallia was said to have been born with two stones in one hand and one stone in the other. He refused his mother's breast and existed from that time forth on his singular diet, augmented only by tobacco and beer. He grew strong enough to be a soldier. Battalia was commemorated as the "Roman Youth" in an engraving by Wenceslaus Hollar in 1641.

Our Stone Eater ate his way to the top of his chosen profession until at least October 1790, the date recorded for his appearance at the felicitously chosen venue of Stone Hall in York. He was immortalized on the stage in the *Stone-Eater's Song* by John O'Keefe, in caricature when King George III was pictured as "The Surprising Stone Eater" in a political satire by William Dent in 1788, and at Joseph Merlin's Mechanical Museum, where an automaton figure in his likeness swallowed stones on command.

22d March, 1788.

Stone Eater.
Wonderful and Extraordinary Phænomenon.

AT the Moment when Philosophers are most distinguished and revered for their Knowledge, and consulted as Oracles, who can interpret all Causes from Effects, and explain the unchangeable Laws of Nature,—Comes this same Nature, and by a single Act o'erturns their Systems in the astonishing Faculty of a Man who Eats and Digests STONES and FLINTS.

Since the above Assertion has staggered the Belief of all who have not had ocular Demonstrations, the Curious are invited to witness the Fact. In the Presence of any Spectator, he Eats the hardest FLINTS that may be offered him; Cracks them with his Teeth like Nuts; Gnaws, Crunches, and Reduces them to the smallest Pieces; at the same Time, by striking him on the Stomach, the STONES resound as in a Sack.

To be seen This and every Day from *Eleven o'Clock in the Morning* till *Four* in the *Afternoon,* at the

GREAT ROOM,
GLOBE TAVERN,
Corner of CRAVEN STREET, STRAND.

ADMITTANCE, HALF-a-CROWN.

Such Persons as please may bring STONES with them.

☞ Door for Carrriages in Craven Street.

Printed by J. DENEW, No. 109, Wardour Street, near Oxford Street.

7¼ x 8⅞

THE MERMAID
"WONDER OF WONDERS"
1789

LOGIC DICTATES THAT IF ONE has seen a mermaid, one has been deceived. One may have seen a fabrication, an actual animal (such as a sea lion, dugong, or manatee) that under certain conditions may appear to be half woman and half fish, or a magician's illusion: a girl in a mermaid costume in a tank, swimming in the company of live fish.

One of the most famous of all attractions was P. T. Barnum's exhibition of the Feejee Mermaid. In 1842, under the auspicious of a British naturalist known as Dr. Griffin, Barnum presented her in New York. When other scientists attacked the exhibition's veracity Barnum responded with advertisements headlined, "Who is to decide when doctors disagree?" Barnum did not reveal that his "doctor," who lectured about the mermaid's live capture off the coast of Fiji, was actually his attorney, Levi Lyman (who also helped promote the Joice Heth imposition; see p. 102). When spectators examined the three-foot-long "mermaid," they saw a most unappealing amalgam of mammal and fish ingeniously sewn together. In spite of frequent protests, including that of Herman Melville in his haunting novel *Mardi*, Barnum's marketing skills persuaded thousands to attend the exhibition. Lest we consider ourselves immune from such appeals, it should be noted that the duck-billed platypus, a real but exotic beast, was once viewed as a fraudulent hybrid.

But Barnum was far from the first showman to present a mermaid. One of the most enduring and universal creatures of myth and legend, the mermaid was a long-established icon in numerous cultures and countries. Medieval manuscripts portrayed peculiar mermaidlike creatures, and Aldrovandi illustrated a seductive version of the half woman, half fish in the seventeenth century. George Cruikshank illustrated a frightening dried and sewn specimen for the publisher Fairburn in 1822. In my files I have accounts of the exhibition of these creatures in every decade from the 1730s to the Barnum show over a hundred years later. Mermaids and mermen were so frequently encountered on stage that a cottage industry was spawned in Japan, where "fisherman found the traffic in mermaids an invaluable means of supplementing their income.... First the mermaid itself was artfully manufactured out of a monkey and a fish. Fishermen would then give out that the creature had been taken alive in their nets, but had shortly afterwards died." In Europe, the trade in such fabrications dated to the sixteenth century.

The woodcut of the mermaid pictured here, for a show at the shop of a London undertaker in 1789, is identical to one that appeared on an earlier eighteenth-century broadside. The example in this playbill, handsomely laid out and set in Baskerville, is altogether more attractive than my earlier version.

Details given of her capture are consistent with a number of contemporary accounts. Here are the particulars: The mermaid was snared alive in 1764 (other versions say 1774) in the Gulf of Stanchio in the Aegean Sea. The merchant captain who captured her attested that the preserved specimen on exhibition "is as perfect at this very moment as when alive." It had a feminine face and fine light blue eyes, a full neck and well-shaped chin, and small teeth, enclosed within thin lips but with rounded edges, "like that of a cod-fish." Its ears, however, resembled an eel's, and behind them were gills for respiration. Its most conspicuous feature was a "beautiful membrane of fin from the temple, gradually diminishing till it ends pyramidically, forming a fore-top like that of a lady's head dress." The body, like the lips, once again is mindful of the codfish. This bill specifically commends the creature's "sweet and melodious voice." According to the *Encyclopaedia Metropolitana*, this "Mermaid was proved to be manufactured chiefly out of the skin of the Angle Shark; and the exhibitor, after making a considerable sum of money, was punished as a rogue and a vagabond."

Wonder of Wonders !!!

1789
or 90

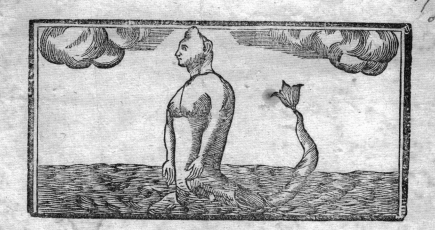

WHEREAS many have imagined that the HISTORY of MERMAIDS, mentioned by the Authors of Voyages, is fabulous, and only introduced as the "Tale of a Traveller;" there is now in Town an opportunity for the Nobility, Gentry, &c. to have an occular demonstration of its reality, in a convenient room, NO. 7, Broad court, Bow street, Covent Garden, at Mr. ELLIOT's, Carpenter and Undertaker.

This Curious and Surprising Nymph, even the QUEEN of the SEA-FISHES, was taken in the year 1764, in the Gulph of Stanchio, on board of a merchantman, called the GOOD LUCK, Captain FORTIER. It is exactly three feet in length, and in form like a Woman from the head down to the lower part of the waist, and half a Fish from thence downwards, and is as perfect at this very moment as when alive, standing in the same position as when it rises at sea between wind and water, in order to make resound the neighbouring echoes of the Archipelago with her sweet and melodious voice. It is to be seen from Ten in the Morning till dusk in the evening.

ADMITTANCE ONE SHILLING.

WM. POWERS

"FEATS OF ACTIVITY"

1789

THIS FOURTEEN-YEAR-OLD LAD from London offered a varied repertoire of stunts for his performance at a coffee house in Baltimore in 1789. He displayed an impressive combination of acrobatics, equilibristics, and contortions.

Powers mastered an early form of gymnastic floor exercises: springing, somersaults, and walking on his hands. He performed a number of variants on the hornpipe by balancing his head on the finial of a chair and dancing with his legs in the air; for a diversion he would provide his own percussion by tapping his feet against his head. He also offered imitations of a porpoise tumbling in the sea.

Powers was an accomplished "posture-master," an early term for what we would today call a contortionist, a very popular act in the eighteenth century. Two especially impressive stunts are described here: "He will lay down a snuff-box in front of his feet, and will throw his head backwards between his legs, and put his nose, two great toes, and thumbs, all in the snuff-box together"; and "He will stick two pins in the stage in front of his feet, throw his head backwards between his legs, and take up the two pins, one with each eye-lid."

As improbable as all this sounds, it was accompanied by a confident precursor of the money-back guarantee: "If the performance is not done agreeable to the above, the money will be returned before any person leaves the room."

Powers proved to be a most elusive subject until I found an almost identical program for a performance in Jamaica by a "William Powers Knight, lately of Charleston in America."

Clearly our fellow, he appeared, according to a newspaper cutting, in August 1791 at Bradley's Tavern in Montego Bay. There is no mention of his age or British origin, but there were a few variations from his Baltimore bill: He no longer provided an imitation of a porpoise, and stunts previously performed with a "copper" now incorporated quarter dollars. In Baltimore he placed a coin on his toes and then threw his feet backward and forward over his head several times without dislodging the money; here he has improved the stunt by doing it with four pieces of change.

In both cities the price of admission was listed in pounds sterling rather than dollars, but in Jamaica there was an unusual two-tiered tariff: Ladies and Gentleman were charged five shillings and "Children and People of Colour," three shillings and sixpence.

The Powers broadside was struck in Baltimore by Samuel and John Adams on October 26, 1789. While one would love to impute political aspirations to the printers, they appear to have had little in common with their illustrious namesakes. They were natives of Wilmington, Delaware, who opened a branch of their business in Baltimore in 1789. They advertised, "most efforts shall be exerted to merit the approbation and favour of their employers, and the public in general.—Hand-bills, advertisements, all kind of blank-work, &c. done expeditiously, with care and on the Most Reason-able Terms." This playbill seems to be one of the first productions from the new concern, and it is otherwise unrecorded.

By Permission.

Wm. Powers,

A Lad of only 14 Years of Age, lately arrived from LON-
DON, will perform a Variety of very extraordinary

Feats of Activity,

*On Wednesday Evening, the 28th inst. The Performance to begin at Se-
ven o'Clock. He will likewise perform at the same Hour on Thursday,
Friday and Saturday Evenings---every Evening there will be a Number
of new Feats.---The Performance will be at the* Old Coffee-House, *lately kept by Mr.* De Witt ; *unoccupied.*

1. HE will go a row of fore springs and back springs.

2. He will stick two pins in the stage in front of his feet, throw
his head backwards between his legs, and take up the two pins, one
with each eye-lid.

3. He will lay down a snuff-box in front of his feet, and will throw
his head backwards between his legs, and put his nose, two great toes
and thumbs, all in the snuff-box together.

4. He will stand on his head on the small knob of a chair, with his
heels up, and dance a hornpipe.

5. He will lay a copper on his foot, throw both feet backward and
forward over his head several times, and never drop the copper.

6. He will lay his left foot on his right shoulder, and let a strong
man take him by his right hand, and another take him by his left foot,
and lift him up from the stage, when he will throw his body round, backward and forward several times, without his hand or leg turning in the
men's hands.

7. He will lay down a copper on the stage behind him, throw his
head backward, and take it up with his mouth, without any use of his
hands.

8. He dances a hornpipe with both feet on the crown of his head.

9. He walks on his hands with both feet under his arms.

10. He shews, with great activity, how a porpus tumbles in the sea.

He, besides these, performs *a variety of feats* too tedious to
mention.---If the performance is not done agreeable to the above, the
money will be returned before any person leaves the room.

⁂ Tickets may be had at Mr. *De Witt*'s, where Mr. *Francis Smith*
lately lived, the second door below the *Old Coffee-House,* and at the
place of performance.------Price for ladies and gentlemen, 2/6 each :
children, 1/6 each.

Baltimore, October 26, 1789.

Baltimore : Printed by Samuel *and* John Adams.

THE FIRST ELEPHANT IN AMERICA

1797

TO HAVE "SEEN THE ELEPHANT" was nineteenth-century slang for having experienced the grittiness of life. The expression was particularly applied to those intrepid folk who prospected for gold or otherwise sought adventure in California in 1849. The fantasy writer Avram Davidson penned a tale called *The Man Who Sees the Elephant* (1971) about a gullible Quaker farmer who, relying on information provided in a broadside, makes a pilgrimage to view the legendary behemoth in the summer of "Eighteen Hundred and Froze to Death." The farmer's objective is amusingly unrequited, but had anyone seen a real elephant in America early in the nineteenth century he might have gazed upon the subject of the illustration here displayed.

This bill advertises the first elephant exhibited in the new land. It was transported from India and arrived in New York on April 13, 1796. The ship's captain, Jacob Crowninshield, made a neat profit. He paid $450 for the animal and sold it for $10,000 to a Welshman. But this too was a shrewd investment, as the elephant was exhibited to paying customers all over the eastern seaboard for a number of years.

The arrival of an elephant on these shores was significant enough to be reported in many newspapers. According to a Philadelphia paper, our attraction "possesses the adroitness of the beaver, the intelligence of the ape, and the fidelity of the dog. He is the largest of the quadrupeds; the earth trembles under his feet. He has the power of tearing up the largest trees and yet is tractable to those who use him well."

This broadside, printed by Carter and Wilkinson in Providence in June 1797, was issued in both illustrated and unillustrated variants. Broadsides also exist for the elephant's appearances in Boston, Newburyport, and Salem during the same summer.

Described here as four years old and weighing about three thousand pounds, the elephant is praised for his size, spirit, appetite, loyalty, and intelligence. His predilection for strong potables is also noted: He "drinks all Kinds of spirituous Liquors; some Days he has drank 30 Bottles of Porter." He pleased onlookers by uncorking the bottles with his trunk. The only negative press generated by our subject was a specific warning not to approach the animal with important documents: "The Elephant having destroyed many Papers of Consequence, it is recommended to Visitors not to come near him with such Papers."

Although he is always described as a male, *he* was a *she*. As the Reverend William Bentley precisely noted in his diary after seeing the pachyderm in Salem on August 29, 1797: "It is female & teats appeared just behind the fore-legs." As no reliable records exist for her after 1799, there is some confusion about her later life and demise. Two others of her species soon landed on these shores, and these beasts are sometimes taken for one another. These three pioneers were followed by many of their compatriots, as elephants soon became a staple feature of the burgeoning menagerie and circus trades.

THE
ELEPHANT,

ACCORDING to the Account of the celebrated BUFFON, is the moſt reſpectable Animal in the World. In Size he ſurpaſſes all other terreſtrial Creatures; and, by his Intelligence, he makes as near an Approach to Man, as Matter can approach Spirit. A ſufficient Proof that there is not too much ſaid of the Knowledge of this Animal is, that the Proprietor having been abſent for ten Weeks, the Moment he arrived at the Door of his Apartment, and ſpoke to the Keeper, the Animal's Knowledge was beyond any Doubt confirmed by the Cries he uttered forth, till his Friend came within Reach of his Trunk, with which he careſſed him, to the Aſtoniſhment of all thoſe who ſaw him. This moſt curious and ſurprizing Animal is juſt arrived from *Philadelphia*, on his Way to *Boſton*.—He will juſt ſtay to give the Citizens of *Providence* an Opportunity to ſee him. He is only four Years old, and weighs about 3000 Weight, but will not have come to his full Growth till he ſhall be between 30 and 40 Years old. He meaſures from the End of his Trunk to the Tip of his Tail 15 Feet 8 Inches, round the Body 10 Feet 6 Inches, round his Head 7 Feet 2 Inches, round his Leg, above the Knee, 3 Feet 3 Inches; round his Ankle 2 Feet 2 Inches. He eats 130 Weight a Day, and drinks all Kinds of ſpirituous Liquors; ſome Days he has drank 30 Bottles of Porter, drawing the Corks with his Trunk. He is ſo tame that he travels looſe, and has never attempted to hurt any one. He appeared on the Stage, at the new Theatre in *Philadelphia*, to the great Satisfaction of a reſpectable Audience.

☞ The Elephant having deſtroyed many Papers of Conſequence, it is recommended to Viſitors not to come near him with ſuch Papers.

⁎ A Place is fitted up for him (ſuitable to receive genteel Company) in a Store back of the Coffee-Houſe; where he will remain till the 8th of *July* only, as he is to be at *Cambridge* at the approaching Commencement.

Admittance, One Quarter of a Dollar—Children, One Eighth of a Dollar.

Providence, June 27, 1797.

Printed by CARTER and WILKINSON.

HADDOCK'S ANDROIDES

C. 1798

AT THE END OF THE EIGHTEENTH CENTURY one of the best-known exhibitors of automata in England was Mr. Haddock. This playbill for his appearance in London included a stylized cut of the telegraph that was to become a kind of trademark for Haddock, who fifteen years after this appearance in London was still using it in provincial advertisements for his show.

This telegraph, unlike the invention of S. B. Morse, used a method of communication based on a system of semaphore, originated by Claude Chappe, a Frenchman, in 1792. Haddock constructed a telegraph house with a seated mechanical operator who displayed the various signals. Haddock's other attractions included an automaton mind-reader in Scottish Highland dress who would strike his shield with his sword to calculate time or various arithmetical problems; "The New Orthographer," in the guise of a young girl who would sit at a table and spell any word selected by the audience; and a "Liquor Merchant," who would stand by a cask and deliver any of sixteen requested beverages.

Although there were even earlier automaton bartenders, the magical distribution of drinks or confections became a staple of the conjuring trade well into the nineteenth century. Its most impressive reincarnation was in the hands of the great French magician Jean Eugene Robert-Houdin, who presented his pastry cook, "The Patissier of the Palais Royal." The mechanical baker not only presented the audience with an assortment of buns and bonbons but also revealed a ring, borrowed from a spectator, baked within a lovely petit four.

Robert-Houdin also created an impressive writing automaton. Mechanical exhibitions often featured figures that could draw or pen phrases. Haddock's "Writing Automaton" was a mechanical boy about the size of a five-year-old who would draw pictures of a lion, tiger, elephant, camel, bear, horse or stag, and "write any word, words, or figures in a round legible hand." The accompanying poem is an actual specimen produced by the figure:

> Unerring is my hand tho' small
> May I not add with truth
> I do my best to please you all:
> Encourage then my Youth.

Haddock's figures remained before the public for decades. When his successor Thomas Weeks died, more than thirty-five years later, the Androides were put on the auction block with this explanation:

This exhibition, the invention of the late Mr. Haddock, was exhibited with the greatest success some years back, in Norfolk Street, Strand, to very crowded audiences. It consists of a number of small figures, and others the size of life, which go through a series of amusing performances; the whole of which is moved by an invisible agent.

For Three Weeks only.

Tele- graph,

EXHIBITED UPON   MECHANICAL PRINCIPLES,

By an   AUTOMATON FIGURE,

AT   THE

ANDROIDES,

Nº 38, NORFOLK STREET, *Strand,*

Opens every Day at Half-paſt Twelve o'Clock, and begins at One ; and Opens every
Evening at Half paſt Seven, and begins at Eight.

BOXES TWO SHILLINGS,———GALLERY ONE SHILLING.

THE LATE VICTORY

Over the DUTCH might, in ſome Meaſure, be attributed to the expeditious Mode of conveying In-
telligence by the TELEGRAPH ; for, on the Arrival of the Lugger with Information that the
DUTCH FLEET were out, the Account was immediately ſent up to *London* by the Telegraph, and in
Five Minutes Orders were returned for

The Gallant Admiral Duncan

To proceed after them with all Expedition ; which Orders he could not have received any other Way
(even by Expreſs) in leſs than Two Days, when perhaps it would have been too late to overtake them.

This Piece of Mechaniſm repreſents the Model of that on the Admiralty, with the Cabin underneath,
where the Officer ſits to work it ; which, by the Combination of Six Swivel Boards, can Spell any
Word, or enumerate any Number of Figures, excluſive of ſeveral occaſional Signals adapted for the Pur-
poſe. Deſcription of the Signals are as follows.

TELEGRAPHIC DICTIONARY.

[Alphabetical Signals.]			[Numerical Signals.]					[Occaſional Signals]		Signals.
Nº.	Let.	Combinat.	No.	Fig.	Combinations.	No.	Combinations.			
1	a	1	25	1	1, 2, 6	35	2, 4, 5	————		To
2	b	2	26	2	1, 3, 4	36	2, 4, 6	————		From
3	c	3	27	3	1, 3, 5	37	2, 5, 6	————		Captain
4	d	4	28	4	1, 3, 6	38	3, 4, 5	————		North
5	e	5	29	5	1, 4, 5	39	3, 4, 6	————		South
6	f	6	30	6	1, 4, 6	40	3, 5, 6	————		Eaſt
7	g	1, 2	31	7	1, 5, 6	41	4, 5, 6	————		Weſt
8	h	1, 3	32	8	2, 3, 4	42	1, 2, 3, 4			Fog
9	i	1, 4	33	9	2, 3, 5	43	1, 2, 3, 5			Arrived
10	k	1, 5	34	0	2, 3, 6	44	1, 2, 3, 6			Sailed
11	l	1, 6				45	1, 2, 4, 5			Convoy
12	m	2, 3				46	1, 2, 4, 6			Packet
13	n	2, 4				47	1, 2, 5, 6			Ship of the Line
14	o	2, 5				48	1, 3, 4, 5			Court Martial
15	p	2, 6				49	1, 3, 4, 6			Fleet
16	q	3, 4				50	1, 3, 5, 6			Sea
17	r	3, 5				51	1, 4, 5, 6			Put back
18	s	3, 6				52	2, 3, 4, 5			Sail
19	t	4, 5				53	2, 3, 4, 6			Execution
20	u	4, 6				54	2, 3, 5, 6			Firſt fair Wind
21	w	5, 6				55	2, 4, 5, 6			Guns
22	x	1, 2, 3				56	3, 4, 5, 6			Wind
23	y	1, 2, 4				57	1, 2, 3, 4, 5			Tranſports
24	z	1, 2, 5				58	1, 2, 3, 4, 6			Commander
						59	1, 2, 3, 5, 6			Port-Admiral
						60	1, 2, 4, 5, 6			Vice Admiral
						61	1, 3, 4, 5, 6			Rear Admiral
						62	2, 3, 4, 5, 6			Admiral
						63	1, 2, 3, 4, 5, 6			Prepare for Signal between Sentence

Small MODELS of the FRENCH TELEGRAPHS now in Uſe;—one between *Paris* and *Liſle*, and the other
between *Paris* and *Landau*, will be exhibited alſo. The other much-admired Pieces of Mechaniſm are as follow :

THE NEW ORTHOGRAPHER,

A Figure about Three Feet high, repreſenting a Female Child, which will be brought to a Table where an
Alphabet is placed, on which it will Spell any given Word.

THE WRITING AUTOMATON,

About the Size of a Boy of Five Years old, will be alſo brought to a Table, and ſet to Write any Word, Words, or
Figures, in a round legible Hand.

THE FRUITERY,

At the Gate of which the PORTER ſtands, and when deſired rings the Bell ; then the FRUITRESS comes out to
attend the Company with any Fruit demanded, at Pleaſure ; it will likewiſe take in Flowers, or any ſmall Articles,
and produce them again as called for. The different Fruits will be given in Charge to a WATCH DOG, which
Barks on their being taken away, and ceaſes on their being returned. Next, the little CHIMNEY SWEEPER
comes from behind the Houſe, enters the the Side Door, preſently aſcends the Chimney and cries " *Sweep!*" ſeveral
Times, then deſcends and goes off with his bag filled with Soot.

THE LIQUOR MERCHANT AND WATER SERVER,

The LIQUOR MERCHANT ſtands at a Caſk, from which it will draw, at the Choice of the Company, any of the
following Liquors : Rum, Brandy, Gin, Whiſky, Port, Mountain, Shrub, Raiſin Wine, Peppermint, Aniſeed, Curraçoa,
and Uſquebaugh. The WATER SERVER ſtands at a Pump to ſupply Water when ordered, and pumps, or ceaſes, at
the Deſire of any Perſon preſent. And

THE HIGHLAND ORACLE,

A Figure in the Highland Dreſs, which gives a rational Anſwer by Motion to any Queſtion propoſed, calculates
Sums in Arithmetic, by ſtriking its Sword on a Targe, and gives the Amount of any Number of Yards, Pounds, &c.
at any given Price ; ſtrikes the Hours and Minutes whenever aſked ; and alſo ſtrikes the Difference of Time between
any Watch and the Time-Piece on which it ſtands ; beats Time to Muſick, &c.
The MACHINE ORGAN will play occaſionally between the Pieces.

THE RUNNING ATTENDANTS

Are deſigned to wait on the Audience in the Gallery with any Thing required from the Exhibition, in Order to
prevent any Inconvenience to the Company in the Boxes.

HADDOCK's new-invented TABLE ORGAN

Will be introduced in the Exhibition, which he makes for Sale, of different Kinds and Prices. The Utility of
that portable and elegant Inſtrument needs no Eulogium, for what renders other keyed Inſtruments an Inconvenience,
is done away in this MULTUM IN PARVO, as it anſwers every intent of a Breakfaſt, a Card, or a Tea Table, and
ſtill can be uſed as an Organ. It might be deemed one of the moſt convenient Inſtruments for ſmall Concert or
Country or Other Parties. He hopes a Sweetneſs in Tone, a Delicacy in Touch, a Portability in Conſtruction, and
a reaſonable Charge, will be an Inducement to Purchaſers. ORGANS of every Deſcription Made and Repaired.

Tickets for the Exhibition, and Places for the Boxes taken, at the Theatre ; which is neatly fitted up, and every Thing
calculated to give Satisfaction to a polite and diſcerning Audience. The Exhibition laſts nearly Two Hours.

GEOGHEGAN, Printer, No. 3, KENT STREET, Borough.

7½ x 19⅞

ASTLEY'S AMPITHEATRE
1799

PHILIP ASTLEY IS WIDELY ACKNOWLEDGED to be the father of the modern circus. In 1766, newly discharged from military duty where he had attained the rank of sergeant major, he set up an arena for equestrian exhibitions near Westminster Bridge. He was a gifted showman and athlete and his offerings, though modest, earned him an enthusiastic following. By 1770 he had built a wooden amphitheater for his shows, and now combined his virtuoso horse riding with variety entertainment: acrobats, rope dancers, clowns, strongmen, magicians—elements of the early circus. He also featured a "Little Learned Horse" that demonstrated its sagacity in a repertoire of mathematical and orthographical stunts.

This playbill, printed on blue paper in 1799, shows a handsome blend of type and illustration. It was once part of the famous Gardner London topological collection; the circus memorabilia were purchased by Fred Martin and later owned by Lord Bernstein. The central image of the learned horse was taken directly from an earlier image of a learned pig that appeared at Astley's a dozen years before. The curtain, background, and figure of the trainer are almost identical. The earlier bill, however, which is preserved in Chetham's Library in Manchester, reveals a pig choosing the letter "A" from a group of cards. The banner, written in French, announces "The famous learned pig of Sieur. Garman" (see p. 76). The broadside features an amalgam of equestrian demonstrations, tumbling, ventriloquism, and theatrical burlettas such as

"The Philanthropic Female" and "Rolla & Cora, Or, The Virgin of the Sun." The special feature of this engagement, however, was the retirement of the "Wonderful Little Horse," pictured in the woodcut performing a card trick. Astley, who by this time had left the management of the circus to his son John, was engaged specifically for this event, the final run of the equine star, who "cannot be exhibited by any other Person whatever, he having been Solely Instructed by Mr. Astley, Sen., who after the Present Season, totally retires from any Public Capacity."

The horse, called Billy, long survived his original trainer. After Astley's death, one William Davis took care of the horse, but entrusted him to Abraham Saunders, who lost his show through debt; the learned horse was auctioned with the rest of his stud and taken by a tradesman who had no knowledge of Billy's accomplishments. He pulled the tradesman's cart until he was spotted by one of Astley's riders, who cued the horse by clicking his fingernails, as he had done in the exhibitions. The horse confirmed his identity by tapping his foreleg. He was repurchased and taken home, where he resumed and even enlarged his remarkable repertoire. In old age, Billy could still ungirth his own saddle and wash his feet. He could serve tea, taking a kettle of boiling water off of the fire and carrying a complete equipage. When he died at age forty-two, his hide was not retired but fashioned into a special-effects thunder-drum, used for many years in the same amphitheater where he had performed.

THIS
Theatre will CLOSE
IN A FEW DAYS.

Royal Amphitheatre, Aſtley's,
Weſtminſter Bridge.

Their Royal Highneſſes the *Prince of Wales,* and *Duke of York's* Servants.

This preſent FRIDAY the 27th, and SATURDAY the 28th of
SEPTEMBER, 1799,
WILL BE PRESENTED,
The Three following diſtinct popular PIECES.
FIRST,
The Military and Naval Spectacle of Action,
CALLED, THE

PhilanthropicFemale

Or, the Britiſh Army in Holland.
SECOND,
The new OPERATIC BALLET of ACTION, by Mr. ASTLEY, Jun.) called

Rolla & Cora,
Or, The VIRGIN of the SUN.
And, THIRDLY,
THE COMIC AND MECHANICAL PANTOMIME OF

Harlequin's Enterprises.

☞ Pleaſe to obſerve, that in the intervals of the above Entertainments, the following Performances will
take Place, viz.

The ſurpriſing VENTRILOQUIST.
VARIOUS FEATS OF
H O R S E M A N S H I P,
With the Grand and Extraordinary
TROOP OF JUMPERS.

*See and believe ! that ſuch extraordinary Performances are poſſible for Man
to accompliſh.*

Ne   Multum

Plus      in

Ultra   Parvo.

Mr. ASTLEY, Sen. with the higheſt deference, begs Leave to inform the Public, that in conſequence of
the many and repeated Applications relative to the Performances of the *Wonderful Little HORSE,* he will
appear at the Theatre, Weſtminſter-Bridge, during the above *Two Nights,* and THEN BE WITHDRAWN
FOR EVER! As this ſingular little Animal cannot poſſibly be exhibited by any other Perſon what ever,
he having been SOLELY INSTRUCTED by *Mr. Aſtley, Sen.* who after the PRESENT SEASON, totally retires
from any *Public Capacity;* he therefore deems it particularly incumbent on him at this time, to comply
with the wiſh of the numerous Viſitors of this Theatre.

The Whole to conclude with the New Superb and celebrated PANTOMIME of the

Dæmon's
TRIBUNAL:

DOORS to be opened at Half paſt Five, to begin at Half paſt Six o'Clock.
BOX 4s.——Second Price 2s.   PIT 2s.——Second Price 1s.   GALL. 1s.——Second Price 6d.
Second Price to commence at Half paſt Eight o'Clock preciſely ——Places to be taken of Mrs. CORNELL at the Box-Office,
Weſtminſter-Bridge, from Ten till Three o'Clock.

Printed by S. TIBSON, No. 7, Bridge-Road, Lambeth.

9⁷⁄₁₆ x 27⁷⁄₁₆

RANNIE'S VENTRILOQUISM

1804

THIS ADVERTISEMENT FOR THE Newport performance of the multitalented John Rannie is an impressive production for an early American broadside. The size, the half-dozen amusing woodcuts, and the uncharacteristic reverse lettering of the word "ventriloquism" contribute to the impact of this piece, printed by the press of the *Rhode Island Republican*. The large image in the lower right corner — presumably, the performer practicing his bird impressions in colloquy with a variety of bipeds suspended on a tree branch — also graces the cover of a contemporary blank book likely used by schoolchildren. The same cut appears on playbills of Richard Potter, the first native-born American conjurer to gain fame in this country. There is speculation that Potter, a New Hampshire mulatto who gained renown, may have been tutored by Rannie.

For a decade at the turn of the century the Scottish-born Rannie plied his skills as a ventriloquist, magician, wire-walker, and theatrical impresario from Maine to New Orleans and to the West Indies. His younger brother James also performed in America for a brief time but apparently returned to Scotland. John is said to have offered the first theatrical performances in English west of the Allegheny Mountains. Rannie was the subject of playbills, advertisements, and reviews in books and newspapers. His act is described in an undated self-published pamphlet, *The European Ventriloquist's Exhibition*, printed in Portsmouth,

and in the first original magic book published in America, William Pinchbeck's *The Expositor* (Boston, 1805). *The Expositor* praises "the ease and dexterity with which he manages his business and the plain manner he has of accomplishing his designs…which renders his exhibitions not only marvelous but amusing."

At times Rannie offered to expose his magic effects to show that they were not the product of diabolic agency, and he also offered "scenes which would serve as a lesson against gambling." His repertoire consisted of a variety of card tricks, including one in which the selections chosen by the audience would be revealed by a "Philosophical Fish" (see the cut, center right). Among his ventriloquil offerings was to make a voice appear to come from "a lady's muff, and the lady was so fully impressed…that she threw the muff away with exclamations of terror and astonishment."

On another broadside in my collection, dated October 24, 1804, Rannie promised to make a coin leap out of a gentleman's hand, swallow a number of forks and knives, discover eight or ten selected cards in a leg of mutton, walk on a slack wire while balancing a table filled with wine glasses in one hand and a "young gentleman" in the other, and catch on the point of his sword a bullet fired at him from the pistol of a spectator. Rannie offered to forfeit a thousand dollars if the "smallest article here mentioned" were not performed.

FOR THREE NIGHTS ONLY.

THEATRE
NEWPORT.

On MONDAY EVENING, June 4, 1804, will be displayed by Mr. RANNIE, the inimitable powers of

VENTRILOQUISM

WHICH is one of the most singular phenomena that has ever been contemplated by the most enlightened age, and have been more than three persons in the known world, since the war between king David and Saul, who have been possessed of the same faculty, which in the scripture is called *familiar* spirit, when the witch at Endor raised the apparition of Samuel, and by the power of Ventriloquism, occasioned a voice to come from the Ghost, which she took to be the voice of the prophet himself, but which the artful woman, no doubt, managed as she pleased, (1st Sam. ch. 28.)—and this will be clearly demonstrated in the course of this evening's exhibition.

Mr. *Rannie* will introduce a greater variety of new and interesting Experiments and Deceptions, than have yet been offered for public approbation.

The long series of 18 years having been devoted to the study of this species of entertainment, it is presumed must entitle him to a preference in the opinions of all those who are capable of forming a just estimation of merit. The mode in which he performs Deceptions comes so closely to reality, that it is almost impossible to distinguish between.

Among the extensive display intended for the evening, the VENTRILOQUISM will be performed —Mr. Rannie will occasion the voice of a child to be heard from all parts of the room, as he has already done on a late occasion, when the voice came from a lady's muff, and the lady was so fully impressed with the idea of reality, that she threw the muff away with exclamations of terror and astonishment. In like manner the notes of a pig's voice was heard to come from a gentleman's pocket, and on his being asked by Mr. R. to set the pig at liberty, he said he would do so, provided Mr. Rannie would insure his hand from being bitten.

[Printed at the Office of the Rhode-Island Republican.]

He will also perform that surprising operation of cutting off the skirts from any gentleman's coat, and in less than a minute the coat becomes whole as before.

Any lady throwing her handkerchief on the floor, it will appear to move to any part of the room Mr. Rannie pleases to direct.

On the same evening, will likewise be introduced NEFIRO'S BOX—The experiments which Mr. Rannie is enabled to perform by the assistance of this box has hitherto caused general astonishment. It may be examined by all the company, and then locked up, after which, any gentleman may write or figure what he pleases, and immediately on opening the box, there will be found the same words or figures written there.

Twenty or thirty ladies and gentlemen may draw cards from the pack, on opening the box the name of each card will be found written therein.

The Philosophical Fish will also perform several curious experiments:—any Ladies and Gentlemen may fix up on a card, and the fish will pick out the same card and hold it to public view.

On the same evening, any gentleman may charge a gun with powder and ball, and on firing it off, Mr. Rannie will catch the ball on the point of a sword.

To which will be added, by Mr. Rannie the younger, a variety of performances, which cannot fail to excite the admiration of enlightened Characters.

To give any further detail of the particular Performances, would far exceed the limits of an advertisement, or even a volume—suffice it to observe, that every degree of attention will be paid to afford the company the greatest satisfaction possible.

*** Doors will be open half past 7 o'clock, and performance begin at 8—Boxes, one dollar—Gallery, half a dollar.—Tickets to be had at both of the Printing-Offices in this town.—Nights of performance, Monday, Wednesday and Friday.

21 15/16 X 17 11/16

MORITZ'S TROUPE

C. 1809

ONE OF THE MORE VERSATILE impresarios of his day, this German-born entertainer exhibited as a conjurer, strongman, equilibrist, and instructor to a troupe of sagacious goldfinch. He fronted shows at theaters and on fairgrounds with circus acts, variety artists, and melodramas. One of the first to present ghost-raising phantasmagoria (p. 52) in England, in 1804, he deserves credit for not claiming to have created the phenomenon. On a bill for a show in London in 1805, Moritz advertised his presentation as "being equal to the original Invention, and not a miserable Imitation like those exhibited here some time since."

In 1807 Moritz returned to London after a successful tour of the provinces and took over the Minor Theatre in Catherine Street, which he renamed for his purposes the Temple of Apollo. For this engagement he hired as a rope dancer a Yorkshire lass named Mrs. Price, who plied her trade as "Signora Bellinda" at the formidable salary of two and a half guineas per week (her husband's services included as a "make weight"). Employer and employee soon argued, and Moritz excused Bellinda, who refused to leave. Moritz exclaimed that as he was "both the Master and Manager," she must obey. As reported in the session of the Court of Common Pleas, February 21, 1808, Bellinda took strong exception to that language and vowed, "You my Master, you little German humbug, I scorn your words; pay me my salary, and I'll never come into your Theatre again."

After Bellinda was paid, she joined the company of Moritz's rival, the magician Ingleby, then performing at the nearby Lyceum Theatre. One might have assumed the matter satisfactorily resolved, but Bellinda sued for wrongful dismissal. Sergeant Best, who defended Moritz, described Bellinda as "a tall powerful woman" who hit the defendant twice with her umbrella. Sergeant Shepherd, who represented Bellinda, said she was only four feet tall and characterized Moritz as a man of Herculean strength and size. According to newspaper accounts, Moritz rose to reveal his "low stature and slight form." The presiding judge, Sir James Mansfield, characterized the proceedings as "a very ridiculous action," that "could answer to no other purpose than putting money into the pockets of the Attorneys," and ruled for Moritz. It was speculated that Bellinda's grievance was prompted by her new employer,

Ingleby, who billed himself as "The Emperor of all the Conjurers." Moritz, calling himself "The King of all the Conjurers," had already challenged "any man in the world" to duplicate his performance for £300, "especially that lump of arrogance at the Lyceum."

Both men exhibited a braggadocio all too common in their profession but were smart enough to realize that their subsequent notoriety was more helpful than damaging at the box office. Ingleby was later magnificently parodied by the popular north-country magician and showman Billy Purvis, and by Charles Mathews, the famous comic actor.

On a bill for the New Circus in Hull in October 1813 Moritz featured staples of the ring such as "The Little Devil," formerly from Astley's Amphitheatre; the Samwell family of equestrians; and a version of the perennial favorite the "Tailor's Ride," which he called "Billy Button's Wild-Goose Chase to Brentford." Still performing in 1817 at the Theatre Royal in Chester, Moritz was presenting classic magic effects—destroying and then restoring a gentleman's watch, a lady's handkerchief, or a banknote; cooking a pancake in a borrowed hat; and allowing anyone in the audience to "take away the Life of any Animal and by one Blast of his Breath it shall rise and Walk as well as ever" (see p. 72). He presented a magic effect with the puzzling but intriguing title "Sticks of Fancy, never attempted by anyone but Himself," and offered to catch a bullet fired from a spectator's pistol on the point of a knife or in his mouth. The last three effects were also offered, almost word for word, on one of Ingleby's playbills.

I am particularly drawn to this broadside, which, while reminiscent of other pieces of the period (likely the first decade of the nineteenth century), exhibits an appealing variety of attractions as well as typographic flare and pleasing layout. (The four small Masonic symbols that may be found at the top of this bill also appear on Ingleby's advertisement mentioned above.) Here Moritz presents Bellinda's replacement, "the unequalled Miss Saunders," on the slack wire and in equestrian demonstrations; offers tight-rope evolutions by the child Charles Evans; and displays his own hand with trained birds and feats of balancing. It is possible that this sheet was used to advertise his show at Brook Green Fair in West London. An aquatint of this venue by Thomas Rowlandson depicts the Moritz booth.

Horsemanship
During the Fair.

Moritz's
TROOP.

MR. MORITZ most respectfully informs the Ladies and Gentlemen, and the Public in general, that he has, at a great Expence, fitted up a spacious Booth, wherein will be brought forward, that kind of Novel Performances, which never fails giving Satisfaction to an enlightened Audience; and where the Lovers of Genius and Merit have an opportunity of seeing the first Performers in the World, as well known in the Vicinity of London.

Horsemanship

By the unequalled MISS SAUNDERS.
MR. MORITZ will introduce his sagacious

Live Birds,

The Sagacity of these Birds, in various Performances, exceeds any thing to be met with in the Animal Species; and will perform several astonishing Manœuvres, that would be thought incredible to those who have never seen them.

HORSEMANSHIP

By MASTER EVANS, *very justly termed the Flying Phænomenon.*

The celebrated Miss Saunders will exhibit several Equilibriums on the

Slack Wire

With the Hoop, Glass, Triangles, Tambourine, Drum, Tables, Chairs, &c. in FULL SWING, never yet equalled in Europe.

Clown to the Horsemanship by the Little Devil's Son, late of Sadler's Wells.

The Polander's Performances
By MASTER EVANS.

Tight Rope
D A N C I N G

By that juvenile Performer, MASTER CHARLES EVANS; Who will exhibit with Baskets at his Feet, also in Fetters, Wooden Shoes, &c. &c. will also jump over a Garter, elevated 6 Feet from the Rope.

The whole to conclude with Feats of uncommon Strength and Agility, by

Balancing

In a most astonishing Manner, by MR. MORITZ, a Coach Wheel, Chairs, a Peacock's Feather on various Parts of the Body; the curious Balance of the Straw, throwing it from Limb to Limb, and on various Parts of the Body, which renders it very amusing and pleasing to Connoisseurs of Natural Genius.

To begin each Day by 12 o'Clock.
Boxes 2s.—Pit 1s.—Standing Places 6d.

[Romney Printer, Lambeth.]

7⅛ x 17¼

THE CELEBRATED MISS BEFFIN

C. 1811

THE ONLY ARMLESS ARTIST to approach Mathew Buchinger's (see p. 24) fame in Great Britain was Sarah Beffin (sometimes "Biffin"). Unlike the "Little Man," she balanced her brush on her shoulder and directed it with her mouth when producing her pictures. She was particularly lauded for miniatures rendered on ivory. She was an attraction at Strood, Edmonton, and Bartholomew Fairs and similar venues, where it was advertised that she was "industrious and astonishing…and practiced in obtaining the use of the Needle, Scissors, Pen, Pencil, &c. wherein she is extremely adroit; she can cut out and make any part of her own Clothes, Sews extremely neat and in a most wonderful manner, Writes Well. The inexpressible improvement Miss Beffin has made in the polite Art of Drawing and Miniature Painting is truly astonishing even to the most eminent Artists." A reward of a thousand guineas was offered, were these claims proved false.

Her major patron was the Earl of Morton, whose portrait she painted. To insure against chicanery he would personally escort the canvas to and from each sitting. Convinced of her skill, he furthered her prowess by underwriting instruction from a master painter and helping her secure royal patronage from George III, George IV, and William IV. Handicapped artists had to endure much from their benefactors. In return for the admittedly magnanimous sum of twenty-five pounds, Beffin suffered this ditty uttered by George IV, "We cannot reward this lady for her

handy-work, I will not give her *alms*, but I request she is paid for her industry."

A very different indignity transpired when she was brought to the theater one night and carried to her seat by her fiancé, who left her to enjoy the show as he went off to attend to business. At the play's conclusion she remained seated until asked by the management to leave the theater, a request with which she could not comply. (With the best of intentions, the house manager offered to help her to her feet, or to take her hand…) Her suitor finally came to her rescue. Her marriage to this man, Mr. Wright, led to her retirement as an attraction. At the death of her husband and the Earl of Morton, however, she was forced once again to exhibit herself. She died in reduced circumstances in Liverpool in 1850.

A talented and resolute woman, Sarah Beffin survived as the subject of prints and poetic tributes as well as less flattering broadside ballads. She was mentioned in novels by Surtees and Marryat, and referred to in three books by Dickens: *Nicholas Nickleby*, *The Old Curiosity Shop*, and *Little Dorrit*.

This broadside is a lovely illustration of the printer's craft at the turn of the nineteenth century. Handsomely produced in red and black, it is an unusually large and striking example of the power of the medium. The prominent misspelling of "Without" was corrected in a much smaller version of the bill that features the same copy.

The Greatest Wonder in the World.
During the Fair.

PATRONISED  **BY THE**

Royal **Family.**

THE CELEBRATED

Miss BEFFIN

Miniature Painter.

WHO WAS BORN

Wtihout Hands & Arms,

IS NOW EXHIBITING

DURING THE FAIR.

Whose Wonderful Improvement since she last had the honor of appearing here, must be seen to convey an adequate idea of her astonishing Powers, and this being the last opportunity the Public will have, being her farewell Visit to the Fair.

Miss **BEFFIN** Writes well, Works at her Needle, Cuts out and makes all her own Dresses, uses the Scissars with perfect ease, Draws Landscapes, Flowers, Feathers, &c. all of which she does principally with her Mouth, and in the Presence of the Company.

EACH VISITOR

Will be Entitled to a Specimen of her Writing.

And in addition to Miss B's. other Accomplishments, she has lately acquired a perfect knowledge of that much admired and elegant Art, China Painting.

Correct Miniature Likenesses taken on Ivory,
From 3 to 10 Guineas Each.

Admission, Ladies & Gentlemen 1s.   Children & Servants 6d.

T. ROMNEY, PRINTER, Bridge-road, Lambeth.

THE HOTTENTOT VENUS

C. 1811

IF THE VIRTUES OF THE EXHIBITIONS here commemorated are, by and large, a healthy combination of entertainment and edification, they are capable, conversely, of exploiting and degrading the anomalous.

The first major ethnological attraction of the nineteenth century featured a Khoi-San woman from South Africa. The Afrikaaner who brought her to London in 1810 called her Saartjie, or Sarah Baartmann, and she was exhibited in London as "The Hottentot Venus." "Hottentot" was a term used to designate a tribe of a low cultural order, thought to be the "missing link" between humans and apes. Even apart from this lack of evolutionary distinction, her appearance alone immediately compelled curiosity, as she was four and a half feet tall and profoundly steatopygic (the medical term for a prodigious posterior), and her genitals—specifically her labia—appeared by European standards to be abnormally enlarged.

For this provincial exhibition in Colchester she was billed as "the only Hottentot ever exhibited in Europe." The particulars are chaste, dealing only with some ethnographic misinterpretations (her "people" are "scarcely ever observed to laugh") and never, beyond dubbing her "the greatest natural curiosity," courting prurience by mentioning physical details:

She is particularly obliged to the Female Sex, who have so liberally patronized her Exhibition; and more especially after the malicious Reports circulated to her Disadvantage after her Arrival in this Kingdom; but which have been long since proved to be groundless.—Over her clothing, (which is suitable to [her native] Climate) are worn all the rude Ornaments used by that Tribe on Gala Days.

The bill ended with hyperbole that, while standard for the genre, had an unlikely ring of truth: residents of Colchester and the vicinity were urged to see her, "as she will positively never make her appearance in this Town again."

The coy gestures of the playbill notwithstanding, Saartjie was displayed with very little clothing, and she aroused considerable concern about servitude and exploitation. Her Dutch-African manager-employer claimed that she came to London willingly, and that he sought through exhibition to secure her fortune. When he was later accused in court of harboring her against her will, she refused to testify against him and the case was dismissed.

Prints depicting Saartjie were sold, and she became the subject of numerous political and satirical caricatures.

She soon defined notoriety. She was visited by the great actors Charles Mathews and John Kemble (who was very moved by her situation) and mentioned by Thackeray, Surtees, and Carlyle (who commented on her "posterial luxuriance").

After her tour of England she was taken to France, where she attracted attention among scientists and satirists alike. She was examined by the anatomist Georges Cuvier, and she was the subject of at least six dramatic sketches. After she died while only in her mid-twenties, an autopsy was performed by Cuvier, who published the results in 1817. From that time until quite recently, Saartjie's preserved brain and genitals were kept in the Musée de l'Homme in Paris.

The modern focus on issues of race, gender, and sexuality has brought Saartjie new attention. Yet other attractions, both in her own time and today, have relied on similar exploitation and curiosity. Ota Benga, a pygmy, was shown in the monkey cage of the Bronx Zoo; Victorian comedies in England advertised "Buffo Real Negroes direct from the cotton fields of America in their inimitable Festivity and Pastimes"; and the tiny feet of Chinese women, the result of painful foot-binding practices (see p. 128), were exhibited (these were also preserved in the Musée de l'Homme).

Was the display of the Hottentot Venus significantly worse than the exhibition of Joseph Merrick, "The Elephant Man," for instance, or Claude Seurat, "The Human Skeleton"? Seurat, a "Jack Sprat" counterpoint to Saartjie Baartmann, was exhibited in the 1820s. His show was described by the British medical journal *Lancet* as "one of the most impudent and disgusting attempts to make a profit of the public appetite for novelty." Yet Seurat countered that he was making money in order to retire in his homeland, and that the exhibitors had saved him "from a profitless, wandering life of self-exposure in France." This sentiment has been expressed to me personally by acquaintances who have been exhibited as "freaks." Should such displays be banned, or allowed as a means of making these individuals financially self-sufficient? It is a debate that continues to this day.

Saartjie has been the subject of recent creative work as well as critical studies, and she has finally achieved some well-deserved closure. In 2002 the French government handed her skeleton and bottled organs to the South African ambassador for burial in her native land.

ARRIVED FROM LONDON,

AND WILL BE EXHIBITED FOR A FEW DAYS,

AT No. 16, HEAD-STREET, CORNER OF HIGH-STREET,

COLCHESTER,

THAT MOST WONDERFUL

Phenomenon of Nature,

THE

HOTTENTOT
VENUS,

The only Hottentot ever exhibited in Europe.

IN viewing this Wonderful LIVING Production of Nature, the Public have a perfect Specimen of that most extraordinary Tribe of Human Race, who have for such a length of Time inhabited the more Southern Parts of AFRICA, whose real Origin has never yet been ascertained, nor their Character, which has been so differently described by every Traveller who has visited those remote Regions of the World;—and considering the natural morose Disposition of those People (who are scarcely ever observed to laugh) she is remarkably mild and affable in her Manners. She has had the Honor of being visited by THEIR ROYAL HIGHNESSES THE PRINCESS ELIZABETH, the PRINCE REGENT, and several Branches of the ROYAL FAMILY, also the principal NOBILITY of both Sexes; and declared by them, to be unexceptionally the greatest Natural Curiosity of the Human Species ever exhibited in England, and well worthy the Attention of the Public. She is particularly obliged to the Female Sex, who have so liberally patronized her Exhibition; and more especially after the malicious REPORTS circulated to her Disadvantage after her Arrival in this Kingdom; but which have been long since proved to be groundless.—Over her Clothing, (which is suitable to this Climate) are worn all the rude Ornaments used by that Tribe on Gala Days.

N. B. Elegant Engravings from the original Drawing of the Venus, by *Lewis,* may be had at the Place of Exhibition.

₊ The Nobility, Gentry, and Inhabitants of this Town and its Vicinity, are most respectfully desired to embrace the present opportunity of contemplating this singular variety of the Human Species, as she will possitively never make her appearance in this Town again.

☞ *Admittance* ONE SHILLING *each.*

Swinborne and Walter, Printers, Colchester.

7⅛ x 9⁹⁄₁₆

THE PIG-FACED LADY

1815

AN ENDURING LEGEND TELLS THE STORY of a female child born with a pig's face. When she comes of age, her wealthy parents try to marry her off with a dowry equal to a king's ransom. No suitor, however, is able to overlook the swinish proclivities of the would-be bride, and the nuptial negotiations are broken off.

Although the tale has been told in many a pamphlet and ballad, and in many a language, an English monograph of 1640 is seminal: *A Certaine Relation of the Hog-faced Gentlewoman called Miss Tannakin Skinke...Who was bewitched in her mother's wombe.* According to the account, an old lady, whose plea for alms was rejected by a pregnant woman, cursed her and her progeny, "as the mother is hoggish, so swinish shall be the child."

Maternal imprinting, the notion that a mother's reaction to unusual events during her pregnancy will affect the child she is carrying, spawned a number of tall tales as well as exhibitions in the world of entertainment. Lionel the Lion-Faced Boy was born covered in hair from head to foot, following a gestational crisis in which a lion supposedly attacked his father. The Elephant Man's mother was said to have been stepped on by a pachyderm during her pregnancy.

What separates Stephan Bibrowski (the Lion-Faced Boy) and Joseph Merrick (the Elephant Man) from the pig-faced lady is that they were of flesh and blood, while there is no conclusive evidence for the existence of a hog-faced wonder. Nevertheless, versions of the story were told and retold over the centuries, and the tale was particularly fashionable when this broadside was published by Fairburn in 1815. The *Times* and various other London papers then printed advertisements soliciting suitors for the porcine princess. Unlike most of the evanescent pieces in this exhibition, this one, riding the tide of the tale's popularity, was impressively produced and designed as a more permanent memento.

Nevertheless, itinerant showmen did, over a long period, advertise and exhibit pig-faced attractions. What, you may well ask, did spectators witness when they paid their money? Usually, the pig was a disguised bear. It had a closely shaven face and was outfitted in a frock, gloves, shawl, wig, and bonnet. So bedizened, she sat in a large chair in front of which was a draped table. She was propped upright and fastened in her seat, and a young boy concealed under the table would prod her as the showman asked questions. The bear's ensuing grunts would be taken for answers.

A newspaper account of 1829 gives one of the more remarkable first-person accounts of the perils of show business. A dwarf named Lipson appeared before a magistrate to obtain a judgment against his employer. He complained about his poor wages and his confinement in a traveling van with the showman's wife and "large family of squalling children." Unconscionable to Lipson, however, was that he was obliged

to sit cheek-by-jowl with a pig-faced lady, which he considered to be a very great degradation, the pig-faced lady being neither better nor worse than a shaved bear; and Mr. Bruin sometimes took it into his head to play off some very rough and uncouth tricks. For instance, when he was seized with a hungry fit, he would not care what uproar he kicked up in the van, and often directed his fury against the poor dwarf on these occasions, who had been frequently under the necessity of jumping out of the vehicle, to the danger and hazard of breaking his neck, to escape the fury of her pig-faced ladyship. "With all these misfortunes, however," said the dwarf, "I would willingly put up, if I was paid my wages regularly; but no, this has not been the case, and my master is now three weeks in my debt; and when I ask him for my money, he refuses it, and taunts me with not drawing the public. When drawing a contrast between the services of the pig-faced lady and myself, master always gives the preference to the former, and it is rather cutting that more attention should be paid to a *hannimal* than a human *cretur.*"

FAIRBURN (SENIOR'S) PORTRAIT

OF THE

PIG-FACED LADY,

OF

Manchester-Square.

DRAWN FROM THE INFORMATION OF A FEMALE WHO ATTENDED ON HER.

SECOND EDITION, WITH ADDITIONS.

DESCRIPTION.

THIS most extraordinary Female is about Twenty Years of Age, she was born in Ireland, and is of high family and fortune; on her life and issue by marriage a very large property depends.

Her body and limbs are of the most perfect and beautiful shape, but her head and face resembles that of a *Pig*. She eats her victuals out of a *Silver Trough*, in the same manner as *Pigs* do; and, when spoken to by any of her relatives or her companion, she can only answer by *a Grunt*.

The female who attends on her and sleeps with her is paid at the rate of One Thousand Pounds per Annum for her attendance; but, although the salary is so great, her late companion has quitted her situation, having been terribly frightened by her.

The following Advertisement, from a young Female to attend on her and be her companion, appeared in the *Times* of Thursday, February 9, 1815:

"A young gentlewoman having heard of an advertisement for a person to undertake the care of a lady who is heavily afflicted in the face, whose friends have offered a handsome income yearly, and a premium for residing with her seven years, would do all in her power to render her life most comfortable; an undeniable character can be obtained from a respectable circle of friends: an answer to this advertisement is requested, as the advertiser will keep herself disengaged. Address, post paid, to X. Y. at Mr. Ford's, Baker, 12, Judd-street, Brunswick-square."

Also the following Advertisement, from a young gentleman of respectability, declaring his sentiments respecting a final settlement (matrimony) with this most Wonderful Female, and stating his intentions to be sincere, honourable, and firmly resolved, appeared in the Morning Herald, of Thursday, February 16, 1815: "Secrecy.—A single gentleman, aged thirty-one, of a respectable family, and in whom the utmost confidence may be reposed, is desirous of explaining his mind to the friends of a person who has a misfortune in her face, but is prevented for want of an introduction. Being perfectly aware of the principal particulars, and understanding that a final settlement would be preferred to a temporary one, presumes he would be found to answer the full extent of their wishes. His intentions are sincere, honourable, and firmly resolved. References of great respectability can be given. Address to M. D. at Mr. Spencer's, 22, Great Ormond-street, Queen-square."

Another advertisement, from a *Fortune-Hunter*, was sent to the *Times* for insertion, offering to *marry her*, however deformed, but which was refused insertion, (although accompanied with a One Pound Note!!) for reasons best known to the editor of that paper.

This prodigy of nature is the general topic of conversation in the metropolis. In almost every company you join the *pig-faced Lady* is introduced,—and her existence is firmly believed in by thousands, particularly by those who reside at the west end of the town.

GIUSEPPE DE ROSSI

1816

GIUSEPPE DE ROSSI, a magician from Bologna, ended his run in an unspecified Italian city by decapitating *"Un Vivo Castrato."* In graphic detail his playbill of July 21, 1816, explained the procedure:

The Professor will have a live steer brought up in the front part of the stage and while holding a sharp blade he will sever its head and will put it on top of a small table. After having moved away from the severed head he intends—in the twinkling of an eye at the order of anyone who will want to give him the honor—to make sure that the head will disappear from above the table and go to join again the body which will be situated in another area of the stage. In this fashion, the castrated steer, while instantly coming back to life, will be able to stand up again, moo and walk, so that everyone satisfied both with their own eyes and the touch of their own hands will be able without fail to decide that this is one of the most surprising acts of White Magic that De Rossi can do.

In an appeal to the delicacy of the women present, our conjurer promised no unsettling display of blood, a bucket of sawdust having been provided to stem the tide of that offending liquid.

Under the auspices of King Francesco, De Rossi was presenting an illusion that dated from the first royal command performance in magic history. In ancient Egypt, according to the Westcar Papyrus of 1700 B.C.E, King Cheops, the pharaoh known for the construction of the Great Pyramid, witnessed the wonder-working skills of one Dedi of Ded-Snefru sometime around 2600 B.C.E. Dedi was reputed to be 110 years of age, with a daily diet of a shoulder of beef and five hundred loaves of bread, washed down with a hundred jugs of beer.

After his repast, Dedi decapitated a goose, placing its head at one end of the pharaoh's great hall and its body at the other. In a Chuck Berry–like duck walk, the head and the body were then reunited. This was repeated with a pelican and an ox. When asked to perform the illusion on his own species—unlike scores of his successors to the present day—he demurred. (The effect is featured in Reginald Scot's *Discoverie of Witchcraft*, the seminal English conjuring text of the sixteenth century, and scores of subsequent works.) One wonders whether his actions were consequent on moral scruples, or his inability to effect the required result on humans without additional preparation.

A number of De Rossi's contemporaries advertised the decapitation of a calf but, I believe, with no intention of actually accomplishing the effect. In 1811 a playbill of a magician named Hunt announced, "He will permit a Gentleman in the company to Cut off a Fowl's Head, Or any other Animal under the size of a Calf, he will command the same on again as perfect as before, and shall afterwards walk round about, to the astonishment of every beholder." In England, in the same year as De Rossi's performance in Italy, Ingleby, the so-called "Emperor of all the Conjurors," would "positively allow any Gentleman in the company to take away the life of any Animal under the size of a calf, and by one blast of his breath, it shall rise and walk as well as ever." As I have never seen evidence that either of these magicians performed the illusion with anything other than a small fowl, I believe the audience was directed, by a procedure known as the magician's choice, to limit their selection.

De Rossi announced his show on a bill composed in beautiful old roman types within a lovely decorative border. Printed on two separate sheets, this is an especially large and elaborate document for its time. De Rossi offered an intriguing repertoire that included "The Lovely Game of the Blindfold," "The Talking Chest," "The Basin of Venus," "The Enchanted Male Dancer," "The Pyramids of Egypt," "The Fountain of the Sybil," "The Fun Boxes," "The Banker from Lisbon," "The Game of the Diamond," and "The Fun Bottle." Until a contemporary account or review of De Rossi's performance is unearthed, one may use artistic license to speculate on the work ethic of the Banker from Lisbon or the costume favored by the Enchanted Male Dancer.

AVVISO
PER IL TEATRO COMUNALE

La Sera di Domenica 21 corrente Luglio 1816.

GIUSEPPE DE-ROSSI Bolognese decorato di Onori da Sua
Cesarea Maestà Francesco Primo

Eseguirà l'ultima definitiva Rappresentazione, la quale sarà singolarizzata
dal secondo

TRATTO DI MAGIA BIANCA

Ed in fine verrà presentato per la prima volta il sorprendente, e non
più veduto Giuoco

DI TAGLIARE LA TESTA
A UN VIVO CASTRATO

E RIATTACCARCELA ALLA VISTA DEL PUBBLICO

SPIEGAZIONE DEL GIUOCO

Il Professore farà portare sul davanti del Teatro un vivo CASTRATO, ed impugnando un tagliente ferro gli disunirà la Testa, e la porrà sopra un tavolino, ed allontanandosi dalla medesima si propone in un batter d'occhio, e al comando di chi vorrà onorarlo far sì che la Testa di sopra al Tavolino sparisca, e vada a riunirsi al Corpo che da un'altra parte della Scena sarà situato, e così il Castrato riprendendo in un istante la vita, potrà nuovamente alzarsi, muggire, e camminare, cosicché ognuno a soddisfazione tanto con l'occhio, che col tatto delle mani potrà immancabilmente decidere esser questi uno de' più sorprendenti tratti di Magia Bianca, che il DE-ROSSI possa eseguire.

L'intero Spettacolo sarà precorso con molte Operazioni in Matematica.

ESEGUIRÀ

1. *Il Grazioso Giuoco della Benda.*
2. *La Cassa Parlante.*
3. *Il Baccile di Venere.*
4. *Le Piramidi d'Egitto.*
5. *La Fontana della Sibilla.*
6. *Le Scatole Simpatiche.*
7. *Il Banchiere di Lisbona.*
8. *Il Ballerino Fatato.*
9. *Il Giuoco del Brillante.*
10. *La Bottiglia Simpatica.*

E dopo avere eseguiti altri piacevolissimi, e incredibili Giuochi, che per descrivere i quali troppo a lungo si anderebbe, onde rendere lo Spettacolo di sorpresa universale eseguirà il già detto Giuoco

DI TAGLIARE LA TESTA AL CASTRATO

E RIATTACCARCELA ALLA PUBBLICA VISTA

In questa guisa terminerà l'ultimo serale passatempo, che avrà l'onore di dare il DE-ROSSI, onde dalla moltiplicità, varietà, e novità degl'incredibili Giuochi, ognuno penetrato possa partire dal Teatro più delle altre sere convinto, contento, e persuaso.

Il Professore previene che nell'eseguire il Giuoco del Castrato, acciò che le Signore Donne non abbiano un qualche ribrezzo

SARÀ RISPARMIATO LO SPARGIMENTO DEL SANGUE

mentre verrà raccolto in un Secchio di Semola, o di Segatura di legno.

Lo Spettacolo sarà preceduto da una brillante Commedia di Carattere.

BOLOGNA TIPOGRAFIA CAMERALE.

24⅛ x 33¼

CHRISTOPHER LEE SUGG
PROFESSOR OF INTERNAL ELOCUTION

1816

THIS DENSE BUT ATTRACTIVE PLAYBILL advertising the ventriloquist Christopher Lee Sugg is printed on rust-colored paper and bears a crest with a lion and a unicorn rampant. The text is a prime example of what has so attracted me to the genre. It explores the most incongruous themes and is rich in artifice and hyperbole.

It is difficult at this distance to imagine what impression the bill would have made on hapless readers who perused the text in search of particulars. Before any such information was imparted, they were told that Mr. Sugg had in 1790 been offered the tremendous sum of a thousand guineas by a surgeon who wished to dissect his body on its demise (presumably to provide the doctor with the opportunity to examine the workings of Sugg's extraordinary ventriloquil mind). Sugg then refused the offer. But "having experienced a great Reverse of Fortune…and being in great Difficulty," he "now respectfully offers himself for Sale."

Only after this arresting preamble are we told that Sugg is a voice-thrower, indeed, "the only Ventriloquist in Europe." But before we are offered encomia about his prowess in the belly-speaking arena, we are promised an exposé of the techniques of "Philosophical and Mathematical Gamesters"—in other words, laying bare the principles of sleight of hand as performed with cards, money, rings, and eggs. His vaunted skill as a conjurer or expertise at gaming is nowhere, to my knowledge, corroborated, but it can be seen that he offers lessons in the art. In an 1813 playbill in my collection, Sugg presented "Spectrology, or new Optical Illusions" and the "Appearance of Disembodied Spirits," clearly to capitalize on the popularity of the phantasmagoria shows (see p. 152) that were then the rage.

Before the magic exposure could fully claim their attention, spectators were to be treated to a demonstration of the "Whimsiphusicon." By way of non-explanatory explanation, it was also dubbed the "Wandering Melodistical," a "Pill to Banish Melancholy," in the form of songs, anecdotes, and recitations. Sugg, like a number of early magicians, was a proponent of theatrical neologism used to entice, or more likely confuse, the public.

Sugg's playbill offers yet more deception in the boldly displayed names of Mr. Kean, Miss O'Neil, Mr. Incledon, and Mr. Mathews, famous actors all—none of whom would appear at the advertised engagement. The small type reveals that they were only to be imitated. Finally, at the end of the broadside Mr. Sugg flaunts his accomplishments in ventriloquism.

In other bills Sugg claims to have taught the technique to "Mr. Mathews," the greatest comic actor of his day, when by most accounts it appears more likely that Mathews instructed Sugg. This feud is discussed amusingly in the *Memoirs of Charles Mathews*, published in 1839. Sugg had billed himself as a "Professor of Internal Elocution," and Mathews did praise Sugg for his "good loud voice," but added that he "bawled out hunting songs of the day with as much effect as a thick impediment and lisp would permit."

Sugg announced that he would display his vaunted skill (on this bill and elsewhere he is more inclined to refer to it as a God-given "power") by placing a burning candle in front of his mouth to confirm the immobility of his lips and the stillness of his breath. Sugg presents the same stunt on other bills and cuttings dating back to the turn of the century, the earliest I have seen this demonstration advertised.

Sugg offered an impressive repertoire of human and barnyard imitations, but his fame seemed more dependent on publicity than prowess. At a time when some authors have been caught red-handed in praising their own work under the banner of impartial reviewers on Amazon.com, it may be worth noting that Sugg was a pioneer in this endeavor. He paid for space in local newspapers and inserted letters that appeared to be from favorably impressed observers. These pieces, signed with "Veritas" or "Rectifier," or some such weighty moniker, extolled the virtues of his show or related amusing anecdotes about the great Lee Sugg.

Sugg was a peculiar character, an opportunist and a late bloomer. He learned ventriloquism in his fifties, and in that same decade of his life had a daughter, who before she was six appeared on his show as a precocious actress, "The Infant Roscius." Katherine Lee Sugg went on to a distinguished career and married the well-known American actor James Henry Hackett. Sugg performed into his seventies, no doubt because of financial imperative, and died on the Isle of Wight in October 1831.

POSITIVELY FOR TWO NIGHT ONLY.

The Ventriloquist in a Coal Hole!!!

Brother LEE SUGG, the Original Ventriloquist, who was in the year 1790, offered by a Surgeon. ONE THOUSAND GUINEAS for his Body, for *Dissection*, which C. L. S. then refused. He now respectfully offers *himself for Sale*, having experienced a *great Reverse of Fortune*, and being now in great Difficulty. The Lot may be viewed, and his Powers heard, with Songs, Necromancy, and Recitations, by the kind Leave of Mr. W. J. RHODES, landlord, in the Long Room,

The Coal Hole & Union Tavern & Chop House,

Fountain Court, near Exeter Change, Strand, London,

On MONDAY Evening, April the 8th, and on TUESDAY Evening the 9th, (only) 1816, precisely at 7 o'Clock, by Tickets 3s. each.

Provincial Performers arriving in London, for Passion Week, may be improved in their Action, Singing, and Theatrical Oratory, by addressing, Post Paid, as above.

JUST ARRIVED, THE CELEBRATED

Br. Christopher Lee Sugg,
VENTRILOQUIST.

The Nobility, Gentry, and Public in general, are respectfully informed, that the above is the only VENTRILOQUIST in EUROPE, who will display his wonderful Powers for the Time specified only.

GOOD FIRES CONSTANTLY KEPT.

PHILOSOPHICAL AND MATHEMATICAL

GAMESTERS;

In which their extraordinary and wonderful Tricks *with Cards, Eggs, Money, Boxes, Rings, &c.*
DISCLOSING THEIR WHOLE SECRETS
TO THE AUDIENCE, GRATIS, A WONDERFUL INFORMATION,
Which on no other Occasion could they attain for the Sum of

ONE HUNDRED GUINEAS.

Never has been performed in this Town,
(And never will be after the Time herein specified)

BY THE WHIMSIPHUSICON,
Or, Wandering Melodistical,

Who respectfully offers to the Public, the following rational Novelties, calculated for rubbing off the Rust of Care, or
A PILL TO BANISH MELANCHOLY ;
Consisting of a great Variety of New Recitations, Songs, Anecdotes, and Chromacy, by the celebrated and wonderful

SAXIOGANIUS

Mr. KEAN !!!

A favorite Song on the above
CELEBRATED ACTOR.
After this a Song,
THE UGLY OLD MAID,
Recitation, Law, or Bullum and Boatum—Recitation. Louis the 18th, or a Trip to Paris—Song, "The Battle of Waterloo."

MISS O'NEIL !!!

A favorite Song on the above
CELEBRATED ACTRESS,
Daniel and Dishclout,—Poached Eggs and Pork Steaks, Song, "The Performer," after the manner of that great Singer

Mr. INCLEDON,

Will sing the Descriptive Horrors of a SEA STORM.
In the Course of which, the most extraordinary, astonishing, singular, and original
VENTRILOQUIST,
Whose wonderful powers surpass all possibility of description ; suffice it to say, that this Professor of
INTERNAL ORATORY,
Will, in an extraordinary a manner, hold conversing with persons seemingly concealed in closets of the room, chimnies, in cellars, under hats, chairs, glasses, in persons' pockets, in the roof and floor of the place of performance, and finally, will converse with seemingly
INVISIBLE BEING,
His Lips closed ; and no Person can discover the least motion of the Performers LIPS, although close to his Mouth is held
A BURNING CANDLE.
Recitation and Song after the Manner of

Mr. MATHEWS, of Covent-Garden Theatre.

Parties of the Nobility, and Public Seminaries, may have a Private Performance, at any Hour either as above, or at their own Mansions.
TERMS.—The Ventriloquist only, £1.—Ditto, with Songs and Recitations, £2.—Ditto, with the Mechanical Games, £2. Ditto, with Explanations, £3.
The Doors will open at Six o'Clock. The Entertainments commence at Seven,
The Public is earnestly requested to be early in their applications for Tickets, as the Great Novelties herein advertised, (and much more will be introduced than the Performer can specify in his hand-bill) cannot be repeated.
Acting, Singing, Ventriloquism, and Conjuring taught, and Private Plays got up,
By Br. LEE SUGG, Ventriloquist to His Royal Highness the Prince Regent.
Bills Printed at an Hour's Notice, by W. Glindon, Rupert Street, Haymarket

TOBY THE SAPIENT PIG

C. 1820

IN THE YEARS SINCE the eponymous Toby graced my book *Learned Pigs & Fireproof Women*, I have been fortunate to secure a number of additional bills advertising his appearances (one favorite boldly dubs him "The Sapeen Pig"). Toby was the most famous of a host of sapient swine that captivated the public in the London of the early nineteenth century. He was originally managed and exhibited by Mr. Hoare, a magician and trainer of a number of sagacious animals. In appreciating Toby's accomplishments, it is good to bear in mind that his handler was well schooled in illusions.

As it is here proclaimed, "The Performances of this Animal are so truly astonishing, his Intelligence and Instinct so great, they appear to be the work of magic." Toby would spell, read, tell time, solve mathematical problems, play cards, and determine the age of any spectator. Most impressive, however, was this:

He will Discover A Person's Thoughts—a thing never heard of before to be Exhibited by an Animal of the Swine Race. The Performances of this truly surprising Creature Must be Seen to be Believed.

Toby was praised for his physical appearance, as "his Colour and Symetry please every beholder." On a different advertisement for Toby, Hoare included these verses to bring home the point:

The silken rob'd peer, and the delicate *belle*,

Are unsull[i]ed by filth, unoffended by smell;
Toby turns all disdainful from deeds of offence,
For what would so blast his pretensions to sense.

This broadside, which heralds Toby as "The Philosopher of the Swinish Race," marks his return to London after a provincial tour. Despite this heightened celebrity, I sense that the cut of our porcine scholar has been rather indiscriminately chosen, almost certainly selected from a printer's cache of agricultural images rather than specifically struck for his appearance here. Nevertheless, Toby graces an altogether neat and pleasing, if not spectacular, printed sheet.

Thomas Jefferson attended the appearance of a scholarly swine in 1786, and American and English audiences were especially attracted to such demonstrations during the last quarter of the eighteenth century. The educated pig has been celebrated by such luminaries as Samuel Johnson, William Wordsworth, Pierce Egan, Mary Wollstonecraft, Samuel Taylor Coleridge, and William Blake. So famous was Toby, however, that he became the standard-bearer for learned pigs. Notwithstanding, one rival showman announced that his pig "was far superior to any thing of that kind, as Sir Isaac Newton, would be to a mere Idiot."

AT HOME for a SHORT TIME,

Toby, the Sapient Pig,
The greatest Production of Nature,
Has JUST ARRIVED from FRANCE,
AND IS NOW EXHIBITING AT THE GREAT ROOMS,
97, Pall Mall,
Which had the honour of Performing before the DUKE and DUCHESS of YORK.

The Performances of this Animal are so truly astonishing, his *Intelligence* and *Instinct* so great, they appear to be the work of magic; his *Colour* and *Symetry* please every beholder, and his *Sagacity* leaves them in a maze of wonder at this extraordinary production of Nature; and he may truly be said to be

The Philosopher of the Swinish Race.

This PHENOMENON will
SPELL and READ, CAST ACCOUNTS, PLAY at CARDS, TELL any person WHAT O'CLOCK it is to a MINUTE by their own Watch; also, TELL THE AGE OF ANY ONE in company; and, what is more astonishing, he will DISCOVER A PERSON'S THOUGHTS—a thing never heard of before to be Exhibited by an Animal of the Swine Race. The Performances of this truly surprising Creature
Must be Seen to be Believed.

He is now Exhibiting every Day, at
The Large Room, 97, PALL MALL,
Where his Performances commence precisely at the Hours of
11, 1, 2, 3, and 4 o'Clock.
ADMITTANCE ONE SHILLING.
N. B. *Any Family can have a private Performance at their own House, by giving Notice at the above.*

TOPPING, Printer, Playhouse Yard, Blackfriars, London.

5½ x 8⅞

GERMAN STRONGWOMEN

C. 1821

JOHANN ENGELBERT, AN IMPRESARIO from Prague exhibiting in Germany in 1821, offered to a "Noble and Notable Public, Two Strong Ladies Never before Presented Here." The best seats cost 24 kroner, the next block sold for 12, and the least favorable for 6. Those viewers who chose standing room paid at their own discretion. The girls were available to perform at any time between nine in the morning and nine at night. The teenaged strongwomen displayed different skills:

The Younger is 16 Years Old and possesses her strength in her hair. The Older is 18 Years Old, 5 Shoes high, and possesses her strength in her bodily power. Both are well proportioned.

The First Lady will lift 900 pounds of weight, consisting of two ship's anchors with her hair from the ground and a third anchor with her mouth, so that all three anchors will be balanced at the same time in the air.

The Second Lady will lay across two chairs where it may be seen that she has her head on one chair and her feet on the other so that her entire body remains free while a 1,000 pound weight will be placed upon her that she will balance with her unbelievable strength.

The First Lady, standing with her toes on two chairs, will lift an anvil of seven hundredweights two shoes off the ground with her hair while still to the astonishment of the audience take up and balance a weight of 100 pounds in each hand. Every member of the audience is free to test and examine the weights.

These women, sadly, are not identified by name or even by nationality. Few fairground entertainers surmount historical obscurity, but perhaps the one circumstance that performers themselves did not anticipate, even at the most modest venues, was anonymity. Why might a showman fail to advertise the name of a performer? The most likely motive would be to substitute another if his attraction should, for instance, seek more money than he was willing to pay.

Were there indeed other performers who displayed similar skills? The stunts advertised on this bill were actually staples in exhibitions of strength. From my archives, I have gathered a few eighteenth-century examples of anonymous strong-folk: In 1740, "The Wonderful Strong and Surprizing Persian Dwarf," a forty-five-year-old man, three feet eight inches tall, performed in London. As part of his repertoire he would dance around the room bearing "a stone of four hundred weight hanging on his hair, above six inches from the floor." Lest you think, all brawn, no brain, he had mastered, it was noted, eighteen languages. In 1751 a "Little Gentlewoman, lately arrived from Geneva" allowed herself to be suspended between two chairs, enduring the collective weight of "five or six Men [standing] on her Body, whom after some time, she flings off." In 1753 an unnamed "Female Sampson" advertised in the *New York Mercury*. She "lies with her body extended between two chairs, and bears an anvil of 300 lbs. on her breast, and will suffer to let 2 men strike it with a sledgehammer." At almost the same time, an "Italian Female Sampson" in London lifted "a large Anvil of 500 lb Weight by the Hair of her Head." Another advertisement promised that "A large block of Marble, of near a Thousand Weight, shall be on her Body, which she will permit to lie on her some Time; after which she will throw it off at about six feet distance without using Hands."

Even acknowledging these spectacular precedents, we may delight in this playbill, with its unique woodcut depicting a woman with anchors suspended from her hair and mouth.

Mit hoher Bewilligung

wird Unterzeichneter bey seiner Durchreise die Ehre haben,
einem hohen und verehrungswürdigen Publikum

Zwey starke Dames,

welche hier noch nie gesehen worden, zu produziren.

Die jüngere ist 16 Jahre alt und besitzt ihre Stärke in ihren Haaren.
Die ältere ist 18 Jahre alt, 5 Schuh hoch und besitzt ihre Stärke in körper-
lichen Kräften. Beyde sind gut proportionirt.

1) Wird die Erste 900 Pfund Gewicht mit ihren Haaren vom Erdboden aufheben, welches in zwey
Schiffsankern besteht, und noch einen dritten Anker mit dem Mund aufnehmen, so, daß sie alle
drey Anker zugleich in die Höhe balancirt.

2) Wird die Zweyte sich auf zwey Stühle legen, wobey zu bemerken ist, daß sie mit dem Kopf auf
dem einen und mit den Füßen auf dem andern Stuhle ruht, so, daß der ganze Körper frey bleibt,
und ein Gewicht von 1000 Pfund auf sich legen läßt, welches sie mit unglaublicher Stärke balancirt.

3) Wird die Erste, mit den Zehen auf zwey Stühlen stehend, einen Ambos von sieben Centnern zwey
Schuh hoch vom Erdboden mit ihren Haaren aufheben, und noch zur Bewunderung der Zuschauer
in jede Hand ein Gewicht von 100 Pfund nehmen und damit balanciren.

Jedem Zuschauer steht es frey, die angegebenen Gewichte zu besichtigen und zu untersuchen.

Der Unterzeichnete schmeichelt sich, auch hier den Beyfall einzuerndten, welcher ihm in vielen großen Städten
Deutschlands zu Theil wurde, und versichert zugleich, daß gewiß Niemand den Schauplatz mißvergnügt verlassen wird.

Diese Stücke sind von Morgens 9 Uhr bis Abends 9 Uhr zu sehen.

Standespersonen bezahlen nach Belieben. Preise der Plätze: Erster Platz 24 kr. Zweyter Platz
12 kr. Dritter Platz 6 kr.

Der Schauplatz ist

Johann Engelbert, aus Prag.

Mr. Handel's Experiments
1823

This broadside is printed on an unusual orange clay-coated paper, and Mr. Handel's name appears reversed out against a black background. The printer, in a capacity we have noted elsewhere in these pages (see p. 140), is listed as a source of tickets to the show, which could also be obtained at the theater and the local hotel. The verbose Mr. Handel appeared on the island of Antigua after successful long runs, if his handbill is to be believed, in London, Dublin, Liverpool, and various provincial towns. The show is the third in a series of performances, implying that he was capable of varying his repertoire. Among his effects were "The Invisible Hen," likely his version of the classic egg bag effect; "The Sympathetic Clock," another popular illusion; and "The Self-Impelled Mill," a favorite example of magicians' automata in which the blades of a mechanical windmill start or stop on a spectator's command (more elaborate versions of this illusion were featured in this century). According to Handel, "This comes the nearest to Perpetual Motion of any invention heretofore seen."

The highlight of the show was an illusion here called "The Celebrated Feat of The Ne Plus Ultra, The most interesting and impenetrable secret in the Arcana of Philosophical illusions." It was indeed impressive: Handel borrowed some personal effects—rings, watches, gloves, handkerchiefs—and made them vanish "before the eyes of the Spectators"; the objects would then "be found in any part of the Town, not exceeding one quarter of a mile, in chimneys, public buildings, apartments, &c., or, in a word, in any place that may be required of the Company." To pre-empt the charge of confederacy,

those deputed for the purpose of bringing the articles from the places so ordered shall be chosen by a majority of the Company, and a carriage will be in readiness at the door to take them to the place desired. To enlarge on this truly surprising and astonishing experiment would be unnecessary, as the idea is incredible. It requires all the dignity of man to believe, after having seen, that there was a possibility of performing it without the aid of supernatural influence.

A version of this remarkable effect was performed by Robert-Houdin before Louis Philippe at St. Cloud in 1845. He borrowed several handkerchiefs from the royal entourage, which he then pressed together into a small package. He asked other spectators to fill out cards suggesting where the parcel might then be found. His majesty was asked to select three cards and make his choice among the locations indicated. Louis Philippe vetoed finding the items under the candelabra in his study as too easy, and thought that the dome at the Hôtel des Invalides was too far away. He settled on a metal box in an orange tree, just outside the palace and he immediately dispatched guards to make sure the spot was undisturbed. Robert-Houdin transformed the hand-kerchiefs into a white turtle dove. Gardeners were sent to the designated spot and after considerable digging they returned with an old iron chest. The key was found on a ribbon around the neck of the dove. In the chest was a note supposedly written some sixty years earlier by the great charlatan Cagliostro, bearing his wax seal. The text predicted that the handkerchiefs of Louis Philippe would be found in his majesty's orange tree that day; and so they were. The effect is described in *The Unmasking of Robert-Houdin*, the embarrassing history of magic by Harry Houdini that was an attack on his former hero, the man from whom he had derived his name.

Houdini mentions precedents for the "flying handkerchiefs" in an illusion called "The Ne Plus Ultra of the Cabalistic Art," performed by Testot in October 1826. He notes that Marriot performed the same stunt with an identical description in 1831, and Buck offered a similar effect with a borrowed watch in a loaf of bread purchased from "any baker's shop in the town" in 1840. Even though it is unlikely that he originated the illusion, it was Mr. Handel who preceded all those conjurers enumerated by Houdini with his version of the "Ne Plus Ultra," performed in Antigua in 1823.

THEATRE ROYAL.

BY PERMISSION OF HIS EXCELLENCY THE CAPTAIN GENERAL.

MOST respectfully begs leave to return thanks to the Public of Antigua, for the Patronage that has been conferred on his First Two Evenings' Performances; and informs them that a

THIRD EXHIBITION
OF A VARIETY OF NOVEL AND EXTRAORDINARY

EXPERIMENTS,

WILL TAKE PLACE ON

SATURDAY EVENING,

THE SIXTH OF SEPTEMBER, 1823.

When every exertion will be used to render the Evening's Entertainment as amusing as possible; and in the course of which he will introduce

THE CELEBRATED FEAT OF THE

Ne Plus Ultra,

The most interesting and impenetrable secret in the Arcana of Philosophical illusions; which drew crowded houses for sixty successive nights in London, Dublin, Liverpool, &c.——Notwithstanding every attempt to develope the means by which the objects were conveyed, it still remains the wonder of the most acute minds.—Mr. H. will borrow from the Company present a number of Articles, such as Watches, Rings, Gloves, Handkerchiefs, &c., which articles, at the command of the Performer, will disappear from before the eyes of the Spectators, and will be found in any part of the Town, not exceeding one quarter of a mile, in chimneys, public buildings, apartments, &c., or, in a word, in any place that may be required by the Company.—To do away with the idea of confederacy, those deputed for the purpose of bringing the articles from the places so ordered shall be chosen by a majority of the Company, and a carriage will be in readiness at the door to take them to the place desired. To enlarge on this truly surprising and astonishing experiment would be unnecessary, as the idea is incredible. It requires all the dignity of man to believe, after having seen, that there was a possibility of performing it without the aid of supernatural influence.

VOLCANIC BASIN.
THE MYSTERIOUS CANDLE,
Which brings to light abstruse Secrets.

The Invisible Hen.
THE TURKISH MAGICIAN.

The Sympathetic Clock.

THE SELF-IMPELLED MILL.

He has, for the inspection of his Spectators, a curious Self-impelled Mill, which will go or stop as any person in company may require. This comes the nearest to Perpetual Motion of any invention heretofore seen.

Tickets of Admission to be had at the Register Printing Office, at Miss Appleby's Hotel, and at the Theatre (where a plan of the Boxes may be seen) from 10 to 4 o'clock, on the day of Performance.—BOXES, TWELVE SHILLINGS GALLERY, SIX.—Children under 10 years, half price to the Boxes.—Doors to be opened at half-past Six o'clock and the Performance to commence precisely at a quarter-past Seven.

BOSCO'S BULLET CATCH

1827

BARTOLOMEO BOSCO, BORN IN TURIN in 1793, was more than a well-known conjurer, he was an international celebrity whose career spanned almost fifty years. An opportunist and self-promoter, he was clearly clever and genuinely skillful but also crude. He was the acknowledged master of the slight-of-hand classic, the "Cups and Balls."

It is said that while serving reluctantly in Napoleon's army during the Russian campaign he was wounded and feigned death on the battlefield. When a soldier leaned over his body to strip him of valuables he simultaneously picked the fellow's pocket, garnering enough money to secure his passage home. Although this story reads like one created by a modern-day press agent, it is repeated by respectable historians and is included here for your amusement.

Bosco was the major transitional figure of magic in his day, his success paving the way for the more elegant and refined sleight-of-hand experts who followed, including perhaps the two most important Continental conjurers of the century, the Austrian Johann Nepomuk Hofzinser (see p. 142) and the Frenchman Jean Eugene Robert-Houdin. We have firsthand accounts of Bosco from both of these men. Robert-Houdin, who witnessed Bosco performing in Paris in the early 1830s, praised his "unequalled manual dexterity in Cups and Balls" but criticized his old-fashioned presentation: his address, his costume, his use of confederates, and especially his cruelty to animals. Robert-Houdin reports that Bosco gave impromptu demonstrations on the street to induce spectators to purchase tickets to his paid shows (this same technique was successfully employed by the great twentieth-century master of impromptu magical performance, Max Malini).

Hofzinser, whose reviews of music, dance, and theater were published in Viennese newspapers, wrote appreciatively of Bosco on at least three occasions. He praised not only his great manual skill but also his humor, psychological insight, and audience rapport. Hofzinser called him the greatest conjurer of the age and declared, "the soul of magic lives only in Bosco."

This playbill features the gun trick (see p. 126), first described in the sixteenth century, which resulted in the death of a number of performers in the intervening three hundred years. It is embellished with a striking woodcut of the blindfolded Bosco about to be fired at by a half dozen marksmen. A sample of his modest analysis follows:

The Extraordinary Test of Invulnerability. Namely, there will be a six-man military detachment set up at the end of the hall, and their guns will be loaded with bullets before the viewers to give every proof to the honorable public in order to demonstrate that they are made of real lead. Additionally, guns and bullets may be brought along by the public. Thus the designated bullets may be loaded into the guns and fired at the prepared subject, who at the same moment will catch all the bullets with his bare hands in the manner of his own invention and hand them to the honorable public for inspection. So that those who may be afraid of the shooting and wish to leave and not wish to feel cheated of the remaining sixteen certainly very interesting pieces of the performance, this great test of invulnerability will take place at the end of the performance, and time will be allowed for them to leave then; it is assured however by the undersigned that this show is neither dangerous for the honored public nor for himself.

The intrepid and ultimately vulnerable Bosco finally expired in Dresden in 1863.

Mit hoher obrigkeitlicher Bewilligung
wird
am Mittwoch den 1. August 1827
im großen Redouten=Saale,
Bischofs=Straße, im Hôtel de Pologne,

Bartholomäus Bosco
eine
außerordentliche Vorstellung
in zwei Abtheilungen zu geben die Ehre haben.

Diese Vorstellung wird unter allen bisher gegebenen die brillanteste seyn, denn nicht nur daß sie sich durch Neuheit und Manigfaltigkeit der zu produzirenden Kunststücke vor den übrigen auszeichnet, sondern sie wird mit einem großen Schusse enden, genannt:

die außerordentliche Probe der
Unverletzbarkeit.

Es werden nehmlich 6 Mann Militair an einem Ende des Saales aufgestellt, und ihre Gewehre mit Kugeln, welche früher zur Ueberzeugung, daß es ächte Bleykugeln sind, und zur beliebigen Bezeichnung dem geehrten Publikum hingegeben werden, laden. Auch können Gewehre und Kugeln nach Belieben mitgebracht werden. Sodann werden die mit den bezeichneten Kugeln geladenen Gewehre auf den Gefertigten losgefeuert, und in demselben Augenblicke wird er alle die Kugeln mit flachen Händen nach seiner eigenen Erfindung auffangen und dem geehrten Publikum zur Besichtigung überreichen. Damit aber diejenigen, welche sich etwa vor dem Schießen fürchten, der übrigen 16 gewiß sehr interessanten Stücke nicht beraubt werden möchten, wird dieses große Probestück ganz am Schluße der Vorstellung geschehen, und Zeit gelassen, damit sie sich entfernen können; es versichert aber der Unterzeichnete, daß es weder für das geehrte Publikum, noch für ihn selbst gefahrbringend ist.

B. Bosco.

Preise der Plätze:
Ein nummerirter Sitz 15 Sgr.   Parterre und erste Gallerie 10 Sgr.   Zweite Gallerie 5 Sgr.

Die Casse wird um halb 7 Uhr geöffnet.
Der Anfang ist um halb 8 Uhr. Das Ende um halb 10 Uhr.

16 X 20

GOUFFE
"THE MAN-MONKEY"
1828

DONNING THE COSTUMES OF MONKEYS, men bounded, leapt, and cavorted on the nineteenth-century stage. Although animal imitation is one of the founding conventions of the drama, the modern man-monkey is usually dated from the ballet-pantomime production "Jocko, or the Brazilian Ape" of 1825. Its delineator was the great comic dancer Charles Mazurier (1793–1828). A remarkably talented fellow, he spawned numerous imitators, and his influence long outlasted his unfortunately foreshortened career. One theory even suggests that Mazurier's ape-like prancing was a significant precursor to the cancan. Not only dancers but also variety-stage acrobats created a following with their aerodynamic turns on this simian theme.

Interest in the burgeoning field of ethnology spawned a pre-Darwinian fascination with the relationship of man to monkey that was often enacted on stage or in fairground exhibitions. In the vernacular of the showman, these displays might be exploited as a missing link, a nondescript, or a "what is it." A marvelous lithograph of Mazurier as Jocko shows him in full monkey regalia reaching out to touch the hand of a small boy in a pose remarkably similar to the likeness of God and Adam on the ceiling of the Sistine Chapel. How would a modern creationist have viewed this parodic blend of entertainment and metaphysics?

A group of internationally respected performers, including Mazilier, Klischnigg, Parsloe, Blanchard, Marzetti, and even the redoubtable wire walker Madame Saqui, all tried their hand at monkey business. In his autobiography Wallett, the "Queen's Jester," related the story of carrying an injured, bleeding prop man to a dispensary while still in full monkey regalia. The proprietress regarded "the apparition of a man-monkey with his tail trailing on the ground and a half-dead man on his back with the blood streaming down. One glance sufficed. She fainted senseless to the ground."

Monsieur Gouffe, one of the more renowned of this ilk, first performed in England in the mid-1820s. Gouffe's name appears on bills with various spellings, and there are conflicting views as to his real name and background. Thomas Frost suggested that his surname was Vale, citing his discovery by John "Muster" Richardson, the theatrical impresario. I have in my collection, however, a playbill for Mr. Vale's

benefit at the New Surrey Theatre on November 15, 1825, at which Gouffe also appeared. He danced "on pint pots, on his hands, in an inverted position." It was just such a display, in the pub at which he worked, that had induced Richardson to sign Gouffe with his company (when Richardson's effects were dispersed at auction in 1836, among the lots were monkey costumes and dresses worn by a "nosdescrit," or wild man). Whatever his true name and origins, both Richardson and Charles Dibdin extolled his virtues but acknowledged his humble intellect. He was, however, remarkably strong and agile and a talented mime. Even Mazurier was said to have admired Gouffe's performance.

This provincial bill of 1828 features his major theatrical vehicle, "The Island Ape." Gouffe, we are told, "will exhibit his Wonderful Tricks, Leaps, Balancing, &c., which have excited the Curiosity and Astonishment of the Metropolis, and raised a doubt in the mind of Thousands Whether He Be A Monkey Or A Man." The large woodblock image of Gouffe in full costume was similar to another octagonal cut featured on a playbill for the actor at the San Souci Theatre in London in 1825. Traveling to America in the 1830s, Gouffe appeared in "The Dumb Savoyard and His Monkey" as well as his signature, "Jocko, the Brazilian Ape."

Perhaps his relocation to America was prompted by the unwanted notoriety of marital strife. In what reporters characterized as a "strong foreign accent," Gouffe described his wife as drunk, incorrigible, and adulterous, and sought legal action against her on the grounds that her public displays of misconduct had cost him employment. When the magistrate told him to seek divorce he replied, "That would be the delight of my heart to get clear away from her; but she refuses to go, declaring that she will stick to me as long as I have a shirt on my back. When I threatened to turn her out the other night after having caught a big fellow in bed with her, she swore that she would get a basket and hawk periwinkles about the different public-houses of the Theatre, and every one who purchased from her should know that she was the wife of 'Monsieur Gouffe, the performer.'"

THE WONDER OF THE AGE,
MONSIEUR
GOUFFE,
Is Engaged for Three Nights,
and will make his FIRST APPEARANCE in Sheffield this Evening.

The spirit and confidence with which MONSIEUR GOUFFE performs his Tricks, Leaps, Escapes from his Pursuers, &c., keep the spectator in constant good humour; nor can any emotion of fear, for one moment, disturb the pleasures excited by his varied Feats, as they are all performed with that apparent ease which characterises the Animal MONSIEUR GOUFFE is so happy in his Imitation of.

On *THURSDAY* Evening, December 18,
Will be Performed, (3d time) the New Petit Comedy of The

GREEN - EYED
Monster.

Baron Spenhausen, Mr. WILTON............ ....Colonel, Mr. HAINES
Marcus, Mr. HAY......Krant, Mr. BLAND
Jerome, Mr. EMDEN.....Petro, Mr. FELLOWS....Antonio, Mr. TELBIN, Jun.
Lady Spenhausen, Mrs. HAINES..Anjelia, Miss CLEAVER..Luise, Miss SHORE

After which, a New Ballet Pantomime, called THE

ISLAND
APE.

Lieutenant Selkirk (shipwrecked on the Island) Mr. HILL
Karaboo (a Savage Chief) Mr. NELSON........Fataboo (a native Warrior) Mr. FELLOWS
Boatswain, Mr. POPHAM..Tom Starboard, Mr. EMDEN
The Island Ape, by Mons. GOUFFE,
Who will exhibit his Wonderful Tricks, Leaps, Balancing, &c., which have excited the Curiosity and Astonishment of the Metropolis, and raised a doubt in the minds of Thousands
WHETHER HE BE A MONKEY OR A MAN.

To conclude with the highly Comic Farce of
ALL THE WORLD'S A
STAGE.

Sir Gilbert Pumpkin, Mr. WILTON....Charles, Mr. ELLIS
Harry, Mr. COURTNEY..........Diggory, Mr. HAY.......Cymon, Mr. BLAND
Timothy, Mr. POPHAM....John, Mr. NELSON..Wat, Mr. EMDEN
Miss Bridget Pumpkin, Mrs. CLEAVER........Miss Kitty Sprightly, Miss CLEAVER

On FRIDAY, by desire, and under the Patronage of the Gentlemen Subscribers to the
SHAKSPEARE CLUB, SHAKSPEARE's Comedy of MUCH ADO ABOUT NOTHING.—
To conclude with SHERIDAN's Farce of the CRITIC.

B. A. BACON, PRINTER, SHEFFIELD.

6¼ x 18¹¹⁄₁₆

SCAPIGLIONE
"THE MODERN SAMPSON"

C. 1828

WHILE MANY PERFORMING ARTISTS have used the epithet "The Modern Sampson," few have exploited such a direct link of hair and strength as the subject of this broadside. From a series of playbills advertising his appearances in France, Italy, Germany, and the Netherlands, we are able to piece together this unauthorized biography: Using the (comic) billing of Scapiglione, our subject, whose given name may have been Valentin Peresinotti, was born around the turn of the nineteenth century on the Barbary coast (this document says he hails from Brischel while other playbills give Tangier) of an African father and a European mother. He was brought to Italy at a young age, and there received his education.

It is unclear which developed first, his singular coiffure or his outstanding physique, but it was this unusual combination that set him apart as an attraction. One German playbill proclaimed that in eight hundred years there had never been a human being with such a beautiful form and such beautiful hair.

His torso and waist were described as regal, with an infinitely broad but hairless chest and powerful arm muscles on his equally hairless arms. It was also noted that he sported only a scant beard—all in contrast to the disproportionately enormous amount of hair on his head (estimates of its circumference ranged from four and a half to five and a half feet). His hair was likened by turns to a Roman helmet, a "handsome circle," or an enormous bearskin. It grew so quickly that every eight days,

one is obligated to cut it. If one neglects to do this, Scapiglione suffers a stinging heat flash, accompanied by hemorrhaging. Medical doctors of different [backgrounds] have been consulted on this subject and their conclusion was that he should have his finger- and toe-nails pulled out; something he never agreed to have done. Some have remarked that if too much of this modern-day Samson's hair is cut, he experiences an intense weakness, and becomes pale and falls prey to headaches as well as a kind of fiery fever followed by cold. To preserve the gaiety of his character and his perfect health, it is necessary that his hair be maintained at the precise length indicated above. Those who honor him with their presence, may, while he [appears] in front of amateurs, inspect his hair and even touch it without fear.…His hair, tousled, and flipped over is not so free such that a single twitch of the head allows it to regain its natural shape, and there is no sign that it was touched. Scapiglione is not sensitive to cold; in all seasons he is lightly dressed and never covers his head. He loses weight in the winter and becomes quite rounded in the summer.

We are told that his strength and appetite were linked, like Samson's, to his hair. When his locks were properly maintained, his strength surpassed that of two men. He also entertained his fans with his strong voice, offering "Italian songs with a Venetian flavor." His oddly foreshortened physique is not mentioned. His peculiar physiognomy attracted an audience ranging from the king of France to civil servants, from students to soldiers—and young women of various classes and callings, attracted to "his song, his words and his noble bearing."

While other broadsides of Scapiglione use woodcuts, this example exploits the technique of lithography, an early use presaging the medium that later in the century would revolutionize the entertainment poster. Combined with an engraved text, the illustration lends an altogether splendid and singular appearance to our hero, as he emerges through the elaborate curtain to command the stage. Scapiglione appeared from noon to four in the afternoon and evenings between six and eleven o'clock at the location formerly occupied by the Théâtre de Mons. Comte (which was vacated by that famous conjurer and ventriloquist in 1827). Finally, he announced his willingness to make house calls to important patrons upon demand.

LE SAMSON MODERNE

De  plus

SCAPIGLIONE,

Phénomène vivant & modèle d'Académie, homme très agréable à voir.

Les raretés de son corps consistent en une chevelure de quatre pieds et demi de circonférence, forment un très-beau cercle. Ses cheveux sont d'un châtain-brun tirant sur le noir; ils croissent si rapidement que, tous les huit jours, on est obligé d'en couper quatre travers de doigt. Si on se néglige sur cela, le Scapiglione, éprouve une chaleur piquante, accompagnée d'une hémorragie. Des docteurs en médecine de différentes contrées ont été consultés à ce sujet, et leur décision a été qu'il devait se faire arracher les ongles des mains et des pieds; à quoi celui-ci n'a jamais consenti. On remarque que si l'on coupe trop les cheveux du Samson moderne, il ressent une faiblesse extrême, devient pâle et est atteint de maux de tête ainsi que d'une espèce de fièvre en chaud suivie de froid. Pour conserver la gaîté de son caractère et sa parfaite santé, il est nécessaire que sa chevelure soit maintenue au point ci-dessus indiqué. Les personnes qui l'honoreront de leur présence, peuvent, lorsqu'il va au devant des amateurs, visiter sa chevelure et même la toucher sans aucune crainte, laquelle, étant extrêmement propre et sans apprêt, forme un superbe casque à la romaine va le plus beau colbak que l'on puisse voir. Sa chevelure, éparpillée, froissée et renversée, n'est pas plutôt libre, qu'un seul secouement de sa tête lui fait reprendre sa forme naturelle, et on ne s'aperçoit plus d'y avoir touché. Il existe enfin, dans cette chevelure, deux particularités dignes d'admiration: la première, c'est que, depuis le haut du front jusqu'à la moitié de l'élévation des cheveux, on la voit hérissés, et la dernière, que, de cette moitié à la surface, ils sont triangulaires. Le Scapiglione n'est point sensible au froid; dans toutes les saisons, il est vêtu légèrement et ne se couvre jamais la tête. Il maigrit en hiver, et devient fort gras en été. Son corps et sa taille sont majestueux; sa poitrine est infiniment large et très-élevée; ses muscles sont athlétiques; son estomac a 54 pouces de circonférence, chacun de ses bras en a 20 de tour, et chacun de ses mollets 22. Lorsque sa chevelure est maintenue, sa force surpasse celle de deux hommes, et son appétit l'égale.

Ce Samson moderne, est celui qui a fait l'admiration de plusieurs Souverains. Il est né à Brischel, en Barbarie, d'un père africain et d'une mère européenne.

La curiosité à laquelle ce Phénomène excite, dispense d'un plus long détail et surtout du moindre éloge. On assure seulement qu'il n'a besoin ni de musique ni d'annonce, pour être visité par toutes les classes de la société. Pères & mères, sachez qu'il n'est rien qui puisse blesser les mœurs. A la fin de chaque séance, le Scapiglione chantera, étant décemment vêtu et comme il parait devant les Empereurs, les Rois, les Princes, les Princesses, les Corps religieux, civils et militaires.

Le Samson moderne est visible de midi à 4 heures, et de 6 à 11 du soir. Passage des Panoramas, ancien Théâtre de M. Comte. **Le prix d'Entrée 3f., et pour les enfans 1,50.**

Son chant, ses paroles et son noble maintien lui ont toujours attiré et valu d'être appelé dans des Couvents de demoiselles et dans beaucoup de pensionnats. Le Samson moderne se transportera chez les personnes qui le feront demander.

Lith. de Ducarme.

CAPPELLI'S LEARNED CATS

1829

UNDER THE DIRECTION OF THE Italian sleight-of-hand artist and impresario Signor Cappelli, animals famous for their intractability demonstrated feats of dexterity and docility before London audiences. This performance in 1829 was held at 248 Regent Street, just a short distance from the Cosmorama Rooms, the venue for a number of attractions represented in this volume.

The exhibition of "The Greatest Wonder in England" featured stunts not usually numbered among the repertoire of performing animals, let alone feline actors: turning a spit, striking an anvil, roasting coffee, and initiating the movement of a machine that would grind rice. The dramatis personae were elsewhere described as a mother, two sons, a daughter, and, the star of the troupe, a "jet-black and maternal-looking negress," who fetched a pail of water from a well. Her image is reproduced on this playbill in a crude but charming woodcut. Cappelli, who performed his conjuring as "The Inimitable Tuscan," took his pampered pets, which also included a domino-playing dog, to venues throughout England, Scotland, and Ireland before again performing in London at Bartholomew Fair in 1832.

Contemporaneous with Cappelli was the clown Dicky Usher's "Celebrated Stud of Real Cats," in which he rode in a carriage whose motive power was four "Thorough-bred Mousers, Tibby, Tabby, Toddle and Tot." As Derek Forbes mentions, Usher not only circled the stage but also paraded through the streets in his feline chariot to generate publicity for his shows. His cats, he claimed, won a wager by traveling almost a thousand yards in just over eight minutes on the Turnpike Road in Liverpool. Usher was also the originator of the geese-drawn washing tub (one is shown on the playbill of the clown Arthur Nelson, p. 108).

One of the more remarkable examples of cat chaos among feline thespians was recounted by the nineteenth-century showman Sam Wild who, at the benefit of his clown Boardman, announced that the jester would be transported across the stage in a carriage drawn by fifty-four cats in a blaze of fire. The troupe was recruited from locals who brought strays and household pets to the stage door in return for a free pass. "Little preparatory training on the part of the feline performers was considered necessary," Wild noted. The cats were very gingerly harnessed to the chariot and led out from the wings. Insurrection was brewing, and the report of gunfire and the blaze of fireworks did not "contribute much toward reassuring the rebels, or towards inspiring them with confidence in the existing state of things. But the rebellion was quelled before serious consequences ensued, and a timely rescue of the revolters was made the instant the curtain closed upon a scene of an unaffected struggle for liberty."

To this day, performances by this recalcitrant species are witnessed with amazement. Antony Hippisley Coxe revealed the key to producing such an act in his classic work, *A Seat at the Circus*. He allowed that the secret was to harness the proclivities of individual animals in determining the tricks each would perform on stage.

April 1829

The Greatest Wonder in England is
The Learned Cats!

THESE REPRESENTATIONS WILL TAKE PLACE
At Signor Cappelli's
248, Regent Street,
Next Door to the Argyll Rooms,
OPEN EVERY DAY.

Signor Cappelli
(FROM TUSCANY,)

Has the honor of informing the Nobility and Gentry, that he has just Arrived in London, where he has opened an Exhibition entirely Novel to the Inhabitants of this Metropolis.

This Exhibition will consist of the Extraordinary and

Wonderful Exercises Performed by CATS.

The entertainment will commence with an Exhibition of some very extraordinary Manœuvres or " Slight of Hand " by SIGNOR CAPPELLI, he inimitable Tuscan. Executed in a style the most remarkable and unknown, in this Country. The Cats will then be introduced and their performance will be to beat a drum, turn a spit, grind knives, strike upon an anvil, roast coffee, ring bells, set a piece of Machinery in motion to grind rice in the Italian manner with many other astonishing exercises.—One of the Cats, the cleverest of the company will draw water out of a well at her masters command, without any other signal being given than the sound of the voice; this command being pronounced both in French & Italian, all who have witnessed her prompt obedience,

Have expressed themselves at once astonished and delighted, with the Prodigy.

To begin at 12 o'Clock, performing at every ½ Hour till 5, and after that Hour, will attend Private Families at their own residences.

ADMITTANCE, Front Seats 2s.—Back Seats 1s. Children under 10 years of Age, Half-Price.

J. W. PEELE, PRINTER, 31, NEW CUT, LAMBETH.

6½ x 10

SPELTERINI'S LIVING ASS

C. 1830

I AM VERY FOND OF SPELTERINI and his ass, but on some level I know less about this broadside than the others in this volume. I certainly knew less about it upon purchase, as I made no conscious effort to acquire it, unlike all but a few of the items included here. It was among a small cache of materials on remarkable characters that I acquired from a well-known New York firm about twenty-five years ago. I was eventually able to determine that the items had been assembled by an early collector of materials on strength and strongmen.

The broadside is, on the surface, undistinguished. The cut is charming but crude, far more primitive than even its seventeenth-century companions in this volume. Although I assume the broadside is from the second quarter of the nineteenth century, it bears no date or printer's mark. The performer is probably Carlo Spelterini who, billed as the "Italian Hercules" or the "Patagonian Sampson," performed at Vauxhall Gardens (see p. 98) and with various circus troupes in the 1820s and 1830s. I am not sure of his relationship to the most famous of his namesakes, Madame Spelterini, who gained fame in 1876 as the first woman to traverse Niagara Falls on a tight wire. She performed the stunt with peach baskets affixed to her feet.

On this broadside we are told that Spelterini "will balance on his teeth a real Living Ass, At the Top of a Ladder at the same time holding in each hand a Fifty Six Pound Weight. Without any Assistance but his own Muscular Power. A Feat never attempted by any one, except himself." Another version of the act was related by Sam Wild, the colorful Liverpudlian showman whose establishment was known as Old Wild's. He presented a juggler and equilibrist called Old Malabar. Known for both strength and agility, Malabar would balance long planks, coach wheels, and, as a special feature, a donkey perched atop a ladder. Wild relates that when not more formally employed, Malabar often plied his trade as a street entertainer. "How much have you got?" he would ask of his wife and the youth who went around "nobbing" (passing the hat) among the spectators. "Ah, we must have another shilling ladies and gentlemen, and then up goes the donkey."

There are also precedents for bad behavior, and perhaps one can be intuited here. I have quoted from letters citing nonpayment of printing charges by individual acts, and some bad blood may have existed between the strongman and his supplier, who did not even include the name of his firm on this advertisement. Perhaps the printer chose to exact an amusing revenge. If one scans the phrase "Signori Spelterini will balance on his teeth a real Living Ass" vertically, instead of left to right, the second column reads "Spelterini, a real Ass."

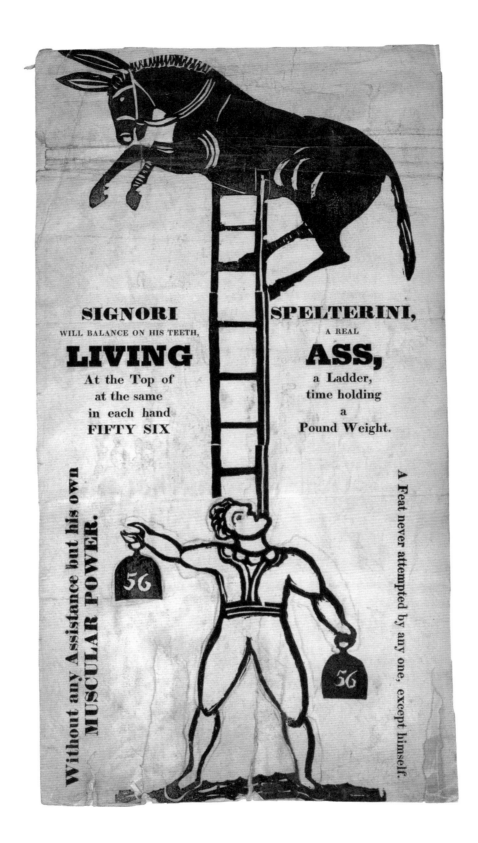

SIGNORI SPELTERINI,

WILL BALANCE ON HIS TEETH, A REAL

LIVING ASS,

At the Top of a Ladder,
at the same time holding
in each hand a
FIFTY SIX Pound Weight.

Without any Assistance but his own MUSCULAR POWER.

A Feat never attempted by any one, except himself.

8¼ x 16⁷⁄₁₆

THE GIGANTIC WHALE

1831

IT IS DIFFICULT TO IMAGINE the skeleton of an enormous whale floating, of its own accord, down the Thames River, but such a specimen was sighted by astonished Londoners in 1702. The discovery was eagerly exploited by showmen, who exhibited the remains in an open field. A number of other whales were displayed in eighteenth-century England; my favorite is an attraction billed in the 1730s as "The largest Thames-Monster or miraculous man-eater, that was ever in the World."

One hundred years later the "Pavilion of the Gigantic Whale" was established in London's Charing Cross. A formidable playbill for the attraction was printed by the firm of T. Brettell in London's Haymarket. A smaller playbill, also in my collection, gives the beast's dimensions:

Total Length of the Animal	95 feet
Breadth of ditto	18"
Length of the head	22"
Height of the cranium	4½"
Length of the vertebral column	69½"
Number of vertebrae	62
Number of ribs, 28, length of ditto	9"
Length of the fins	12½"
—— of the fingers	4½
Width of the tail	22½"
Length of ditto	3"
Weight of the animal, when found	240 tons or 480,000 lbs
Quantity of oil extracted from blubber	4000 gallons, or 40,000"
Weight of the rotten flesh buried in the sand	85 tons, or 170,000"

The last entry, rotting flesh buried in the sand, was a not inconsiderable problem, and one with which Londoners were all too familiar. When another whale had been shown a generation earlier, the *Times* noted, "the stench was intolerable," and spectators were urged to come armed with handkerchiefs dipped in strong vinegar.

Our "Gigantic Whale" was found floating in the North Sea by a fisherman on November 3, 1827. He solicited the aid of two vessels to bring the enormous carcass to shore at Ostend, Belgium. The towing cable and the creature were "cast on the sands on the East end of the harbour." The exhibitors claimed that the famous anatomist Baron Cuvier (who had examined the Hottentot Venus; see p. 68) calculated the whale's age as somewhere between nine hundred and a thousand years.

Viewing the attraction cost one shilling, but for double the price the spectators were invited "to inspect and sit inside the belly of the whale where twenty-four musicians performed a concert." On a platform inside the ninety-five-foot skeleton, customers sat at tables listening to their favorite tunes and perused a guest book to admire the signatures and *bon mots* of notables who had already attended. *The Mirror of Literature*—cited by Richard Altick, who describes many of these giant mammals—pronounced it "one of the pleasantest places we have visited this season."

PAVILION

OF THE

GIGANTIC

WHALE,

OPPOSITE THE

NATIONAL REPOSITORY,

Charing Cross

The Proprietor of this Cetaceous Animal, **95 Feet in Length and 18 in Breadth**, which has been admired by the Learned and most Distinguished Personages of a part of Europe, having been proclaimed by the Naturalists and Professors of *Paris*, as the Largest in the possession of Man, respectfully informs the Public, that HIS PAVILION is

NOW OPEN

and will continue OPEN DAILY (Sundays Excepted), from TEN o'Clock in the Morning, till EIGHT at Night.

ADMISSION, - - - *One Shilling.*

Persons desirous of being admitted into the Saloon, to inspect and sit in the BELLY OF THE WHALE, where Twenty-Four Musicians performed a Concert; and to examine the Album, which is already one of the most remarkable in Europe, by the respectability of its Signatures, will Pay. - - - - - *Two Shillings.*

Children under Twelve Years of Age, Half-Price.

PRINTED BY T. BRETTELL, RUPERT STREET, HAYMARKET

19¹³⁄₁₆ x 29⅞

MENAGERIE OF LIVING ANIMALS

1832

THIS BROADSIDE IS A SIGNIFICANT document in the history of the American circus. It is graced with a wonderfully crude anthropomorphized woodcut of a Bengal tiger, fashioned by R. G. Harrison, which appears under the bold heading "Purdy, Welch, Finch & Wright's Menagerie of Living Animals."

The group that presented the tiger and a host of other animals was an impressive quartet. Ed Finch was an experienced animal exhibitor and manager who had featured "Little Bet," the third elephant to be shown in America. Charles Wright, who was responsible for "Bet," was better known as the first lion tamer in America. Eisenhart Purdy was one of the foremost menagerie men of his time and, according to the historian Stuart Thayer, "none were more admired and well thought of by their contemporaries than was Rufus Welch."

The moral rhetoric surrounding these early menageries is quite surprising to the modern ear, long accustomed to negative press about the treatment of wild animals. While clergymen were inclined to see the trick riding, clowning, and acrobatics in the ring as tools of the devil, they were favorably disposed to the menagerie, describing it as a religious spectacle revealing the dominance of man over God's brute creations.

This show offered a widely varied group of animals: the camel, the red alpaca, the zebra, the jaguar, the African porcupine, the black wolf, apes, monkeys, baboons, talking parrots, and Shetland ponies. Also featured were three major attractions—an elephant, a tiger, and a pair of lions.

The tiger was an especially impressive beast that was both elegant in its appearance and terrible in its ferocity.

The elephant, which joined an earlier version of this show in 1831, was the first of that breed to be placed in a menagerie. The story of the elephant's arrival had already become legend. Brought over from India on the ship *Caroline*, the elephant had to swim to shore when the vessel ran aground on a shoal in the Delaware River. Named after the ship, "Caroline" was thereafter featured as "The Shipwrecked Elephant."

Most impressive was the display of the "Asiatic Lion and Lioness" because their trainer, Charles Wright, entered the cage with the animals. No American had ever performed this stunt that we now take for granted (only the French lion tamer Henri Martin [see p. 100] had accomplished it before Wright). Consistent with the moral imperative of the show, Wright entered the cage every afternoon at three o'clock to demonstrate

[t]he domestication of the above animals [which] exemplifies at once the master spirit of the creation, where it is said that the brute shall be subject to the will of man. Their docility pleases and instructs, though it be viewed through the prejudice of danger. The cages being perfectly secure, no fear need be apprehended from the Exhibition. A performance so novel in itself, has, as was to be expected, excited various rumours and speculations; some doubting its reality, and others affirming its danger. This is to assure the public that the performance is reality, and that the most fastidious need not be apprehensive of the result.

PURDY, WELCH, FINCH & WRIGHT'S

MENAGERIE

OF LIVING ANIMALS,

Will be exhibited at *A. H. Welch's Hampton Village*

on *Monday the 1st day of October 1832 for one day only* the

☞ The Proprietors, in having the pleasure to invite the Public to visit their Menagerie, feel a degree of confidence that it contains the most rare, gigantic and beautiful Collection of Living Animals that has ever been exhibited in this place; and they assure visitors that every attention shall be paid to render the Exhibition agreeable, which is from ___ in the morning until ___ in the afternoon.

AMONG THE COLLECTION ARE THE FOLLOWING:

Shipwrecked Elephant,

Recently imported from Calcutta. The above animal was wrecked in the Bay of Delaware, in December, 1831, and if any thing could add to the well-earned reputation and the known sagacity of this most extraordinary of all quadrupeds; or, if the prejudices of mankind are not too deeply rooted to admit of reasoning qualities in the brute, we will refer him to the peculiar case of the animal above-named. The third day after the wreck had been deserted by every thing human, and at a time when nothing was to be seen or heard but the tempestuous roaring of the troubled billows, a long boat hove in sight, manned by some of her old associates. Upon arriving at the wreck they found her writhing in agony, occasioned by the loneliness of her situation and want of food; she showed evident signs of recognition, and suspending her proboscis from its elevation, drew her deliverers on board. Upon being lowered into the water, she made her way to the nearest landing, with a sagaciousness that would have done credit to humanity.

ASIATIC LION & LIONESS.

The Keeper will enter the Cage with them at 3 in the afternoon.

The domestication of the above animals exemplifies at once the master spirit of the creation, where it is said that the brute shall be subject to the will of man. Their docility pleases and instructs, though it be viewed through the prejudice of danger. The cages being perfectly secure, no fear need be apprehended from the Exhibition.

A performance so novel in itself, has, as was to be expected, excited various rumours and speculations; some doubting its reality, and others affirming its danger. This is to assure the public that the performance is reality, and that the most fastidious need not be apprehensive of the result.

ROYAL BENGAL TIGER,

Lately arrived from Calcutta. Of all the animals of the cat kind, the Tiger is the most beautiful; their skin is rich beyond description, consisting of a jet black stripe over a ground of a brilliant yellow, disposed in such an elegant manner, that the beholder would imagine that art had actually been employed in the arrangement; their ferocity in a wild state is terrible; in size and strength they compete with the Lion, and often surpass him; travellers describe the contests between the two to be most awfully grand; they inhabit the East Indies, and frequent the most secluded and remote parts of the forest. The present is a male, of a gigantic size, and is admired by all who have viewed him.

THE RED ALPACHA,

A native of South America; said to be the fleetest animal on the continent.

AN IMMENSELY LARGE

North American Panther.

THE ZEBRA,

From the Cape of Good Hope; the most beautiful animal of the horse kind.

BRAZILIAN TIGER,

OR JAGUAR,

A very striking resemblance of the Leopard, though much larger.

A BEAUTIFUL PAIR OF

PERUVIAN LAMAS,

MALE AND FEMALE.

HISTRIX CRISTATIA,

OR WONDERFUL PORCUPINE OF AFRICA.

The quills are from 10 to 15 inches in length, and they are capable of repelling even the Lion and Tiger. The present is the first brought to this country.

A PAIR OF

Arabian Pack Camels,

MALE AND FEMALE.

Ravenous Black Wolf

OF THE ROCKY MOUNTAINS.

The orange-crested COCKATOO; pair of MACKAW BIRDS of South America; and several ENGLISH FERRETS.

The Fisher Animal of the Weasel genus.

A PAIR OF ICHNEUMONS,

OF EGYPT.

A GREAT VARIETY OF

Apes, Monkeys, Baboons, Talking Parrots &c.

Together with the interesting Performances of the

Semi-Equestrians on their Shetland Ponies,

Who seldom fail to gain applause.

☞ The Menagerie is accompanied with a Splendid **BAND OF MUSIC**, far superior to any with similar Collections, who will execute various new and popular airs, &c. *For particulars, see large bills.*

YOUNG, PRINTER, PHILADELPHIA.

Admittance 25 cents children under ten years of age half price

17¹⁵⁄₁₆ X 23³⁄₁₆

THE AUTOMATON CHESS PLAYER

1833

THE AUTOMATON CHESS PLAYER was, according to a Philadelphia newspaper of 1840, "seen by more eyes than any terrestrial object ever witnessed." Even allowing for hyperbole, this mechanical wonder was doubtless one of the most provocative attractions ever presented. Constructed in 1769 by the Hungarian inventor Wolfgang von Kempelen to please the Empress Maria Teresa, it enjoyed a spectacular but erratic career until its demise, by fire, in the Chinese Museum in Philadelphia eighty-five years after its debut. Considered by many the first great thinking machine, it was actually a magician's illusion that relied on the principles of mechanics, misdirection, and showmanship. The very possibility of a device that could play chess, however faulty the presumption, led indirectly to the invention of Cartwright's power loom and Babbage's calculating machine.

A slightly smaller than life-size figure, dressed as a Turk, sat behind a cabinet on which a chess set had been placed. The compartments were opened to reveal a complex series of wheels and gears. After the exhibitor wound the machine, the Turk would lift his arm and move the pieces in match play with a panoply of distinguished opponents, including Benjamin Franklin and Napoleon. The automaton was rarely defeated. Numerous theories were propounded to account for its motive power. A recent bibliography lists more than four hundred references to the apparatus.

When Von Kempelen died in 1804 the Turk was purchased by Johann Nepomuk Maelzel, a talented but unscrupulous showman. He was a mechanic, musician, and inventor (he took credit for the creation of the metronome, which he merely improved, but he did fashion earphones for his friend Beethoven). He refurbished the Chess Player and even enabled it to articulate the word "check [echéc]" when his opponent's king was in jeopardy.

Maelzel took the Turk to America in 1826. Although he achieved initial success, he was soon battling debunkers and competitors with rival chess- or whist-playing machines. In order to stay ahead of them, and to continue to draw crowds in cities where he had already appeared, he exhibited the Chess Player with a roster of other attractions. This broadside announces a run at Concert Hall in Boston commencing in May 1833. It featured an impressive assortment of automata, mechanical music, and his diorama, "The Conflagration of Moscow." The show was very favorably reviewed in the *Boston Advertiser*:

This remarkable exhibition of ingenuity and mechanical talent opened Monday and it was received with the same gratification which it has afforded in former years. In fact any one of the ingenious pieces, the chess player, the melodium, the trumpeter, the rope dancer and the "Burning of Moscow" would be sufficient in itself. Nothing in the way of mechanism can exceed the "Burning of Moscow." All the sights and sounds, which must have given sublimity and horror to the scene itself are here represented with a power and accuracy which almost deludes us into the belief of their reality.

At Concert Hall in Boston in 1835, Maelzel was praised by a young showman who called him "the great father of caterers for public amusement." Maelzel in turn recognized in this youngster the qualities necessary for a successful impresario. He was especially impressed that his colleague understood the value of the press. The tyro then presenting his first attraction across the hall—Joice Heth, billed as the 161-year-old nursemaid to George Washington (see p. 102)—was P. T. Barnum.

MAELZEL'S EXHIBITION,
CONCERT HALL.

PART FIRST.
THE ORIGINAL AND CELEBRATED
AUTOMATON
CHESS PLAYER,
Invented by DE KEMPELIN, improved by J. MAELZEL.

☞ The CHESS PLAYER has withstood the first Players of Europe and America, and excites universal admiration. He moves his head, eyes, lips, and hands, with the greatest facility, and distinctly pronounces the word "*Echec*," (the French word signifying "*Check*") when necessary. If a mis-move is made, he perceives and rectifies it.

THE MELODIUM.

This INSTRUMENT differs in many respects from the Panharmonicon of Mr. Maelzel. The Music it produces is not military, but of the most sweet and melodious description, and particularly calculated to gratify the connoisseur. It will perform on each evening two select pieces from the most celebrated compositions of Rossini, Bethoven, Cherubini, and other great masters.

After Part First, the Interlude of
THE MECHANICAL THEATRE,
Purposely introduced for the gratification of Juvenile Visitors,

IT CONSISTS OF THE FOLLOWING PIECES:

1. The *Amusing Little Bass Fiddler.*
2. The *French Oyster Woman*—who bows to the Company, and performs the duties of her station, by opening and presenting her Oysters to the Audience.
3. The *Old French Gentleman*, of the ancient Regime, who drinks the health of the Company with great glee.
4. The *Chinese Dancer*, accompanying the Music with his Tambourine.
5. The *Little Troubadour*, playing on several instruments.

PART SECOND.
The Automaton Trumpeter.

The Trumpeter is of a full size, and dressed in the Uniform of the French Lancers. The pieces executed by this Automaton are performed with a distinctness and precision unattainable by the best living Performers; the measurement of time, being from the nature of the Mechanism, absolutely perfect. In doubletongueing, his superiority is particularly manifested, not only in the clearness of the tones, but also in the number of the notes which are sounded. All the sounds are actually produced in the Trumpet, there being no pipes whatever within the Figure. The Pieces he plays were written expressly for him by the first Composers.

The Speaking Figures,
AND AUTOMATON
Slack Rope Dancers,

These are the only Figures known that produce distinct articulation by mechanical means. A small Automaton will, in the hands of any person, say "*Mamma*," and "*Papa*," with the French accent, and the most perfect distinctness. One of the Rope Dancers uses the French exclamation, "*Oh! La! La!*" when on the Rope, as well as in the hand. The performance on the Slack Rope is unrivalled; the most surprising Feats being executed with the greatest agility, and without any apparent mechanism.

TO CONCLUDE WITH THE
CONFLAGRATION
OF
Moscow;

In which Mr. M. has so combined the Arts of Design, Mechanism, and Music, as to produce by a novel imitation of nature, a perfect fac-simile of the real scene. It is taken at night, and the moon observed aloft, is rendered pale by the glare of the blazing and smoking Ruins below, the combined reflections of which, strike upon the distant Buildings, clothing them in gloomy splendor. The View is from an elevated Terrace of the Kremlin, the Imperial Palace, at the moment when the inhabitants are evacuating the Capital of the Czars, and the French Columns are commencing their entry.

They advance in the following order:

The Vanguard with its Artillery, | Regiment of Flying Artillery, followed by their Cannon, Ammunition and Baggage Wagons, &c.
Regiment of Voltigeurs, |
The Imperial Foot Guard, | Regiments of Cuirassiers, &c.

Amid the din and hurry, and confusion, the Incendiaries who fired the City, are seen with blazing Torches, passing to and fro among the flying inhabitants, in the precincts of the Kremlin.

The rapid progress of the Fire, spreading from the Centre to the extremities of the City, the hurrying bustle of the Fugitives, the eagerness of the invaders, the Tolling of Alarm Bells, the sound of Trumpets and other Military French Music, the roar of Cannon, the brisk discharge of Musketry, the explosion of a Mine, which demolishes what the Fire had spared, and the Kremlin falling into Ruins, will tend to impress the Spectator with a true idea of a Scene, which baffles all powers of description.

Performance Every Evening, (Sunday's Excepted.)
Doors open at 7 o'clock—Performance to commence at 8 o'clock.

The Three Front Benches are exclusively appropriated for Children.

Admittance 50 Cents, Children Half-Price.

Tickets obtained during the day at the Exhibition Hall, or at the Door in the Evening

☞ *N. B. MAELZEL'S METRONOME, (or Musical Time Keeper) may be had on application to the Proprietor.*

PRINTED AT THE EVENING GAZETTE OFFICE, 14 CONGRESS-ST.

8¼ x 22⁷⁄₁₆

SIMPSON AT VAUXHALL GARDENS

1833

FOR ALMOST TWO HUNDRED YEARS, commencing in 1661, Vauxhall Gardens (originally called Spring Gardens) was a major showplace in London. Situated on the Surrey side of the Thames, it comprised twelve acres of walks and arbors. Samuel Pepys was an early habitué, and Jonathan Swift attended in 1711 to hear the nightingales for which it was justly famous. From its early days it was also known as a venue for assignations. Although Vauxhall could at times attract a rowdy element, it enjoyed noble patronage almost to the end. The historian Warwick Wroth observed of its classless character, "the place was never exclusive or select and at no other London resort could the humours of every class of the community be watched with greater interest or amusement."

Spectators who strolled the Gardens in the eighteenth century were treated to displays of art and music. On view were movable and mechanical pictures and trompe l'oeil paintings, pavilions, and statues. Hogarth provided scenes for some of the viewing-stand boxes and designed some of the season tickets, which were struck in silver. In return he received a gold ticket granting him entrée in perpetuity. Orchestras and singers were often engaged to divert the patrons. In 1822 Vauxhall was re-christened "The Royal Gardens," a gesture approved by George IV, who before he ascended the throne had been a frequent visitor.

By the early nineteenth century Vauxhall Gardens became London's major center for outdoor entertainment. Commencing in 1816 Madame Saqui, the famous Parisian tight-rope artist, kept audiences spellbound for a number of seasons. At noon each day she mounted a platform sixty feet in the air and walked the cord for three hundred and fifty feet. Her "masculine and muscular" figure was bedizened in spangles and plumes and bathed in blue light, until she descended the rope in a tempest of fireworks. As one observer noted:

> Amid the blaze of meteors seen on high,
> Etherial Saqui seems to tread the sky.

One could also witness an odd device called the Heptaplasiesoptron, which produced mirrored reflections of "revolving pillars, palm-trees, twining serpents, coloured lamps and a fountain." In 1822, Ramo Samee, the most famous of a troupe of Indian entertainers, performed magic and sword swallowing. Shadow pantomimes, operettas, puppet shows, balloon ascensions, and spectacles such as "The Battle of Waterloo," said to feature a thousand men and horses, were presented.

One of the Garden's most notorious figures, however, was an unpaid attraction. Although his name was determined to be Joseph Leeming, he referred to himself as "The Aerial," with various subtitles: "The Paragon of Perfection," "The New Discovery," "The God of Beauty," "The Phoenix," and "The Grand Arcana of Nature." In July of 1825 he appeared in Vauxhall sporting flamboyant attire: a close-fitting blue and white jacket, short breeches that ended some three inches above the knee, silk stockings, blue kid gloves, a collar ruff, and a wristband trimmed with lace. He distributed printed cards, or challenges, exhorting the crowd to "find a man that can in any way compete" with him, and offered himself "for inspection to artists and surgeons as a model of bodily perfection." He insisted on being billed at exactly his true height—five feet and one-quarter inch—as five foot one was too tall, and five feet too short, for perfect proportion. After creating a small fracas for some days, he was permanently denied admission to the Gardens.

Among the curious attractions of Vauxhall was Simpson himself. A fixture as master of ceremonies at the Gardens for thirty-six years, he was known for his "florid humility" in his addresses and his writings. A short fellow with a smallpox-scarred face, he always affected the attitude captured by the artist George Cruikshank, which is pictured on this handsome broadside: with his right leg extended straight behind him and his pointed toe touching the ground, he tips his hat in an obsequious gesture. He holds a silver-headed cane in his left hand, a top hat in his right.

This broadside commemorates Simpson's only benefit in thirty-six years of service, at which the sixty-three-year-old impresario hoped to receive funds adequate for his future comfort. He hereby implores "the most noble and puissant Princes, and other illustrious Ambassadors" to that end. For this occasion his effigy was constructed in Vauxhall in colored lights forty-five feet high. Thackeray called him "the gentle Simpson, that kind, smiling idiot." He died on December 25, 1835.

UNDER THE ESPECIAL PATRONAGE OF HIS MAJESTY,

ROYAL GARDENS, VAUXHALL.

AN INTERESTING AND UNIQUE
GALA

WILL TAKE PLACE

ON MONDAY, 19th of AUGUST, 1833,

FOR THE BENEFIT OF

MR SIMPSON,

MASTER

OF

THE CEREMONIES

OF THE

Royal Gardens, Vauxhall,

UPWARDS

OF

THIRTY-SIX YEARS.

MR. SIMPSON'S OWN ADDRESS TO THE PUBLIC.

To the most illustrious Princes and Princesses of the British Empire; to their Excellencies, the most noble and puissant Princes, and other illustrious Ambassadors of the Foreign States, now residing in London, and their truly noble and accomplished Ladies; to the most noble and distinguished Nobility of the United Kingdom, and their truly noble and accomplished Ladies; and also to all the other respectable classes of distinguished Visitors, that so kindly honor and grace the Royal Gardens every Season with their distinguished presence, and their amiable and lovely Ladies.

To all those truly illustrious, noble, and distinguished Visitors of the Royal Gardens, Vauxhall, their truly humble and very devoted Servant, C. H. SIMPSON, Master of the Ceremonies of those Gardens for Thirty-six Years, most dutifully and most respectfully begs to inform all the illustrious, noble, and all the other respectable classes that visit the Royal Gardens, that, for my humble services, for so long a period, in the truly honorable service of the Public, the very kind generosity of the worthy Proprietors of these Gardens have been pleased to permit (on my own sole account) an unprecedented occurrence, that never in the whole annals of the Gardens took place at the Royal Gardens before, namely, (a Benefit.) I therefore, with all due and humble submission, and filled with the most dutiful and sincere expressions of heartfelt attachment, presume, with all becoming awe, to approach such illustrious, noble, and distinguished Personages, and with every sense of the most profound humility, confidently relying on the paternal disposition of the generous Public to an old servant, at one of the first places of Public Amusement in the first City in the Empire, this celebrated splendid ancient Temple of loyalty, where the most lovely British and Foreign beauties congregate under the same happy roof to enjoy the pleasure of each other's company; and where I have had the HIGH HONOR of receiving his late Majesty, George IV. when Prince of Wales, and Royalty, Rank, Fashion, and Elegance, to the present moment, and am now in the Sixty-third Year of my Age.

On this gratifying conviction, most illustrious, noble, and distinguished Personages, and all the other respectable parts of a generous Public, I very humbly rest my hopes, that your well-known unparalleled goodness of heart will graciously receive, not only with indulgence, but with favor, the humble yet earnest request, which I now, in the most dutiful manner, presume to lay at your feet.

Such condescension of such illustrious, noble, and distinguished Patrons, I should hail as the sure harbinger of my future happiness, assured that the patronage and the presence of such truly-illustrious, noble, and distinguished Visitors, on the 19th of AUGUST, the Night of my Benefit, would essentially promote the prosperity of my future days as long as I live.

I also very dutifully beg to make known to the distinguished Visitors, that neither pains nor expense will be spared in putting the whole Gardens into a state of unequalled splendor, and fitting-up every part in order to render the Night worthy of their illustrious patronage; and every Device worthy of such a distinguished occasion.

I also very respectfully beg leave to make known, that I am one of the very few survivors, at the present day, of that bloody and furious battle, that lasted from day-light in the Morning until dark, fought by Admiral Rodney, in the West Indies, on the 12th of April, 1782, when the British standard completely annihilated and destroyed the whole French Fleet, and, among the captured ships, was the celebrated Ville de Paris, a tremendously high red-sided, 90 gun ship, with a gilt Lion at her head, and took their grand Commander in Chief, the Count de Grasse, a fine tall stout athletic man, about 5 feet 11 inches high, prisoner. For like His present Majesty, and at the same time as His Majesty, I began some of my earliest days in the honorable profession of the Royal Navy; for when I was eleven years of age, the Gallant Captain Sir James Wallace, who was a friend of my father, took me on board of his ship the Warrior, 74 gun ship, as an acting Midshipman, which was then at Portsmouth, and immediately set sail for the West Indies, to every Island of which we were cruising about, until the great battle took place on the 12th of April, 1782. We then went to North America, then back to the West Indies. When at St. Lucia, on the 10th of March, 1783, a Packet of Peace arrived to inform us that a ratification of Peace had taken place between Britain, France, Spain, and America, when our ship immediately set sail for Old England, with joyous hearts, and arrived at Portsmouth the latter end of April, 1783. The ship was paid off; and I was, like other young gentlemen in my situation, honorably discharged in the thirteenth year of my age; and had been always very much beloved and respected by all the officers on board the ship, and so much so, that Captain Stone of the Royal Navy, the brother of Mr. Stone, the Master of our ship, wrote a letter to his Brother from the East Indies, stating that he would give all the world if he could but have me with him on board his 74 gun ship in the East Indies.

All these reasons will, I earnestly hope, induce all the illustrious, noble, and distinguished Visitors to be graciously pleased to condescend to patronise my earnest prayer for your distinguished support on the Night of my Benefit; as I do assure you, most illustrious, noble, and distinguished Ladies and Gentlemen, it will truly gladden the heart, for the remainder of his days, of your most submissive, humble, and devotedly faithful Servant, at your command, in the Sixty-third Year of his Age; and shall never, while I live, cease to testify my gratitude for the same.

I have the honor to remain, most illustrious, noble, and distinguished Personages,
With every sense of the most profound respect,
Your very grateful and devoted humble Servant,
C. H. SIMPSON,
Master of the Ceremonies, Royal Gardens, Vauxhall.

ROYAL GARDENS, VAUXHALL,
August, 1833.

Tickets, at the usual Price of Admission; FOUR SHILLINGS each, may be had of Mr. SIMPSON, 31, Holywell Street, Millbank; at Mr. EBERS's Library, Bond Street; Mr. SAMS', St. James's Street; Mr. CHAPPELL, Royal Exchange; Mr. THRESHER, 24, Haymarket; 23, Ludgate Hill; 141, Fleet Street; and at the Gardens.

☞ FULL PARTICULARS OF THE GALA WILL BE DULY ANNOUNCED.

BALNE, PRINTER, GRACECHURCH STREET.

10⅛ x 15⅝

MARTIN THE LION TAMER

1834

THIS BROADSIDE FOR THE animal trainer Henri Martin is embellished with a decorative border of the kind found almost exclusively on Continental bills of the period. In strong roman types it informs the public that, under the aegis of the mayor, Martin will present his show, hopeful of receiving the same unanimous approbation he had obtained in the capitals of Europe, most recently in Paris and London.

Martin displayed the largest boa constrictor that had ever appeared in France and a striped hyena that he declared so tame that "the audience will have nothing to fear," even though the ferocious beast was tethered only by a slender leash. Martin ended his performance by feeding his animals to show a more frenzied side of their demeanor. In their natural state, without their advanced training at his hands, the animals would clearly be vicious as well as voracious.

The featured attraction was Martin's appearance in a cage inhabited by the lion, Neron, and the tiger, Atir. Martin had trained these two natural enemies not only to accommodate his presence but also to live together peaceably in the same cage. They exhibited the kind of obedience usually obtained only with the most docile species. He taught Atir to sit up and lie down and to execute other movements on command. According to historian Stuart Thayer, Martin first entered the animal's cage, although only for a few minutes, in a show in Nuremberg in 1819, "apparently the first such event in menagerie history." Gradually he was able to spend longer intervals in the cage, scratching the animals through the bars, then sitting in a separate cage adjoining the tiger's half of the den. He introduced his head and shoulders into the tiger's cage, and after these cautious approaches he entered fully.

The first American to enter a cage with wild animals was Charles Wright (see p. 94). A short time later, another American trainer, Isaac Van Amburgh, sat in a cage with a lion and a lamb before Queen Victoria. The display of several natural enemies in the same cage, a tableau often called "The Happy Family," was most closely associated with John Austin, who displayed his diverse brood in London for nearly forty years. "The Happy Family" was a much sought after attraction and a favorite of P. T. Barnum, who frequently featured it on his shows at his American Museum.

Martin, who was born in Marseilles in 1793, escaped an unwanted family apprenticeship to a perfumer by running away to join a circus. He worked as a trick rider and acrobat but showed an early predilection for animals. In 1820 he married the daughter of the great menagerie proprietor Van Aken and, with her dowry, formed his own animal show. In the course of a long and successful career he received numerous honors and royal patronage and, unlike many in his chosen profession, died in his bed on April 8, 1882. He is shown below with Neron and Atir.

M. MARTIN,

Natif de Marseille,

A l'honneur d'informer le Public que, se rendant à Paris, il profitera de son passage en cette ville, pour offrir à ses habitans ses exercices.

Aujourd'hui **1834,**
UNE SEULE SEANCE, à Heures

M. MARTIN

Paraîtra dans une Cage où sont réunis

LE LION NERON
et LE TIGRE ATIR.

Le propriétaire de ces deux terribles animaux a su les dompter à un tel point que non-seulement il est parvenu à faire vivre en paix dans la même cage ces deux féroces carnivores, que la nature a créés ennemis, mais encore à obtenir de leur obéissance des exercices qu'on obtient quelquefois difficilement des animaux les plus dociles.

M. MARTIN fera paraître

UNE HYENE BARRÉE

De l'espèce la plus féroce, qu'il a su maîtriser de telle sorte que, quoiqu'elle ne soit retenue que par un faible lien, les spectateurs n'ont rien à redouter.

LE SERPENT BOA CONSTRICTOR,

Le plus grand qui ait paru jusqu'à présent en France,

La SEANCE sera terminée par

LE SOUPER DES ANIMAUX

Les assistans pourront juger de la patience, des soins et des précautions qu'il a fallu mettre en usage pour rendre dociles et soumis des animaux à qui le repas rend toute leur férocité naturelle.

Les succès unanimes et non contestés que ces exercices ont obtenu dans les diverses Capitales de l'Europe, et tout récemment à Paris et à Londres, font espérer à M. MARTIN qu'il sera accueilli avec la même bienveillance par les Amateurs de cette Ville.

La Séance aura lieu dans

PRIX D'ENTRÉE : 4 Fr. -- Demi-Place pour les Enfans.

MARSEILLE, Imprimerie de Feissat aîné et Demonchy, Imprimeurs de la Ville et du Commerce, rue Canebiere, n° 19. — 1834

18 X 24⅞

JOICE HETH
AGED 161 YEARS!

1835

IT IS EASY TO SEE WHY one might overlook this simple, unillustrated broadside from 1835 without a second thought. At first glance it appears a dreary plea to witness just another anomaly: a very old woman who is obviously in such terrible shape that her mere survival is her calling card. On closer inspection, however, the broadside becomes a document of almost endless fascination.

Joice Heth, the bill proclaims, is 161 years old, born in 1674 (the same year as Mathew Buchinger; see p. 24). Formerly a slave to Augustine Washington, she had been nursemaid to his son George, "The father of our country," the broadside proudly announces. She was the first to put clothes on young George. "She raised him," we are told (according to another account, she even suckled him).

The prolific Heth had fifteen children, the verso of the bill noted, quoting the *Providence Daily Journal*, and she had outlived them all. The last of her progeny survived only until age 116, and had died two years previously. Her five great grandchildren, it was reported, were "now the slaves of Wm. Rowling, Esq. Of Paris, Kentucky, to the purchase of whose freedom the proceeds of this exhibition are to be appropriated," a ploy later used by Henry Box Brown (see p. 130).

Not one of these statements was true. The man responsible for this playbill, and for this exhibition, was the then twenty-five-year-old Phineas Taylor Barnum. It was his first foray into the business that would eventually make him one of the most famous figures in America.

When Heth died a few months after this appearance, an autopsy was conducted to determine her age. Barnum charged fifty cents to attend, double the fee Heth commanded when alive. Almost fifteen hundred people crowded into the amphitheater of the City Saloon in New York to find that Heth had in all likelihood died before reaching the age of eighty. Richard Locke of the *New York Sun* called the Heth affair "one of the most precious humbugs that was ever imposed on a credulous community."

To this day Barnum's role in this convoluted story remains murky. At one point he claimed to have devised and fabricated the age and provenance of Heth; at another that when he purchased the attraction from the previous exhibitor he was himself completely duped. Both of these scenarios are implausible, but there is no doubt that Barnum turned a moribund attraction into a money-making one. In the course of marketing Heth he honed the techniques of prevarication and equivocation that would serve him well in later life. By starting rumors that Heth was not human but an automaton whose voice was supplied by a ventriloquist, by charging people to view her autopsy, by suggesting the dead woman was not Joice Heth but an imposter, he created an interest in her that was sustained (and generated income) even after her demise. Yet Barnum evolved from an unsympathetic exploiter, and perhaps even owner of the slave Heth, to become a staunch abolitionist.

An exponent of contradictions, he embodied an odd but always compelling combination of showmanship and public service, hubris and humbug, entertainment and edification. Barnum became not only synonymous with a particular kind of audacious American genius but also a symbol for how the rest of the world viewed Americans. Perhaps that is why James Cook has written that we might regard the moment of Barnum's exhibition of Joice Heth as "the birth date of modern American popular culture."

GREAT ATTRACTION

JUST ARRIVED AT CONCERT HALL.

☞ FOR A SHORT TIME ONLY. ☜

JOICE HETH,

NURSE TO

Gen. George Washington,

(The father of our country,) who has arrived at the astonishing age of **161** years ! will be seen at Concert Hall, corner of Court and Hanover streets, Boston, for a SHORT TIME ONLY, as she is to fill other engagements very soon.

JOICE HETH is unquestionably the most astonishing and interesting curiosity in the World ! She was the slave of Augustine Washington, (the father of Gen. Washington,) and was the first person who put clothes on the unconscious infant who in after days led our heroic fathers on to glory, to victory and freedom. To use her own language when speaking of the illustrious Father of his country, "she raised him." JOICE HETH was born in the Island of Madagascar, on the Coast of Africa, in the year 1674 and has consequently now arrived at the astonishing *(1835)*

Age of 161 Years !

She weighs but forty-six pounds, and yet is very cheerful and interesting. She retains her faculties in an unparalleled degree, converses freely, sings numerous hymns, relates many interesting anecdotes of Gen. Washington, the red coats, &c. and often laughs heartily at her own remarks, or those of the spectators. Her health is perfectly good, and her appearance very neat. She was baptized in the Potomac river and received into the Baptist Church 116 years ago, and takes great pleasure in conversing with Ministers and religious persons. The appearance of this marvellous relic of antiquity strikes the beholder with amazement, and convinces him that his eyes are resting on the oldest specimen of mortality they ever before beheld. Original, authentic and indisputable documents prove however astonishing the fact may appear, JOICE HETH is in every respect the person she is represented.

The most eminent physicians and intelligent men both in New York and Philadelphia, have examined this *living skeleton* and the documents accompanying her, and all *invariably* pronounce her to be as represented 161 *years of age* ! Indeed it is impossible for any person, however incredulous, to visit her without astonishment and the most perfect satisfaction that she is as old as represented.

☞ A female is in continual attendance, and will give every attention to the ladies who visit this relic of by gone ages.

She was visited at Niblo's Garden New York, by *ten thousand persons* in two weeks.————Hours of exhibition from 9 A. M to 1 P. M. and from 3 to 10 P. M.—Admittance 25 cents—Children 12½ cents. ☞Over

MADAME WOOD'S
DISTAFF DECEPTIONS
C. 1839

FOR THE PAST FEW CENTURIES there has been a small but steady flow of women working their wonders on the stages of Europe and America. Among them have been creative and entertaining performers who commanded respect, sizeable salaries, and devoted fans. Yet not one of them has achieved the status of a first rank star or sensation—no conjuring equivalent of Jenny Lind or Sarah Bernhardt. It was therefore unusual to find an early-nineteenth-century American playbill devoted entirely to the performance of a woman conjurer.

Madame Wood, "formerly Mademoiselle Adrien," is most likely the offspring of the French conjurer Monsieur Adrien, who plied his trade in America from the 1820s to the 1840s. Adrien also had a son who appeared as a magician and a juggler. Monsieur Adrien was appearing at Niblo's Garden in New York in June 1835 when he announced his farewell performance, and its climax, in which Mlle. Adrien would "appear and disappear in a wonderful manner, never before attempted." She did, in any case, appear again for a benefit only a few days later. These are the only notices I have been able to find for the girl before she assumed the name of Madame Wood.

She is here introduced as "The Magic Queen," presiding over her "Temple of Enchantment," with "Hindoo Magic, Thaumaturgics, and Necromancy." Only seventeen, she offered a varied and evocative bill, rich in the verbose vernacular of the medium. The effects are difficult to identify from their dramatic names alone: "The Chinese Electric Fan, or the Magician's Dream of Death," "The Rose of Milan," "The Handkerchief of Ava," and "The California Gold Box" (perhaps a version of an effect her father called "The Sociable Box"). She offered a "Feast of Enchant-ment," whatever that was, and "Supper with the Immortal Dr. Faust." She promised to live up to "the delight and admiration of thousands who have visited her Entertainments…under the patronage of the first circles of society." She dispensed presents for members of the audience, thereby qualifying her performance as an early "gift show." All this for an admission charge of only twelve and one-half cents!

On this bill, with its full array of nineteenth-century typefaces, Madame Wood does not inspire confidence. She is pictured in front of an antiseptic stage setting of elaborate magic props. She appears every bit the gawky teenager, and even looks somewhat elongated, as if viewed through a carnival mirror. She stands almost expressionless under an elaborate chapeau, wielding a long scepter. Two rabbits seem equally out of place at the base of her table.

AT GOTHIC HALL!
On TUESDAY EVENING, Jan. 29th.

GRAND
HINDOO FESTIVAL,
OR
FEAST OF ENCHANTMENT,
BY THE DISTINGUISHED
MADAME
WOOD,
FORMERLY
MADEMOISELLE ADRIEN,

THE MAGIC QUEEN.

Whose beautiful, instructive and fashionable
HINDOO ORIENTAL SOIREES,
Have been the delight and admiration of thousands who have visited her Entertainments and under the patronage of the first circles of society.

The Stage will be fitted up as a grand
TEMPLE OF ENCHANTMENT,
And she will offer a series of Wonders pronounced by different Professors and other competent judges, superior to anything ever attempted in this country—including a variety of her most Wonderful feats in

Hindoo Magic, Thaumaturgics and Necromancy,
Which have never failed to deceive as well as amuse the most critical observers.

This youthful and accomplished artist,
(being but 17 years of age)
will have the honor of appearing in her
TEMPLE OF MAGIC,
And perform Feats after the manner of Wizards and Soothsayers of Old, and trusts that the unqualified approbation bestowed upon her amusements will ensure her the patronage of the Public.

PROGRAMME OF WONDERS.
READ AND PONDER.---This Evening Madame
W. will perform
THE CHINESE ELECTRIC FAN,
—OR THE—
MACICIAN'S DREAM OF DEATH.

Fortune Telling,	Flying Money,
Mysterious Hat,	The Enchanted Target,
The Rose of Milan,	Coins of Enchantment,
Handkerchief of Ava,	The Flying Glove.

Letters from the Ærial World, or a Visit from the Angel of Love.

THE CALIFORNIA GOLD BOX,
The favorite Experiment of the Extra Superstition, or the Royal Feast of the
HINDOO MAGIS.

Gifts for the Ladies and Gentlemen.
The Enchantress will distribute among the audience delicious Refreshments, Free of Charge.

A SUPPER WITH THE IMMORTAL
DR. FAUST,
With a variety of other Feats too numerous to mention on this sheet.
☞ COME AND SEE. ☜

SUPERB FINALE.

Tickets to accommodate all, only 12 1-2 cents.
☞ Doors open at 7—The Sybil will appear at 7 1-2 o'clock precisely. ☜

6⅛ x 20⅛

An Enormous Head

C. 1840

IT MAY BE DIFFICULT TO GRASP the glee that I felt upon first seeing this playbill. To me, the "Wonderful Remains of an Enormous Head" shares the same exalted echelon of phraseology as "The Giant Hungarian Schoolboy" (p. 150). It was impossible for me to resist this placard, printed on yellow paper and boldly set in both serif and sans serif types. It has been displayed in my home for years.

I must confess that another aspect of the appeal of this piece is not knowing with any certainty what was exhibited. We are told that the "enormous head" was 18 feet in length, 7 feet in breadth, and weighed 1700 pounds. A whale might seem the most likely species for a skull on this scale, but this is not consistent with the apparent provenance of the remains, which according to the bill were discovered in the interior of Louisiana, "160 miles from the sea." The complete skeleton of the animal was excavated from a depth of 75 feet by a crew building a railroad.

There is something in the prodigious size of the head that recalls a seventeenth-century broadside ballad in the collection of Samuel Pepys, *A description of a strange (and miraculous) fish*. This song told of a monstrous sea-dweller supposedly cast upon the shore in the sand of the meadowlands in Chester. I quote the fifth stanza, with the spelling modernized:

His lower jaw bones five yards long,
  The upper thrice so much,
Twelve yoke of oxen stout and strong,
  (The weight of it is such)
Could not once stir it out of the sands
Thus works the all-creating hands.
  O rare
    beyond compare,
  in England ne'er the like.

A contemporary pamphlet was issued for those who preferred a more detailed version of the fish story.

The exhibition of the giant head took place every day but Sundays in the Cosmorama Rooms on Regent Street, the home to the Singing Mouse (see p. 114) and other unusual attractions chronicled in these pages. I am familiar with only one eyewitness description of the show. It appeared in George Mogridge's *Old Humphrey's Walks in London and Its Neighborhood* (1843), cited by Richard Altick in *The Shows of London*. Mogridge thought the remains most likely those of a whale. The show's impresarios, two Frenchman, were, says Altick, "cautiously noncommittal," describing the remains as those of an obviously gigantic bird, fish, or lizard.

Wonderful Remains

OF AN

ENORMOUS HEAD,

18 Feet in Length, 7 Feet in Breadth, and Weighing 1700 Pounds.

The complete Bones of which were discovered in excavating a Passage for the purpose of a Railway, at the Depth of 75 Feet from the Surface of the Ground in LOUISIANIA, and at the Distance of 160 Miles from the Sea.

This great Curiosity is now to be seen any Day (Sundays excepted) from 10 in the Morning until 6 o'Clock in the Evening, at the

Cosmorama, No. 209, Regent Street.

Admission 1s. each.—Children 6d.

Baynes and Harris, Printers, 9, Clement's Lane, Lombard Street.

6 7/16 x 4 1/4

NELSON THE CLOWN
C. 1842

THIS LARGE DOUBLE-SIDED PLAYBILL was sent to John Procter to be reset for a performance in Hartlepool. It features an impressive combination of unusual display type, striking illustration, and evocative text. It announces a benefit performance for Arthur Nelson the Clown who, acknowledging the need for patronage at this event in his honor, jokingly thanked "the tradesmen and factors, who have kindly consented to close their shops and factories at the usual hour."

For this engagement of Cooke's Circus, the printer was instructed to replace the drama of "Lucky Horse Shoe" with the perennial classic "St. George and the Dragon." A line was also drawn through the phrase "CIRCUMGLOB-ULARANTISTEAMPROPELLINGOmnibus," some sort of conveyance that had been exhibited by Mr. Nelson in the ring. Apparently inoperative before the show reached Hartlepool, the machine was revealed to be a somewhat less formidable circum-globular-anti-steam-propelling contraption. Undaunted, Nelson promised such "a budget of quirps, cranks, conundrums, witticisms, humorous odds and ends, anecdotes and sayings, that the facial muscles of the veriest stoic must needs relax into a smiling expression of good nature." The laughter would be limitless, "Under the influence of his never-failing pleasantry, which...elicits such loud and repeated an[d] reverberating peals of side-splitting cachinnation, as to have earned for him the appellation of Momus the Comic Thunderer!!!"

The name of Jenny Lind, the greatest singing attraction of the day, is set large in the center of the bill, but the smaller type above and below contains the following caveat: "In consequence of the Great Expense attending an Engagement with JENNY LIND, she will not appear." Even though this is presented tongue-in-cheek here, verbal subterfuge with the intent to deceive was not uncommon on playbills, and the admonishment to "read the small print" was as prudent for a broadside as for a contract.

The major attraction, as pictured on the bill, was the comical sight of Nelson in a washing tub being drawn across the river by "Four Real Geese," although the actual motive power was a small steamboat whose towline was concealed beneath the water. This stunt, according to Robert Wood, originated as a publicity scheme for the newly constructed Astley's Circus in 1842, and was the brainchild of the clown Dicky Usher, who rode from Westminster Bridge to Waterloo Bridge in a wash basket drawn by four geese named Gibble, Gabble, Gobble, and Garble.

The stunt went off without a hitch in the billed performance, but it was to be the cause of a major disaster in Yarmouth in 1846, one of the worst in the annals of the circus. Nelson was to promote the arrival of Cooke's Circus with the geese-drawn tub. Some five hundred spectators, many of them children of dire poverty who were unable to buy a circus ticket, crowded on to a suspension bridge that spanned the Yare River. The bridge collapsed under the added weight and, according to the town register, at least seventy-nine people were killed. The surviving townsfolk were infuriated when they learned that the motive power of the conveyance was mechanical rather than avian.

10⅞ x 30

Rabbi Hirsch Dänemark

Mnemonist

c. 1842

Among the earliest entertainers recorded in antiquity were those who gave demonstrations of prodigious memory, and exhibitions of mnemonic techniques remain popular to the present day. In the mid-nineteenth century, the scholarly diversions of Rabbi Hirsch Dänemark were advertised in the German press. For a performance in Wurzburg in April 1846, he was billed as "The Renowned Mnemonist." We are told that he is "famous across all of Europe for his incomprehensible wondrous gifts which lead to the greatest astonishment, and about which he possesses the most excellent references from many of the foremost authorities of Europe." The details of his entertainment were not enumerated. Only a few weeks later a similar advertisement appeared in the *Neue Wuerzburger Zeitung*, mentioning that Dänemark's skills were demonstrated by "tests," but once again the particulars were not revealed. At this show his thirty-six-kroner fee was reduced by half for high school or university students.

I am aware of a Hasidic tradition in which rabbis displayed skills closely aligned to their spiritual concerns to supplement their incomes. These might include the making of amulets, the conducting of séance-like exhibitions, or the demonstration of effects that resemble what we might now regard as mind reading. There were also exhibitions of scholarship. A nineteenth-century rabbi might, for instance, request that a pin be inserted into a book of Talmudic readings. The rabbi would then correctly predict each letter pricked by the pin on the subsequent ten or more pages. Even more impressive was a stunt based on the selection of twenty or thirty biblical verses by knowledgeable spectators. A rabbi would then extemporize a sermon addressing all of the passages chosen. It was said that those individuals who suggested the verses felt as though the completed sermon, much like the readings of a modern mentalist, had touched them in some very specific and personal way.

The bill displayed here was beautifully printed in Fraktur types on a luxurious mold-made paper with generous margins. It advertised the performance of Hirsh Dänemark in Stuttgart, probably in 1842. With the permission of the local magistrates, the Rabbi gave his demonstration at a building he had apparently dubbed the "Museum of Mnemonic Art." In the elaborately deferential language of the broadside, the Rabbi notes that he was well received in other major cities and hopes to win the approbation and applause of the honorable public of Stuttgart. He then lists testimonials of the royalty and nobility of Europe: His Majesty the King of Saxony, His Highness the Archduke Franz Karl of Oettingen-Spielberg, and the Duke Metternich, who averred: "The achievements of Rabbi Hirsch Dänemark are as peculiar as they are surprising and prove a rare ability…to solve unbelievable tasks, while the ability itself is inexplicable." Perhaps Dänemark's most unexpected endorsement came from "his Holiness the Pope."

Stuttgart.

Mit hoher obrigkeitlicher Bewilligung

wird

Rabbi Hirsch Dänemark,

Künstler und Wundermann,

die Ehre haben

Donnerstag den 30. Juni

im kleinen Saale des obern Museums

eine große

mnemonische Kunst = Vorstellung

zu geben.

Der ergebenst Unterzeichnete, dessen Vorstellungen in allen großen Städten mit dem ungetheiltesten Beifall aufgenommen wurden, schmeichelt sich auch hier die Zufriedenheit eines verehrlichen Publikums zu erlangen. Oeffentliche Blätter, sowie die rühmlichsten Zeugnisse höchster Personen, namentlich Seiner Durchlaucht des Fürsten Metternich, dessen Zeugniß mit den Worten schließt:

„Die Leistungen des Rabbi Hirsch Dänemark sind eben so eigenthümlich als überraschend, und beweisen eine „seltene Orientirungs= und Zurechtfindungsgabe, welche unglaubliche Aufgaben löst, während sie selbst räthsel= „haft bleibt;"

ferner Sr. Heiligkeit des Pabstes, Sr. Majestät des Königs von Sachsen, Sr. Hoheit des Erzherzogs Franz Karl, Erzherzogs Fer= dinand, Fürsten von Taris, Fürsten von Oettingen=Spielberg und anderer hohen Personen, sprechen über seine Leistungen die schmeichelhaftesten Urtheile aus.

Rabbi Hirsch Dänemark.

Eintritts = Preise: Erster Platz 1 Gulden. — Zweiter Platz 36 Kreuzer.

Die Kasse wird Abends um 8 Uhr geöffnet.

Anfang halb 9 Uhr. Ende 10 Uhr.

17¼ x 21⅛

ROBERT AND HIS WIFE

1842

WHILE THESE PAGES ARE PEOPLED with resourceful, eclectic, and intrepid performers, it is difficult to imagine many who would have had the fortitude to advertise their engagements beneath the phrase "Death to the Savage Unitarians." Such, however, was the exclamation impressed upon this juggler, magician, and dog trainer named Robert, who appeared in Buenos Aires, with his wife, in November 1842.

While I must confess to limited knowledge of the life and opinions of Mons. Robert, I think it unlikely that the sentiments "Long Live the Argentinian Confederation" and "Death to the Unitarian Savages" were suggested by his publicist. Both slogans, however, were used by the dictator Juan Manuel Rosas, who must have insisted upon their inclusion on this broadside. Rosas was a wealthy cattle rancher, businessman, and equestrian who became the governor of Buenos Aires and the head of the Federalist faction during the bloody Argentinean civil wars. He was opposed by the Unitarians, who fought for a more liberal "rule of law" and a strong central government.

Robert and his wife seem to have thrived in spite of the volatile atmosphere, and with the permission of the chief of police were staging a benefit for themselves before departing. In an expression of gratitude for their reception they decided to offer a varied farewell extravaganza. They hoped "the public will be pleased, because no expense has been spared to present the most brilliant and difficult tricks. If you attend, your desire will be met, since that is the principal reason we are producing this event." A symphony with full orchestration enhanced the evening's festivities,

and Robert presented his show in three acts: First was a comic piece offered by the dramatic company. This was followed by a full hour of magic in which Robert promised to "execute a great variety of tricks, proofs, physical dexterity, sleight of hand, conjurings, magic, transformations, metamorphoses, appearances and disappearances, of the most extraordinary kind." The third act featured juggling: Robert's wife performed "the new trick of the ceramic plates that will very much please the spectators." This was followed by a cascade of six Oriental daggers. Eight bronze rings were then manipulated, followed by a fire dance and "the lovely balancing act of the two dogs dressed as a Marquesa and a Marquis."

The illustrated and climactic attraction showed Robert defying gravity with "five rifles whose weight will be borne by a single bayonet placed upon a single tooth." (A Mr. Adams balanced five such intertwined guns, although in a less appealing configuration, with the point of one bayonet resting on his chin, for the Nathan Howes Circus in Lebanon, Pennsylvania, in 1832.) The program concluded with Robert suspending the national flag with a child dangling from the end of the pole. While we have no idea of Robert's level of skill, it is difficult to imagine that he did not provide, as the English are wont to say, "value for money."

This playbill is distinguished by its size, its multiple woodcuts, and its very unusual colored decorative border. (Astute observers will note that the richly caparisoned performing dogs here pictured graced the masthead of the first issue of *Jay's Journal of Anomalies*.)

¡VIVA LA CONFEDERACION ARGENTINA!
MUERAN LOS SALVAGES UNITARIOS!

TEATRO ARGENTINO.
Gran Funcion Estraordinaria, á Beneficio del Sr.

Robert y su Esposa.

El *Jueves 3 de noviembre* de 1842.

El Sr. ROBERT y su ESPOSA, deseosos de manifestar á este respetable público los sentimientos de gratitud y reconocimiento de que están animados por la feliz acogida que siempre han merecido de él, han dispuesto una gran funcion. Si en, las anteriores han merecido captarse la benevolencia de sus espectadores, esperan no desmerecer de este concepto, pues ofrecen hacer cuanto el arte ha enseñado de mas difícil en esta clase de espectáculos, tanto en las suertes de física y destreza, como en los equilibrios y transformaciones, habiendo convinado una funcion enteramente variada.

La Compañia Dramática contribuirá por su parte con la representacion de una de las mas graciosas peti-piezas.

Los agraciados esperan que el público será satisfecho, pues no han omitido gasto alguno para presentar las mas brillantes y difíciles pruebas. Si lo consiguen, sus deseos serán colmados, pues es el principal interés que llevan en presentar ésta escogida funcion.

Se tocará una armoniosa sinfonia á toda orquesta, y en seguida se dividirá el espectáculo en tres partes y en el órden siguiente.

PARTE 1.ª

Esta será desempeñada por la Compañía Dramática, exhibiendo la graciosa y divertida pieza cómica, riginal de *D. Manuel Breton de los Herreros,* que obtuvo la general aceptacion, cuando por primera vez se puso en escéna; y que hoy se repite á instancias de varios inteligentes y favorecedores del Establecimiento, su título—

LA PONCHADA.

PARTE 2.ª

UNA HORA DE MAGIA.

Monsieur Robert Prestidijitateur tendrá el honor de presentar por la segunda vez su gabinete, y ejecutará una gran variedad de suertes, pruebas de *Física recreativa,* juegos de manos, magia, transformaciones, metamórfosis, apariciones y desapariciones, las mas estraordinarias, &a. &a. Concluyendo esta primera parte por la aparicion del gran Màgico *ROTOMAGO.*

PARTE 3.ª

Ocupará la escèna la Sra. *Robert* y desempeñará otras difíciles y raras pruebas, entre éllas los juegos de Malabar; y el nuevo juego de los——

PLATOS DE LOZA,

que agradará mucho á los espectadores.

Despues se introducirá el manejo de los seis *Puñales orientales,* el de los *ocho aros de bronce,* un hermoso vuelo amplificado, y varias suertes que no se espresan.

El baile de la

TRANGA

con fuegos artificiales en cada estremidad.

El gracioso equilibrio de los dos *PERROS,* vestidos de Marqueza y Marquez.

El de los cinco fusiles de municion, cuyo peso será apoyado en una sola bayoneta puesta sobre un diente.

Finalizará el todo de la funcion por el estraordinario equilibrio de la——

Bandera Nacional

con un jóven en el estremo del palo.

NOTA— Los Beneficiados teniendo en consideracion los muchos gastos que han impendido para la presente funcion, y recabado el permiso del Sr. Gefe de Policía, han hecho la variacion siguiente en los precios de las aposentadurias y entradas—á saber—— PALCOS de primer órden 30 ps.—id bajos 25 LUNETAS 6 ps. id. de CAZUELA, 1.ª linea 7 id. de 2.ª 5— ENTRADA—cuatro pesos.

A LAS 8.

Imprenta de la LIBERTAD—Buenos Ayres.

THE SINGING MOUSE

1843

WITHIN A SHORT BUT AUSPICIOUS interval, the Cosmorama Rooms on London's Regent Street, home to a host of unusual attractions since the 1820s, exceeded the expectations of even its most loyal patrons. It offered a canary that spoke like a parrot and a mouse that sang like a nightingale. The canary, according to a playbill, possessed "the power of imitating the sounds produced by the human voice, to a degree infinitely surpassing that which exists in the Parrot tribe, the Jay, and the Starling." He performed from ten until half past four at an admission price of one shilling, but customers were alerted, "The earlier the hour the more advantageously the Bird is heard." The following annotation appears on my copy of the broadside: "£500 was offered for this talking wonder but refused—it died shortly after."

The mouse, clearly a more spectacular attraction, was exhibited for the same fee, which may have been more modest than expected because of—get this—the competition of another crooning rodent.

Accounts of trained rats and mice, it should be noted, are not uncommon in the annals of unusual entertainment. A more irregular, though still generic, strain, puts rodents through their paces in prison, as in the accounts penned by George and Austin Bidwell, the nineteenth-century financial scammers. Their memoirs of incarceration, *Forging His Own Chains* and *From Wall Street to Newgate*, respectively, spoke of training a mouse in a jail cell. The pièce de résistance of this repertoire was doubtless the mouse's imitation of the state of rigor mortis.

The mouse at the Cosmorama Rooms was far more impressive. It was advertised as a "truly remarkable Phenomenon, which has by its musical powers succeeded in exciting the admiration of all who have heard it." This rather plainly printed, unillustrated playbill—except for the sans serif title type and rule identical to one in the Harvard Theatre Collection—felt compelled to warn its potential audience that no deception was involved. This, in spite of the rumors that the singing was manufactured by "some mechanical contrivance or Ventriloquist." The *Atheneum* reported that the tiny songster vocalized for a full quarter of an hour in a manner not unlike the nightingale. The *John Bull* was initially skeptical: "we had a strong suspicion when we found this zoological phenomenon actually advertised to be exhibited to the public, that there must be some deception, and that the singing would turn out to be mere *humming*, as in this world of wonders we know, in spite of the old proverb, seeing and hearing is not always *believing*." The periodical, however, was won over, extolling the virtues of the "veritable little vocalist," the "wonderful little quadruped."

Lest our soloist be tempted to retire on his laurels, however, he was soon to face an adversary. His challenger surfaced at Palmer's Hair Cutting Rooms in the Strand. Billed the "Greatest Wonder of the Age," this mouse, according to the *Family Herald*, had the advantage of his rival in "that it warbles its notes sufficiently loud to be heard across a room." How this affected Mr. Palmer's tonsorial customers, whose admission charge for the concert was waived, is unclear, as the mouse continued to sing "for several hours in succession…until weary from exhaustion."

THE SINGING MOUSE!

This truly remarkable Phenomenon, which has by its musical powers succeeded in exciting the admiration of all who have heard it, is

NOW EXHIBITING,

AT THE

Cosmorama Rooms

209, REGENT STREET,

BY MESSRS. WHITE AND AUNGIER.

The majority of the persons who have inspected the little animal, have come fully convinced that the notes must be produced by some mechanical contrivance, or Ventriloquist; but all, even the most sceptical, have departed fully convinced that there is not the least deception whatever.

From the John Bull, Aug. 12.—"THE SINGING MOUSE.—We had a strong suspicion when we found this Zoological phenomenon actually advertised to be exhibited to the public, that there must be some deception, and that the singing would turn out to be mere *humming*, as, in this world of wonders we know, in spite of the old proverb, seeing and even hearing is not always *believing*. It was therefore with some surprise, that on bringing this curiosity to the absolute test of our ears and eyesight we found ourselves listening to a veritable little vocalist, whose notes though low and soft, were sufficiently distinct to entitle him to be received among the disciples of Hullah. We were half inclined to believe that a mountain having in days of old brought forth a mouse might be something more than a fable, and that this wonderful little quadruped that runs so merrily round its rolling cage, might, peradventure, be one of the progeny of that miraculous birth.

Admission, 1s. *Children half-price.*

OPEN FROM 10 TILL 6.

For the convenience of Parties residing in the City, it will be Exhibited at 24, REDCROSS SQ., JEWIN ST., *from 7 till 9 every Evening.*

Francis Shanly Printer, Redcross sq. City.

PROFESSOR FABER'S EUPHONIA
C.1846

JOSEPH FABER, A SHY AND RETIRING German scientist and professor, was the inventor of the speaking machine known as the Euphonia. Even in the era of entertainment and edification introduced by P. T. Barnum, Faber was an odd choice to grace the showman's museum and the various stages of Europe and America. When artists were typically touted as "the greatest hoop roller in the world" or "the king's conjurer," he was billed as "The Premier Calculator and Land Surveyor to the Emperor of Austria."

Faber's machine actually articulated human speech. It had the misfortune to appear in the wake of various exhibitions of faux speaking machines, usually presented as a doll suspended from a doorway that would answer questions whispered by spectators. This effect, most often labeled "The Invisible Girl," was a magic illusion from the late eighteenth century that took many forms and continued to appear long after it was exposed as a trick. Because this apparatus was still being exhibited with "The Albino Woman" and other less dignified attractions, Faber's legitimate speech machine was often dismissed. Nevertheless, his invention was critically acclaimed and widely exhibited for many years.

Its convoluted history includes stewardship by Faber's niece and her hustler husband, and even an interlude in the possession of Alexander Graham Bell. The Euphonia is an important link in the story of how an eighteenth-century magician's illusion, "The Automaton Chess Player" (see p. 96), led to the invention of the telephone (I relate this tale in *Jay's Journal of Anomalies*).

For a booking of Faber's machine at London's Egyptian Hall, another playbill in my collection offers encomia from various notables, including the Duke of Wellington and Lord Spencer. Perhaps more salient was the blurb from W. Vesalius Pettigrew, lecturer on anatomy and physiology:

Sir—When visiting the private exhibition to-day of your "Euphonia," coming as I did by invitation to inspect an Instrument, previous to its exhibition before Her Majesty, I could not but feel that I (as well as others) was bound to use every exertion to detect a fraud if such there should be; I, therefore, perhaps have to apologize for having asked you to move the Figure to another part of the room; and also to make the Figure pronounce the word *Lingua*, which I wrote in pencil and which was not uttered by any individual save the Automaton. Upon further examination and reflection since my visit, I cannot look upon the Figure as a mere piece of mechanism; I consider it as the successful result of a mind gifted with the strongest reasoning and calculative powers, and I cannot but think it is the country rather than yourself that is honored by its exhibition.

"Professor Faber," the bill announced, "will cause the instrument to speak any word or sentence in any Language which may be suggested by the Audience, thus proving the Speaking Automaton to be The Only Universal Linguist." For those who cared less for edification, the machine would render a rousing version of "God Save the Queen."

The broadside chosen for inclusion is, I believe, the most appealing of the many used to advertise the attraction. The text was also printed on white paper, but that background seems less compelling than this rich green. Although the speaking figure occasionally appeared in the garb of a Turkish man, the wonderful engraving is a faithful representation of the machine, as corroborated by a contemporary photograph.

PALAIS ROYAL,

Argyll Street, Oxford Circus, W.

WONDERFUL
TALKING

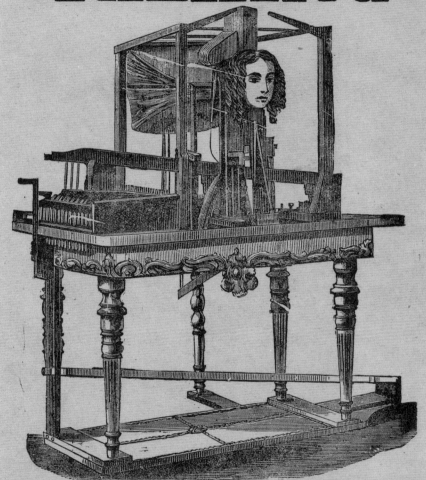

MACHINE

The Exhibition is not limited to simple talking, but is enhanced by an explanatory description of the method of producing the various sounds, words, and sentences, visitors also being allowed to inspect every part of the Machine. It is not only interesting to the Scientific as illustrating the theory of acoustics, but to the public in general, and especially to the young,—to whom it offers an inexhaustible fund of wonder and amusement.

EXHIBITING HOURLY. From 12 noon, till 10 p.m.

Admission, 1s.   Reserved Seats, 2s.   Children, 6d.

TOM THUMB AT EGYPTIAN HALL
1846

TOM THUMB WAS ONE OF THE most famous human attractions ever exhibited. Though he died more than a hundred years ago, he remains a synecdoche for small people.

Born Charles Sherwood Stratton in Connecticut on January 4, 1838, he was contacted by P. T. Barnum before his fifth birthday. The boy weighed fifteen pounds and was twenty-five inches in height, but fearing the public would not view a youngster of that age as a dwarf, Barnum pronounced him an eleven-year-old. He then claimed that Tom was English to appropriate what he elsewhere called American audiences' "disgraceful preference for foreigners."

After great success in America, Barnum took Tom to England in 1844. He created such a furor over the "General" that he was able to orchestrate a command performance before Queen Victoria. She was so taken with the little fellow that she requested another visit within a few days. This royal reception alone guaranteed Barnum a box office triumph. He exhibited Tom at a major venue for unusual attractions, London's Egyptian Hall. The General was a sensation. He was charming, and particularly appealing to women, who outnumbered male attendees throughout his career at a rate of ten to one.

Barnum and the General enjoyed similar success on the Continent. This playbill of 1846 announces his third return to Egyptian Hall, and his farewell appearance in London before his departure for America. The playbill boasts the patronage of the monarchs of England, France, Belgium, Spain, and Russia, who were all captivated by the little fellow. The diminutive broadside reveals a fashionably attired Tom Thumb standing on a chair, and ends with a marvel of advertisement: "Reader! The General is exactly four times the length of the Bill you are reading." The playbill measures 6¼ inches, which multiplied four times would just equal his advertised height of 25 inches. Handing this tiny sheet to passers by could not help but create enormous interest in attending the show.

At the same time that this playbill enticed the multitudes to see Tom Thumb, Benjamin Robert Haydon, one of the most famous artists in England, exhibited his paintings in another room of Egyptian Hall. In 1820 Haydon had used the venue to display his talents and launch his career by showing a massive historical canvas. Although critics compared him to a raree-showman, Haydon generated fame and money with a number of successful exhibitions at Egyptian Hall. His openings typically attracted hundreds of the most important and fashionable people in town. This time, however, with public interest in history painting waning, his epic portrayals of *The Banishment of Aristedes* and *The Burning of Rome* did not attract the crowds, funds, or attention he hoped to garner. As Haydon witnessed the ever increasing crowds attending the General, he grew more and more depressed with his financial crisis deepening. He pled his case succinctly in an advertisement in the London *Times: "Exquisite Feeling of the English People for High Art*—General Tom Thumb last week received 12,000 people, who paid him 600 pounds." "B. R. Haydon," he continued, "who has devoted 42 years to elevate their taste, was honoured by the visits of 133½," which netted him a little more than five pounds. This comparison, although it did stir some controversy, did not produce the desired result. In May, still losing money, Haydon closed his show, and a few weeks later he shot himself in the head. This too failed to produce the desired result, and so he then finished the job by slitting his throat with a razor. That Barnum and Tom Thumb were held responsible was reflected in an article in the *Times* of June 26: "The display of a disgusting dwarf attracted hordes of gaping idiots, who poured into the pockets of a Yankee showman a stream of wealth one tithe of which would have redeemed an honourable English artist from wretchedness and death." The following week Tom Thumb ended his engagement at Egyptian Hall.

EGYPTIAN HALL, PICCADILLY.

FAREWELL LEVEES OF
Gen¹ TOM THUMB

Previous to his Final Departure for America,

Positively for a SHORT TIME ONLY.
EVERY DAY and EVENING.

Under the Patronage of

Her Majesty, Prince Albert, The Queen Dowager, The King and Queen of the French, The King and Queen of the Belgians, The Emperor of Russia,

The Queens of Spain, the Royal Families and Nobility of England, France, Belgium, and Spain, and visited during the last two years by

More than 2,000,000 Persons.

The little General is in fine health and spirits, symmetrical in his proportions,

and he has not increased One Inch in Height, nor an Ounce in Weight, since he was Seven Months Old!
He is 14 Years old, 25 Inches high, and weighs only 15 Pounds!!

The little GENERAL will appear in his various Extraordinary Performances and Costumes, including SONGS, DANCES, ANCIENT STATUES, the NAPOLEON and HIGHLAND COSTUMES, CITIZEN'S DRESS, &c. &c.

Hours of Exhibition 12½ to 2;—3½ to 5;—and 7½ to 9 o'Clock.

Doors open half-an-Hour previous.

ADMISSION, ONE SHILLING.

CHILDREN UNDER TEN HALF-PRICE.

The General's Miniature Equipage will Promenade the Streets Daily.

The General will, at the conclusion of his Evening Performance at the Egyptian Hall, appear *every evening* at the *Lyceum Theatre* (opposite Waterloo Bridge, Strand), in a *New Burlesque*, written expressly for the occasion by *Albert Smith*, Esq., entitled "*Hop-o'-my-Thumb; or, The Ogre and his Seven League Boots.*" The part of *Hop-o'-my-Thumb* by the *General*, being his first appearance at that Theatre.

☞ READER! The GENERAL is exactly four times the length of the Bill you are reading.

PRINTED BY T. BRETTELL, RUPERT STREET, HAYMARKET.

4 1/16 x 6 3/16

CARL HERRMANN

1848

THIS LARGE BROADSIDE FOR Carl Herrmann, with its highly unusual display types, must be one of the first to advertise a matinee. (The establishment of the afternoon performance was later credited to another magician, John Nevil Maskelyne, for an engagement at London's Egyptian Hall.)

Herrmann's London appearance garnered approbation that was not entirely deserved, but it set a precedent for a long and prestigious career and initiated a dynasty of magicians that was patronized by the public for three-quarters of a century. He was hailed in the London Press as more original than his famous contemporaries, Anderson, Jacobs, and Philippe (see nos. 126, 140, and 136); but the new illusions that most excited the critics were actually those of Robert-Houdin, whom he immediately preceded in London (ironically, Robert-Houdin took up residence at St. James' Theatre, in direct competition with Herrmann, the very week of this advertisement). On this bill Herrmann illustrated and featured an illusion in which a young woman was administered ether (its medical application was just then achieving credibility). This potion, he explained, allowed for her suspension in air. Herrmann offers exactly the same presentation Robert-Houdin had created to captivate Parisian audiences.

The only major piece on this bill not derived from the French magician was Herrmann's imitations of birds. Surprisingly, this accomplishment garnered his earliest royal performance, for King Louis Philippe, when Carl was just a schoolboy.

Even the admirers of Robert-Houdin praised Herrmann more than any of his other rivals. To his credit, Carl eventually dropped the big set pieces from his show and employed primarily sleight of hand. He often relied on inventions of his friend Johann Nepomuk Hofzinser (see p. 142), but these were added to his repertoire with permission. Hofzinser, who reviewed Herrmann in the Austrian press, gave him high praise for his manner and performing skills, and singled out his ambidexterity as well as his ability to throw playing cards with great speed, height, and distance.

By the time he arrived in America in 1861, Carl had become one of the most honored conjurers in history. The jewels he had received as tokens of esteem from monarchs and patrons were so dazzling that they were exhibited at Tiffany's during his New York run. His debut at the Academy of Music was performed before three thousand delighted spectators. New York newspapermen promulgated his legend. My favorite story appeared in the *Times*: Herrmann stopped at the most fashionable hair salon in the city for a shave. About to pay, Herrmann asked the manager if he had been well served. The manager saw Carl sporting three-days' growth and called for the barber, who was completely baffled, having just shaved the man. "Shave him again," said the manager, who suddenly recognized his customer, "and when you are finished, give Mr. Herrmann a second bill," for "when conjurers grow their beards at such a rate, it is but fair they should pay each time they require them to be removed."

Carl came out of retirement when his fortune was dissipated in the Panic of 1874. He again conquered the stage, performing for another full decade before his death in 1887. His younger brother Alexander (see p. 154) carried on what was to become a family dynasty: Alexander was heralded as the most famous magician in America by the end of the century.

THEATRE ROYAL,

HAY-MARKET.

Mr. B. WEBSTER, Sole Lessee and Manager, Old Brompton.

MORNING
PERFORMANCES

MATINÉES
MAGIQUE

Commencing at Two o'Clock.

THE

WONDER OF THE WORLD!

THIS MORNING,

FRIDAY, May 5th, 1848,
AND TO-MORROW, (SATURDAY).

M. HERRMANN,

(OF HANOVER)

PREMIER PRESTIDIGITATEUR OF FRANCE,

AND THE ACKNOWLEDGED

FIRST PROFESSOR OF MAGIC IN THE WORLD,

Respectfully announces to the Nobility, Gentry and the Public in general, that he will give

TWO
Farewell Performances,

Previous to his departure to the provinces, and will introduce

Six New Extraordinary Tricks,

NEVER BEFORE EXHIBITED!

L'Album Hanoverien; **The Hanoverian Album.**
Les Chapeaux Diaboliques; **The Diabolical Hats.**
Le Coffre infernale; **The Infernal Chest.**
Le Vase d'Armide; ou, l'horlogerie de Geneve; **Armida's Vase; or, The Geneva Clock work.**
Le Multiplication des Indes; **Indian Multiplication.**
Les Mysteres de Paris; **The Mysteries of Paris.**

L'ESCAMOTAGE,

De Madame HERRMANN,

As performed some weeks since at the Theatre Royal, Adelphi.

MADE. HERRMANN

Will also exhibit her extraordinary powers of

SECOND SIGHT;

OR,

ANTI-MAGNETISM

By divining, with Closed Eyes, any objects that may be submitted
to this proof, which has astonished the most scientific.

PROGRAMME.

Le Volage des Cartes; **Illusions with Cards.**
Le Miroir des Dames; **the Lady's Looking Glass.**
LA BOUTEILLE INEPUISABLE; **THE INEXHAUSTIBLE BOTTLE.**
Robin le Sorcier, (*piece mecanique*); **Robin the Sorcerer.**
La Poche Marveilleuse; **the Marvellous Pocket.**
Le Noces de Canaes; **the Nuptials of Cana,**
Satan et son Mouchoir; **Satan and his Kerchief.**
Les Coloubes Sympathetiques; **the Sympathetic Doves.**
LE CADRAN MATHEMATICIEN; **THE MATHEMATICAL CLOCK.**
Le Timbre Isole, (*piece mecanique*); **the Isolated Clock Bell.**
Le pain de sucre Magique; **The Magic Sweetcake.**
Plusieurs tours de Cartes nouveaux et de magie blanche; **New Illusions with Cards and White Magic.**
La naissance des Poissons rouges, execute en habit de ville; **The Birth of Gold Fish; performed in an Evening Dress.**

GRAND NEW ILLUSIONS
FROM INDIA,

Le SUSPENSION ETHEREENNE
BY ETHER.

SUSPENSION ÉTHÉRÉENNE.

LE DOUBLE VUE!
Or, Second Sight,

BY

MADAME HERRMANN.

WITH VARIOUS NEW

ILLUSIONS WITH CARDS

AND

MAGIE BLANCHE!

AND

A CONCERT,

IN IMITATION OF VARIOUS BIRDS,

BY

M. HERRMANN.

Stalls and Boxes 5s.   **Pit 3s.**   **Gallery 2s.**

Doors open at Half-past One; the Performance to commence at Two o'Clock.
Private Boxes to be had at the Box-office, & at the Libraries of Mess. Sams, Mitchell, Ebers, Hookham, Andrews, Bailey, & Allcroft.
Tickets and Places to be had of Mr. J. T. ARCHER, at the Box-Office, which is open daily from 10 till 5.

W. S. Johnson, "Nassau Steam Press," 60, St. Martin's Lane.

QUIRIN MÜLLER
ARM WRESTLER
C. 1848

THE DEMONSTRATION OF great strength was an act of almost universal popularity. The dominant image of this playbill was also fashionable. A rival athlete, Julius Stark (whose surname means "strong" in German), displayed a similar woodcut in which he lifts six men and a hundred-pound weight suspended from his teeth for a performance in Donaueschingen in 1844. This playbill features Quirin Müller, who lifted six men, the same weight with his teeth, and an additional two hundred pounds suspended from his shoulders. His show, presented with official sanction, was introduced as "A Great Extraordinary Herculean-Athletic-Academic Art and Strength Demonstration in Four Parts."

Müller and his cohort Louis Frederic proudly noted that their accomplishments had often been praised in the press. This broadside enumerated their heroics. Both the first and second parts of the show featured extraordinary feats of strength by Müller. To end the second section dramatically, he provided demonstrations associated with Milo of Crotana (the legendary ancient Greek wrestler whose crowning achievement was that he hoisted an ox on his shoulders, carried it for a furlong, and then ate it). The next section featured a vignette called Simpson's Weapon, and the third part presented "The fighting Herculeses, performed in living-academic images by Quirin Müller and L. Frederic." These were most likely versions of the popular art known as *tableau vivants,* in which actors assumed poses, often based on famous paintings or statuary. The fourth section displayed the "Great attack (with Daggers and Swords) fought by the athlete Quirin Müller and the academic fencing master L. Frederic. All admirers of the arts of weaponry are politely invited." Prices ranged from 18 to 48 kroner. The performance began at six o'clock, with the box office opening an hour prior. An orchestra—and good heating—were promised.

Müller personalized the large and impressive playbill, printed in Mannheim, with a challenge: "That I may have the honor of showing my prowess in Boxing on the great stage…I thus invite all strong men from here and the vicinity to present themselves and to wrestle with me; you will be given assurance that nothing bad will happen to you, and whoever defeats me in wrestling will be given a prize of 500 Francs….A prize of 50 Francs will be awarded to whoever can pull me two strides from where I stand while I hold a rope firmly in my teeth." In what seems a modern touch, Müller ended his text by extending the same offer of 50 francs "to whoever can beat me at arm wrestling."

Mit Obrigkeitlicher Bewilligung.

Dienstag den 22. Februar:

Große

außerordentlich herkulisch-athletisch-
academische

Kunst- und Kraft-Production

des in mehreren öffentlichen Blättern rühmlichst erwähnten Herkules und Athleten

Quirin Müller und Louis Frederic

im

Aula-Saale

in 4 Abtheilungen, wobei ein großer Assaut (auf Stoß und Hieb) statt finden wird.

1. Abtheilung.

Herkulische Tändeleien, ausgeführt von Quirin Müller.

2. Abtheilung.

Außerordentliche Kraftproben des Quirin Müller, zum Schlusse der Abtheilung außerordentliche Stärke des Milo von Crotana, eines der stärksten Athleten seines Jahrhunderts.

Simsons Wappe,
eine Kunstleistung des Athleten Quirin Müller.

3. Abtheilung.

Die kämpfenden Herkulesse, dargestellt in lebend-akademischen Bilder, von Quirin Müller und L. Frederic.

4. Abtheilung.

Großer Assaut, (à la pointe et Spatons) gefochten von dem Athleten Quirin Müller und dem akademischen Fechtmeister L. Frederic.

Alle Liebhaber der Waffenkunst werden höflichst dazu eingeladen.

Preise der Plätze:

Parquet	36 kr.
Ein gesperrter Sitz darin	48 kr.
Parterre	24 kr.
Gallerie	18 kr.

Kasseneröffnung 5 Uhr.
Anfang 6 Uhr.

Da ich meine Fertigkeit im Ringen auf den größten Schaubühnen zu zeigen die Ehre hatte, so wie auch wegen meiner Muskelkraft in den berühmtesten Akademien als Muster aufgestellt war, so lade ich alle starken Männer von hier und der Umgebung ein, sich einzufinden und mit mir zu ringen, es wird ihnen die Versicherung gegeben, daß ihnen nichts Leides geschieht, und erhalten einen Preis von 500 Francs der mich im Ringen besiegt. Bitte vorher ihre Adresse persönlich in meiner Wohnung, Gasthaus zum deutschen Hof No. 25 gefälligst einzureichen.

Einen Preis von 50 Francs erhält derjenige, der mich mit stetem Ziehen 2 Schritte von der Stelle bringt, ich halte blos ein Tau (Seil) ganz frei in den Zähnen fest, und gestatte einer jeden Person nach allen möglichen Kräften zu ziehen.

Denselben Preis von 50 Francs erhält auch derjenige, der meinen gekrümmten Arm, welcher an einem Sei befestigt ist, gerad zu ziehen vermag.

Quirin Müller,
Athlet und Ringer.

Billette zu der Vorstellung sind in der Musikalienhandlung des Hrn. Heckel so wie Abends an der Kasse zu haben. Für gut besetztes Orchester und Beheizung des Locals ist bestens gesorgt.

Buchdruckerei von G. Schweter in Mannheim.

CANTELO'S INCUBATOR

1851

EGGS HAVE BEEN A STAPLE PROP of the magic profession for hundreds of years. A number of the magicians whose broadsides are featured here significantly enhanced their reputations by conjuring with eggs. Among the most famous effects of the eighteenth century was one that may still be found in the repertoire of modern mystery workers: the production and vanish of eggs from a simple bag. The finale of the effect, as in Isaac Fawkes' performance in the 1720s (see p. 26), often included the startling production of a live chicken.

Other conjurers, such as Pinetti, Ingleby, and Lane (see p. 46), dispensed with the bag and just produced birds from eggs in an act sometimes called "Palingenesia." The most improbable of the early egg tricks was described in the playbills of Sieur Boaz, who invited a spectator to select two eggs from a quantity. From one he supposedly withdrew a set of bed linen and from the other the concomitant child. Another conjurer featured an effect called "The Egg in Labour" in the 1820s, and the famous Scottish wizard John Henry Anderson (see p. 126) offered hatching eggs by magic two decades later.

The creation of life from the egg, in a somewhat less exotic mode, was also the major appeal of Cantelo's Hydro-Incubator, exhibited in London in the mid-nineteenth century. It cost one shilling to view this scientific marvel. An earlier incubator had been shown in London's Egyptian Hall in 1824. It hatched the eggs of chickens, ducks, and emus. A Frenchman named Vallée showed his invention at the Jardin des Plantes in Paris in the 1840s. In addition to producing a wide variety of fowl from eggs, he had success with vipers, yellow lizards, and tortoises.

Cantelo's machine was said to be an improvement over earlier models, and it clearly captured the imagination of the public. He announced "Poultry for the Millions" for a showing at the Cosmorama Rooms in 1848. By the time of the Leicester Square appearance billed here he was announcing "The Greatest Wonder of the Age." The subject of poetic ditties and satires, he was summoned to a command performance for Queen Victoria and Prince Albert at Windsor Castle. "Why," posed an unidentified newspaper scribe in 1851, "is the celebrated Cantelo a perfect liberator of the feathery tribe?"

"Because he makes ex-empt chickens!—turns them to shape and gives to little feathers a local habitation and a name"—the process is a triumph of study and art of the simplest nature—the incubation has been viewed in Leicester Square by wondering thousands, and can only be seen to delight—patronized by…all the élite of London.

I have a half dozen Cantelo playbills featuring three different illustrations, but this is the only one I have seen printed on pink paper. It features a number of bold sans serif types. The engraving portrays not only the machine, the chicks, and the spectators but also the fashions of the well-dressed clientele.

The progeny of these edifying devices are still popular with visitors to modern museums, including the much-beloved incubator in the Museum of Science and Industry in Chicago.

7¼ x 9¹⁵/₁₆

J.H. ANDERSON
"THE WIZARD OF THE NORTH"
1851

JOHN HENRY ANDERSON, the famous Scottish conjurer, was dubbed "The Wizard of the North." It is probable that Anderson's shows were seen by more people than those of any other contemporary conjurer. He attracted audiences in numbers that would be impressive on Broadway today. He acted in his own shows and produced them for others, and he built the largest theater in Scotland. The periodical press avidly followed the ups and downs of his career, yet he was no doubt his own best promoter. Houdini, who would inherit his title as the pre-eminent magic publicist, pronounced him the "greatest advertiser" the world of conjuring had ever known. According to Milbourne Christopher, he "plastered his gaudy showbills all over the world, even on the sides of the pyramids in Egypt and on the cliffs of Niagara Falls."

Anderson flooded cities in which he was appearing with written accounts of his life and papered whole towns with his lithographs and playbills. His likeness streamed into people's homes, printed on the covers of sheet music and impressed into pats of butter. Anderson kept himself perpetually in the public eye: he distributed newspapers, conducted contests, lectured on fraudulent spiritualism, displayed props made of costly silver, managed Chinese acrobats and Aztec Lilliputians, and sold novelties — even hair dye. He courted his audiences with gifts, and he advertised this unusual provision for their physical comfort: "The Theatre will be Nightly Ventilated by an Improved Form of the Great Hindostanee Punkah Scented with Frangiapanni and diffusing Odoriferous Coolness through the House."

Anderson was merciless in attacking competitors who encroached upon his presentations but never hesitated to appropriate material from skilled rivals. For an act performed at the Standard Theatre in Shorditch in 1851, Anderson copied not only major illusions from the repertoire of the great French conjurer Robert-Houdin but the basic design of his posters as well. This one was patterned after a bill produced by the Frenchman in 1849 that similarly featured distinctive colored borders surrounding woodcut vignettes of the magician. In Anderson's version, four pieces were lifted from Robert-Houdin's show: "The Fantastic Portfolio," "The Ladies Favorite," "The Shower of Gold," and "The Inexhaustible Bottle."

Anderson's originality lay not in his magical effects but in his creation of humorous and engaging scenarios that cleverly alluded to contemporary cultural preoccupations. In the Hercules Traction Trick, "an interesting looking Child of 7 years of Age, can pull to the Ground 1000 Strong Men." Anderson would then have spectators "Test your Strength against the Cable-nerved Child, whose Magic Touch Cures Rheumatism, Sciatica, Neuralgia, Gout, Spasms, and all the ills which Flesh is heir to. One Touch of the Child is equal to 37,000 Boxes of the best puffed Pills." On this show he also featured the Great Gun Trick (see p. 74), in which a bullet was apparently fired directly at him, but his claim to have originated this effect was belated by hundreds of years. Charles James Mathews, in a sketch featuring "The Wizard of the South-South-West-by-East," lampooned Anderson's presentation of invulnerability.

Anderson's career had great highs and cataclysmic lows. His bombast and his bluster were the source of ribbing, parody, and criticism, but he was a true star of magic. E. P. Hingston, a contemporary author and publicist who penned a biography of the great American humorist Artemus Ward as well as one of Anderson, awarded the latter the laurels of publicity and promotion. "Other men have sought to entrap fame by dint of large type and bold pictures," he said, "but they are bunglers in comparison with Professor Anderson. The invention, the variety, the fancy of his posting-bills, entitle him to the praise of being uncontested head of the mural literature and art of this metropolis." The wizard's bills and advertising were so varied and extensive that they may be said to epitomize the history of the medium in this era. Even his passing was commemorated in a broadside, "The Death and Memoir of Prof'r. Anderson." It encapsulated his career, from debut to demise, and concluded with the verdict of the presiding physician, who pronounced the cause of death "a general decay of nature."

STANDARD THEATRE

Proprietor] Opposite the Eastern Counties' Railway, SHOREDITCH. [J. DOUGLASS.

THE GREAT WIZARD OF THE NORTH.

The Theatre will be NIGHTLY VENTILATED by an Improved form of the GREAT HINDOSTANEE PUNKAH Scented with Frangipanni, and diffusing Odoriferous COOLNESS through the House.

IMMENSE SUCCESS!
NOTHING LIKE IT IN LONDON
THE THEATRE FULL AND THE STREET FULL EVERY NIGHT.

PROFESSOR
ANDERSON
EVERY EVENING, in his MAGICAL DRAMA, A
Night in Wonder-World
OR, MAGIC, MIRTH, AND MYSTERY!

Produced on a Scale of Grandeur far surpassing anything that has yet been attempted on the Stage.

RESULTS
FIRST WEEK!
3,762 visitors on Monday,
3,954 ditto on Tuesday,
2,931 ditto on Wednesday,
5,071 ditto on Thursday,
5,134 ditto on Friday,
5,504 ditto on Saturday.
26,246 visitors in One Week.

ON MONDAY, JUNE 22nd,
AND EVERY EVENING at Half-past Seven,
A NIGHT in WONDER-WORLD
Or, a DRAMA of the WONDEROUS!
IN THE COURSE OF WHICH, THE FOLLOWING
GORGEOUSLY SUPERB APPARATUS WILL BE USED:—

The Casket of the Alchemists
The Wand of Rosicrucius
The Umbrella of Magic
Glass Goblets of Giraldus
Conch of the Genii
Paradoxical Fan
Cabalistical Candles
Clairvoyant Wand
Coffres du Diable
Anderson's Own Phylophligicom
The Ampulla Vitrea Inexhausten
Cagliostro's Carraffa
Dr. Dee's Mirror

Anderson's Own Metamorphic Tables
The Dioptric Puzzle
Mystic Cards—Devil's Punchbowl
Magic-made Canaries
Mysterious Travelling Trunk
Oracle of Pasmatolines
Lavatory of Necromancy
Bewitched Flowers
Chair of Comus
Enchanted Target
Anderson's Rite
The Electric Box
Magneto-Electric Vase

The Spirit Rapping Table
The Mechanical Magician
The Magnet of the Pyramids
The Key of Thibe
Cards Endowed with Volition
Effervescent Ink
Tocsin of the Invisibles
Sketch-book of Sathanas
Bell of the Invisibles
Mystical Tripod
Vitreo Textile Problem
The Enchanted Doves
The Globes of the Hindoos

EXCITEMENT UNPARELELLED AT
THE HERCULES TRACTION TRICK
By means of which, an interesting looking Child of 7 years of Age, can pull to the Ground
1000 Strong Men.
Test your Strength against the Cable-nerved Child, whose Magic Touch Cures RHEUMATISM, SCIATICA, NEURALGIA, GOUT, SPASMS, and all the ills which Flesh is heir to.
One Touch of the Child is equal to 37,000 Boxes of the best puffed Pills.

THE PROGRAMME.

Act 1.
THE BIRDS OF FIRE!
Act 2.
MONEY MADE BY WISHING IT
Act 3.
MAGICAL INTROVISION.
Act 4.
WILLIAM TELL AT HOME.
Act 5.
GREAT GUN TRICK
Act 6.
The Tocsin of the Invisibles.
Act 7.
CLEOPATRA'S WEDDING RING.
Act 8.
THE ORACLE of the SIBYLS!

Act 9.
THE COUCH OF THE GENII
Act 10.
THE WINE VAT OF BACCHUS
Act 11.
MAGIC WOVE HANDKERCHIEFS
Act 12.
The Casket of the Gnomes!
Act 13.
CHAIR of THE WITCHES
Act 14.
Trunk Mysteriously Corded!
Act 15.
TO AUSTRALIA In Ten Minutes!

Between the Parts of the Entertainment,
Mr J. G. FORDE
WILL GIVE HIS
MONOLOGUE ENTERTAINMENT,
IN THE
Great Eastern Panama-Railway-High-Pressure-Hydrogen Style
DESCRIPTIVE OF
The Earth—Sea—Air—Love—Ladies—Law—Marriage—Mirth—Old Men—Young Ladies—All things that are, and everything else besides—with Facetious Power, and more than Chas. MATTHEWS' volubility of expression.—Unrivalled by any Artist living.

☞ NO ADVANCE IN PRICES!
BOX OFFICE OPEN FROM 10 TILL 4. SECURE SEATS BEFOREHAND.
New Private Boxes, Centre Circle. 3s. each Person. Stage Boxes, 2s. 6d. each Person. Private Boxes on the Dress Circle. 2s. each Person. Private Boxes on the Upper Circle. 1s. 6d. each Person. The Centre Box has been fitted up quite private, 2s. each Person. Centre Circle, 1s. 6d. each Person. Lower Circle. 1s. Upper Circle, 9d. Orchestra Stalls. 1s. Pit. 6d.
GALLERY, (First time during Professor Anderson's Expensive Engagements) THREEPENCE
DOORS OPEN at 7, to COMMENCE AT HALF-PAST.
Half-Price to Boxes and Stalls at 9 o'Clock. Bill Inspector...Mr W. PHILLIPS.
NO CHILDREN IN ARMS ADMITTED.

19⅛ x 29⁹⁄₁₆

THE CHINESE LADY

1851

A SMALL BUT NICELY SET HANDBILL, ornamented with a few lines of rubricated type, heralds the 1851 exhibition of "The Chinese Collection," a famous assemblage of Asian curiosities amassed by the wealthy American trader Nathan Dunn. Originally shown in 1838 at Peale's Museum in Philadelphia, the collection had its first London exhibition in a specially constructed two-story pagoda three years later. After the departure of this show the pagoda was home to a number of movable panoramas, and to the first exhibition of a Pre-Raphaelite painting, Rossetti's *The Girlhood of Mary Virgin*.

A sign proclaimed "Ten Thousand Chinese Things," but in spite of lavish groupings of life-size figures and authentic artifacts (weapons of war, costumes, vessels, dwellings, and ornaments), the pagoda housed far fewer than the advertised number of treasures. The irrepressible P. T. Barnum brought the show to his American Museum on Broadway and subsequently took it back to London for the exhibition that is advertised on this playbill. It now contained fewer than half the items originally displayed, but it was augmented by live performance.

Although I take pleasure in the prudently hyped "Two Interesting Chinese Children," the featured player was Pwan-Ye-Koo, a seventeen-year-old girl who sang with accompaniment on native instruments. Hector Berlioz, who was in London for the Crystal Palace exhibition that same year, attended and commented on her recital. What made Pwan-Ye-Koo most marketable, however, were her "Small Lotus Feet, only 2½ Inches in Length!"

The custom of foot binding existed in China for more than a millennium. The process of breaking and confining the foot usually began when girls were about six years of age. They endured this incredibly painful ordeal in order to fit into tiny, beautifully embroidered shoes that were thought by some to be the height of fashion. The standard sought was the "golden lotus," measuring no more than three inches. Prospective grooms might be shown the slippers of a proposed mate, while the bride's family leveraged her dowry. According to a nineteenth-century English missionary, who purportedly authored the first Western commentary on the subject, "the girl with a three-inch sole and an ugly face has a better chance in the matrimonial market than a five-inch-sole shoed girl who might have a face like a madonna."

While most observers recoil in horror at such a custom, some would point to the Western insistence, in former centuries, on pulling the waist painfully tight with corsets, or to the current devotion to high heels so confining that women are surgically modifying their toes to wear them. There is almost no part of the human body that has not been objectified and tormented in some culture, and the Chinese practice of foot binding encompasses a wide range of complex and evolving social and sexual issues. Beyond the fetishistic veneration of the foot, the binding expressed a pledge of fidelity and docility. Status, too, was involved, as women so altered could not easily walk and had to be transported (a certain low class of men known as "tortoises" evolved specifically to transport privileged prostitutes with lotus feet). When these foot-bound women did manage to walk, their "lotus gate" changed the musculature of their thighs, buttocks, and genitals and enhanced their value as objects of male desire.

1851.

"One of the Chief Lions' of the Day."—Times.

THE CHINESE LADY,

PWAN-YE-KOO,

With Small Lotus Feet, only 2½ Inches in Length!

HER NATIVE FEMME DE CHAMBRE,

CHINESE PROFESSOR OF MUSIC,

TWO Interesting CHINESE CHILDREN,

Male and Female—5 and 7 Years of Age,

AND SUITE,

Exhibiting Daily from 11 till 1, 2 till 5, and 6 till 10,

AT THE

CHINESE COLLECTION,

ALBERT GATE, HYDE PARK.

The LADY PWAN-YE-KOO will sing

A SELECTION OF CHINESE AIRS,

And will be accompanied by the Professor, on Chinese Musical
Instruments, each Hour during their Exhibiting.

ADMISSION TO THE

TWO EXHIBITIONS,

ONE SHILLING.

R. S. FRANCIS, Printer, Catherine Street, Strand.

5 11/16 x 8 15/16

H. BOX BROWN
FUGITIVE SLAVE

1854

THIS PLEASANT PLAYBILL IS PRINTED in black ink on gray paper with almost a dozen varied but compatible types—a reserved but nonetheless effective design for a moving-panorama show of the mid-nineteenth century. The conventional appearance of this provincial advertisement, however, belies the remarkable story behind it.

The impresario Henry "Box" Brown was at the time of this 1854 performance perhaps the most famous fugitive slave in the world. He had escaped from Virginia to Philadelphia in a packing case bearing the inscription "This side up with care." In spite of the warning he was, during this twenty-four-hour ordeal, tossed about in body-jarring terror. He rode for long periods while upside down and on more than one occasion almost expired from the extreme heat and lack of oxygen. The story of his personal intrepidity spread far and wide and he became one of the most recognized icons of the abolitionist movement. Brown was a much sought after figure at anti-slavery rallies and conventions, and lithographs depicting his emergence from the packing case were sold in large quantities—even though the illustration was strikingly similar to something from a magician's catalog. Although Brown never learned to write, his memoirs were recorded, and he parlayed his skills as a church singer and his speaking engagements into a most unlikely career.

Panoramas that rolled across the stage accompanied by some basic lighting effects and a live commentary were then the rage. John Banvard, the painter and cicerone of a canvas voyage down the Mississippi River, became the most commercially successful artist of his time and a major theatrical attraction. With a group of writers and artists in Boston, Brown launched his "Mirror of Slavery" panorama. The show he presented was a semifictional look at the history of slavery that also told the story of his own escape.

It was the first time such a highly charged political subject found its way into this popular format.

With the black man who had helped seal him into the case in Virginia, James Smith (now nicknamed Boxer), Brown took the panorama, and the crate, on the road. When the Fugitive Slavery Bill was passed, however, they feared capture and prosecution, and they departed for England, where they were enthusiastically received. But success, it seems, changed Brown. He quarreled with his partner and fired him, and was accused of betraying the anti-slavery cause. On stage he dressed in outlandish outfits (he donned, according to one respected black abolitionist, a green coat and a white hat, and wore gold rings on every finger). He called himself "The African Prince" and led parades with a brandished sword. He abandoned the wife and child he had vowed to liberate from slavery with his earnings and instead married an Englishwoman, who later bore him a child. Even though this playbill announces his "farewell exhibitions…previous to his embarkation for America," he stayed on in Great Britain for another twenty-four years.

To court the public, he modified his panoramas and, after using a hypnotist as an opening act, added this skill to his repertoire. By 1864, his transformation complete, he was billing himself as "The King of all Mesmerists." Eventually he added conjuring to his list of accomplishments. Almost thirty years after his flight in a pine box, this modest seeker after freedom, this recipient of the accolades of Wendell Phillips, William Lloyd Garrison, and Frederick Douglas, was back in America "destroying and restoring" handkerchiefs, performing the "inexhaustible hats," and offering card and coin tricks in "The African Prince's Drawing Room Entertainment." His wife demonstrated mind reading, and his daughter exhibited "the wonderful sack trick," a bizarre parallel to his own escape so many years earlier.

NEW MARKET HALL, STOKE.

FOR FOUR NIGHTS ONLY.

Wednesday, Thursday, Friday, & Saturday,

FEBRUARY 1, 2, 3, and 4, 1854,

MR. HENRY BOX BROWN

Will exhibit his celebrated American Moving Tableaux, or

PANORAMA

OF

AFRICAN AND AMERICAN SLAVERY!

Mr. H. B. BROWN while exhibiting in the various towns in England has met with the greatest success, being under the patronage of some of the most eminent Clergymen and Mayors of this country. He is also in possession of Testimonials and Credentials of the highest authority.

MR. HENRY BOX BROWN begs to inform the public that he is giving his farewell exhibitions in England, previous to his embarkation for America.

MR. JACOB SAMES,

The most renowned and successful performer on the ACCORDEON and FLUTINA that ever appeared in this country, will give some of his most admired Airs in the course of the Evening.

MR. THOMAS FRODSHAM

Will also perform, and accompany Mr. Sames on the Accordeon and Flutina.

ADMISSION,—Reserved Seats, 1s.   Unreserved Seats, 6d.

DOORS OPEN AT SEVEN, TO COMMENCE AT EIGHT.

8 x 9¼

BOSCO AT BALMORAL CASTLE
1855

THIS PLAYBILL WAS ISSUED TO commemorate the performance of the great magician Bartolomeo Bosco (see p. 82) for Queen Victoria at Balmoral Castle on Monday, September 24, 1855. Perhaps as ephemeral as the broadside itself was a pamphlet describing the engagement, issued some forty-four years after the event. It was authored by Bosco's impresario, W. J. L. Millar, and entitled *How an American Brought the Great Italian Wizard before H.M. Queen Victoria*. Millar explains that he undertook the management of Bosco on the rebound: in August 1855, he was exhibiting the conjoined twins Millie-Christine (see p. 146) in Dundee, Scotland, when "they were stolen from me by a body of prizefighters hired from London for that purpose." Even though he was earlier accused of purloining the twins, he indignantly pronounced that to book an act under another's management is a "most contemptible thing for anyone to be guilty of." Millar joined forces with Bosco, promising to book the conjurer in Aberdeen. This too proved a little dicey as that city was the home of John Henry Anderson, the Scots "Wizard of the North" (see p. 126), but the wiley Italian was able to meet the challenge.

The document gives us unusual insight into the techniques of mid-nineteenth-century promotion, although through the self-serving eyes of Millar, who reveals mastery and chutzpah in equal measure. Bosco's stellar ability is almost taken for granted—not even one effect from his show is described. We can tell from the bill, however, that Bosco presented a mixed program showcasing his manipulative skills. The first act ended with "a variety of table feats," which almost certainly included his legendary performance of the classic "Cups and Balls." For the second set he featured intimate conjuring accompanied by music and a demonstration of ventriloquism. Millar, in his pamphlet, did report the royal reaction: "At each of his most wonderful illusions all seemed astonished and highly delighted, particularly with his card tricks and his bewildering sleight of hand, of which he was a most complete master." For Millar himself the highlight came the next day, as he received a letter pronouncing Her Royal Highness' satisfaction and an unexpected payment, the hefty sum of fifty pounds.

Millar described the printing of this particular broadside, which he took some pains over, intending it to be "something out of the common." He secured the services of Keith and Guild, "Lithographers and Engravers to the Queen," and the result was indeed impressive. The new castle at Balmoral, then still under construction, was depicted "within an elegant border and [with] a representation of Bosco performing some of his illusions, struck off on white satin with fine lace." The bill, shown here, is a variant printed on a delicate clay-coated paper.

Signor Bosco's
Programme
of Magic & Ventriloquism

BALMORAL CASTLE,
Monday Evening, 24th September, 1855.

Part 1st

THE CHINESE PLATE & DISH DANCE.
THE MAGIC MONEY. — THE ENCHANTED HANDKERCHIEFS.
THE MAGICIAN'S CHAMPAGNE
LE CARTE DU DIABLE. — THE SPANISH KING'S KNOTS.
TO TELL WHAT THE AUDIENCE THINK.
THE SHOWER OF MONEY.
MOUNT VESUVIUS OR THE PARISIAN MANUFACTURER.
THE INCOMPREHENSIBLE CHAIN.
THE BIRD FROM SEBASTOPOL OR RUSSIAN EAGLE.
A VARIETY OF TABLE FEATS.

Part 2nd

THE INEXHAUSTIBLE HEN. —— THE WONDERFUL RINGS.
THE ASTONISHING SNUFF BOX. — THE MAGIC PISTOL.
IMITATION OF A CLARIONET,
A SELECTION FROM THE OPERA OF NORMA WITH BAND ACCOMPANIMENT.
THE MYSTERIOUS FLOWER POT. — THE INEXHAUSTIBLE HAT.
THE RING AND THE STICK. — THE MAGIC CARD DANCE.
VENTRILOQUISM.

Professor Millar, Manager.

Keith & Gibb, Draftsmen, Lithographers & Engravers To The Queen.
15 Union Buildings, Aberdeen.

9⅛ x 16½

SAVREN
"ARTIST IN EXPERIMENTAL PHILOSOPHY"
1855

ONE OF THE MORE MYSTERIOUS FIGURES of Victorian magic, James Savren performed successfully as a conjurer but was not distinguished for technical accomplishment or originality. His most important contribution to the art may have been to preserve the memorabilia of other magicians. It is said that he was a barber who, infected with the magic bug, would close his shop to offer assistance to such notables as Cornillot, Carl Herrmann, Ludwig Doebler, and John Henry Anderson (see nos. 120 and 126). Houdini endorsed this account but historians have questioned it, and a healthy skepticism is doubtless appropriate.

In the nomenclature of the broadside, this piece seems to bridge a gap between the poster and the playbill. Posters, of course, are printed for general purposes and playbills for specific events. This bill promotes an appearance in April 1855 at the Corn Exchange in Maidstone, but the large, wonderfully crude woodcut was also used by Savren for a number of other shows, with the date appropriately altered.

The piece is also notable as a shameless copy of a lithograph by Pruche that was used in advertisements for the great French illusionist Jean Eugene Robert-Houdin. On view here are many effects performed by Robert-Houdin in his "Soirées Fantastiques": "The Pastrycook of the Palais Royal," "The Ladies Favorite," "The Surprising Silk Handkerchief," "Pierrot in the Egg," and so on—none of which I have ever encountered among the effects on Savren's programs (it is unlikely that he even owned these illusions). In this illustration Savren is pictured with a beard and sporting evening clothes (as was Robert-Houdin in the original), while on other playbills—even for the same engagement on the same day—he is portrayed clean-shaven in an Oriental robe.

Many conjurers stole the creations of the Frenchman. Thus the woodcut itself may have been generic. Popular illustrations were available for purchase by any performer: woodcuts, but especially lithographs, manufactured for this purpose, were called "stock posters." I have seen this particular cut, however, in only three broadsides, all for Savren.

After David of Bordeaux, Savren is one of the first conjurers known to have sought and acquired, deliberately and even passionately, advertising materials from fellow performers. He and Henry Evans Evanion, the other pioneer English magician-collector, are even thought to have exchanged treasures. Evanion stated that Savren acquired playbills directly from Robert-Houdin. Savren's appropriation of designs and effects from someone he so admired seems peculiar homage, but sadly, it is all too prevalent in the magic profession.

CORN EXCHANGE, MAIDSTONE.

FOR TWO NIGHTS ONLY !!

Admission, 1s. each. Reserved Seats, 2s.

EASTER MONDAY & TUESDAY.

Gallery, 6d. Particulars, see Small Bills.

MR. JAS. SAVREN

ARTIST IN EXPERIMENTAL PHILOSOPHY

NATURAL MAGIC !!

PROFESSOR PHILIPPE'S DELUSIONS

1858

PHILIPPE TALON WAS BORN IN Alais, near Nimes, in 1802. He proceeded to Paris to pursue the trade of a confectioner, but having little success he went to England and then Scotland. In Aberdeen in the 1830s, in dire straits, he suggested a lottery in combination with a local pantomime company in a scheme to dispose of his unsold bonbons. Talon not only marketed the show, he also appeared in it. He had been an amateur conjurer and this performance was successful enough to launch him instantly on a new career.

Talon learned the secret of two impressive effects done by Chinese magicians, the production of large bowls of water filled with goldfish and the linking and unlinking of a series of brass hoops or rings, both of which he presented in a sketch called "A Night in the Palace of Pekin." These effects and the presentation of some pieces of magical automata became the staples of his show. He may also have obtained some illusions from John Henry Anderson (see p. 126). He toured in Scotland and Ireland before coming to London, where his offerings were well received, some critics saying he outdid all the contemporary British magicians. He did not perform in his native France until 1841. After striking success on the Continent he returned to Britain for the 1845-46 season and garnered rave reviews. He is generally acknowledged to be the pre-eminent French conjurer before the advent of Robert-Houdin.

All this by way of saying that the playbill here displayed is advertising not Talon, but another who purposely usurped his name and reputation. The imposter was a fellow called Henry, or Harry, Graham, who made a career of impersonating foreign magicians and capitalizing on their fame. Such imitators usually fade away and rarely attract analysis in posterity, but Graham was clearly an amusing and audacious character, and his chutzpah qualified him for enduring renown in three of the major showmen's biographies of the nineteenth century.

G. Van Hare, in his *Fifty Years of a Showman's Life,* recounts hiring Graham as "the notorious Conjurer, Monsieur Philippe"—whom he knew to be a tragedian and circus clown who had earlier assumed the identities of the figures like Frikell, Robin, and Robert-Houdin. David Prince Miller, the well-known Victorian showman who performed as a conjurer early in his career, called Graham "one of the most barefaced professors of magic I ever encountered...whenever a foreign or celebrated conjuror

appeared in London, and acquired fame there, the gentleman I have named above would in a provincial excursion, assume the cognomen of the celebrated professor." The great magician Carl Herrmann (see p. 120), Miller reports, came energetically to the defense of his friend Philippe when he realized that an imposter was performing in his stead. Herrmann left Graham with a "bleeding proboscis, and discolored optic, to proceed as well as he could to entertain his audience."

C. W. Montague, in his *Recollections of an Equestrian Manager,* reports that he had known Graham during a stint as a clown on Ginnett's Circus. At a low point in 1859, when Graham was performing magic tricks at a "miserable booth" in Whitechapel, he had persuaded Montague to produce his show. Montague, although not generous in his assessment of Graham's conjuring, did take him on tour.

How Graham appraised his own skills as a conjurer is not known, but he fantasized that he was a great Shakespearean actor and that his Richard III was rivaled only by the renowned Edmund Kean. When Montague gave him an opportunity to play Richard on his benefit night, he could not have anticipated mortal consequences. After the announcement, "the excitement caused by the realization of this dream of years was too much for him; he died, poor fellow, a few days afterwards."

The real Philippe, meanwhile, suffered a reversal of fortune and was forced back on the boards long after his retirement. For almost two decades after 1860 he presented his illusions in a wearying succession of venues. A letter to his wife, now in the collection of Christian Fechner, describes his travails on the road from Boukharat, Turkey, only a few weeks before his death there in May 1878.

This large bill, printed in red and black, features two woodcuts. A juggler named Pio Whautkins is shown demonstrating his version of Japanese top spinning. The other illustrates a performance of "spirit rapping." The Mulholland Library has an undated Philippe playbill for a show at Guildford with this same cut. A note, likely in Houdini's handwriting, reads "graham Bogus Phillippe." The text mentions the present of a gold box from the queen for a performance at Windsor Castle (that Graham never gave). Van Hare reports that Graham had a "magnificent looking...box, set in diamonds (duffers, of course) which he represented to the audience as being presented to him by the Emperor Napoleon."

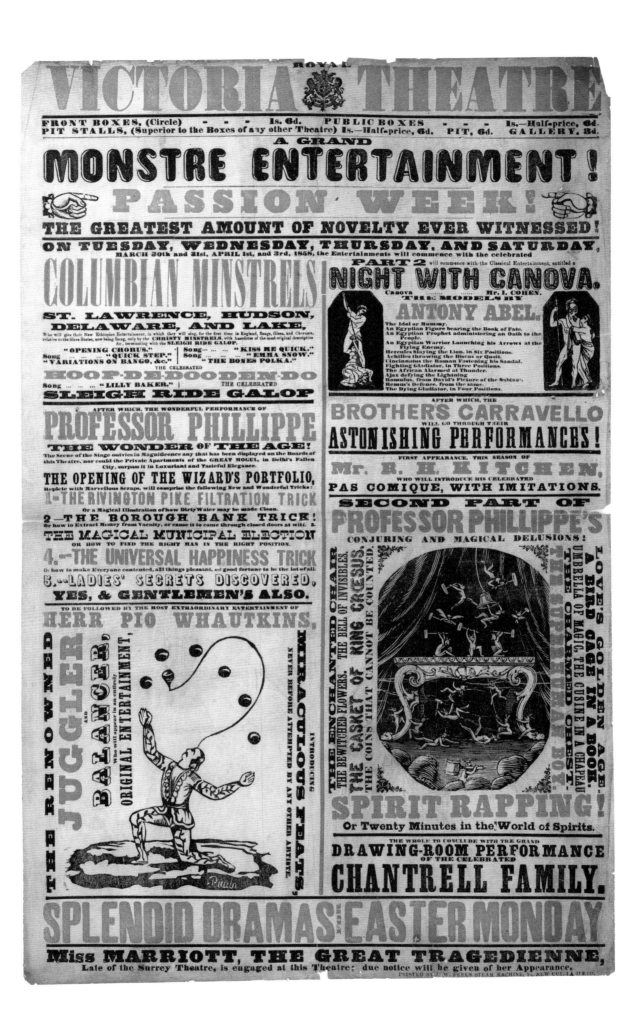

16⅛ x 26¼

GEORGE ANDERSON
"THE LIVING SKELETON"

C. 1862

ATTENUATED AND EMACIATED attractions billed as "living skeletons" had their precursor in the ancient poet Philotus, said to be so thin that he "fastened lead on his shoes to prevent his being blown away." George Anderson was one of a number of rail-thin figures who commanded attention in the nineteenth century. According to this formidable placard with its startling woodcut and unusual display types, he had been reduced from a robust two hundred pounds to a mere sixty-five. He boldly offered a reward of a thousand dollars for any physician able to explain and reverse this trend.

Anderson speculated on his condition in a document sold at his exhibitions, *The Life of George Anderson* (the usual warnings about questionable veracity are hereby invoked). It reveals that he was born in New Boston, New Hampshire, on February 1, 1831, and considered a normal child. He was an expert swimmer who, until afflicted with his anomalous condition, weighed 165 pounds—not the inflated 200 advertised on the broadside. It was his endless hours in the water, he thought, that stripped him of his health. The last line of the biography, which he sold for five cents, admonished: "My appearance should be a terrible warning to all young persons, causing them to avoid excessive bathing, and especially in fresh water." (The only comparable diatribe with which I am familiar is one by his contemporary Jonathan H. Green, the former card cheat and "Reformed Gambler," who railed about the dissolute life sure to ensnare tykes who were excessively fond of playing marbles.)

While one would not think to associate the exhibition of living skeletons with the kinds of subterfuge used by crooked gamblers, deception in the wide arena of performance abounded. Prince Puckler-Moskau, an indefatigable visitor to a wide variety of British attractions, recalled paying a modest fee to witness a mixed bill consisting of a German dwarf and his diminutive children, a fat woman, and a human skeleton. The prince dubbed the show, "the most impertinent 'charlatanerie' exhibited that I ever witnessed. The living skeleton was a very ordinary sized man, not much thinner than I. As an excuse for our disappointment, we were assured that when he arrived from France he was a skeleton, but that since he had eaten good English beef steaks, it had been found impossible to curb his tendency to corpulence."

Why, one might ask, would anyone be interested in witnessing a display such as Anderson's? Yet our subject himself mentions other famous attenuated attractions, Calvin Edson, John Battersby, and Isaac Sprague, all of whom were at some time exhibited by P. T. Barnum. The most famous of the living skeletons was Claude Seurat, a Frenchman who did not come to America but visited London in 1825. The *Lancet*, the major British medical journal, was horrified at the display of Seurat, calling his exhibition "one of the most impudent and disgusting attempts to make a profit of the public appetite for novelty, by an indecent exposure of human suffering and degradation, which we have ever witnessed." Yet Seurat himself seemed grateful for the opportunity to make a good living. His biography concluded with this passage:

We have witnessed many curious and wonderful mortals. Men and women with extraordinary powers of strength—others distorted most hideously—eaters of fire, and consumers of stone—dwarfs and giants—women with horns on their head, and men with three arms—beings that could live without food, and gluttons who could consume a lamb at a meal.—We have instances of persons who have slept for weeks without sustenance, and seen blind persons make clocks, watches, and repair organs—boys without hands painting pictures, and women cutting watch papers with their toes—but we never before beheld so great a curiosity as "the living skeleton."

Perhaps the controversy surrounding such exhibitions prompted George Anderson to launch an ancillary career as a magic-lantern projectionist. Like many such itinerant showmen, he presented traditional scenes and combined these with views of recently fought Civil War battles (most of which took place in 1862, enabling us to date this bill). We are able to include in our show a remarkable survival, a piece of canvas likely from a tent in which Anderson's exhibition took place, on which stenciled scenes are still visible.

GEORGE ANDERSON,
THE LIVING
SKELETON!

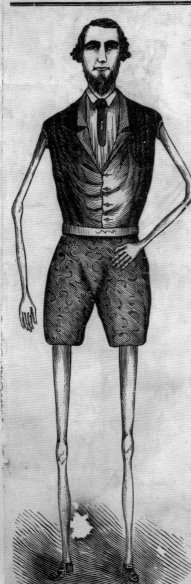

George Anderson, the Living Skeleton, invites the Ladies and Gentlemen of this place and vicinity, to visit his Great Exhibition of late

BATTLE SCENES,

Of surpassing beauty and interest, in connection with himself. He is Five Feet Eight Inches in Height, and now

WEIGHS ONLY SIXTY-FIVE POUNDS!

And is the Greatest Curiosity in the World as a SKELETON.

Will exhibit at _____

On _____ For _____

At the age of 20 years he weighed 200 pounds, and never has been sick for one day, always enjoying perfect health; but by some mystery he has become as he is. WEIGHT, 65 Pounds; and

THIRTY YEARS OF AGE.

$1000 REWARD!

This sum is offered to any Physician who will solve the mystery of his becoming as he is, and restore him to his original form.

BATTLE SCENES.

The Wagon Trains of the Army of the Potomac, en route from the Chickahominy to the James River, Va., during the Seven Days' Fight.

Battle of Williamsburg.   Battle of Pittsburg Landing.
Battle of Malvern Hill.   Battle of Pea Ridge, Ark.
Battle of Fair Oaks.   Battle of Fort Donaldson.

Washington as Colonel. Surrender of Cornwallis Grand Plaza de Armas. Surrender of Burgoyne to Gen. Gates. Destruction of Sebastopol. Santiago de Cuba. The Deluge. Battle of Arcole. Washington Crossing the Delaware. Washington as a Farmer. Trinidad de Cuba. View of the Great Eastern Steamship. Destruction of Jerusalem. Bonaparte's Return from Elba. Napoleon at Waterloo. Death of Napoleon. Marriage of Washington. Death of Washington. General View of the City of Mexico. Trial of Effie Deans for Child Murder. Festival of the Virgin Mary. Great Fire in New York. Milan Cathedral. Burning of Charlestown.

ADMISSION, only 15 Cents.

COME AND SEE!

Doors open at 9 o'clock in the Forenoon, and will remain open until 9 in the Evening.

From the Daily Mirror Mammoth Steam Job Printing Establishment, 85 Merchants' Exchange, Manchester, New Hampshire.

33 X 50

PROFESSOR JACOBS
"WIZARD OF WIZARDS"

1862

JOSEPH JACOBS WAS BORN IN Canterbury, England, in 1813. A prominent Jewish conjurer, he had a long performing career that took him to destinations as far-flung as Australia and America. He was a versatile if not original performer, and the major British competitor of John Henry Anderson (see p. 126). He was probably more renowned as a ventriloquist than as a magician. Among his favorite effects were covering his assistant with a large cup and transforming him into a goose, and turning a clear basin filled with ink into a bowl of water with goldfish. He was one of the first Westerners to present the famous "Chinese Linking Rings."

This particular bill revealed the performer in a number of capacities. As "The Wizard of Wizards" (alluding to Anderson's epithet "The Great Wizard of the North"), he featured costly silver apparatus. He highlighted his portly assistant Goblin as his comic foil. He extemporized songs with subjects suggested by the audience, and closed with a ventriloquil sketch in which he played all twelve parts. (He probably presented "Alderman Gobble and his Curious Family," a comic piece influenced by the monopolylogues of Charles Mathews and by "The Rogueries of Nicholas" of the great French ventriloquist Mons. Alexandre.) Jacobs offered a roster of his accomplishments in this paragraph:

Thus it will be observed that Professor Jacobs concentrates, in himself, the qualities of three distinct Entertainments. Whether he is looked upon as an Ambidexterous Prestigiator an Improvisatore, or a Ventriloquist, the result is the same, in each he is successful; and, above all, he is scrupulously careful, while carrying out these various interesting Performances, that nothing of an offensive nature is introduced.

While his playbills often featured lively illustrations that would have been intriguing to reproduce, I have chosen to include this broadside, printed by T. and W. Birtwhistle of Halifax, because it was accompanied by a letter to another printer, John Procter. Jacobs asks Procter to change the date and venue on the poster to reflect his upcoming show. He is sure of the necessary revision to the date, from March 6 to March 20, but much less so about the place; both the name of the hall and its location—is it in Harltepool or West Hartlepool?—quite escape him. He relies on Procter to fill in the blanks. Procter's establishment will also replace Birtwhistle's as the source for both tickets and information. The corrections seem to have been added to the playbill in holograph after the printer received it. Both the bill and the accompanying letter are punched through with holes where they were likely thrust onto large spike files.

Another letter to Procter is more revealing of the promotional strategies of the era. It offers any shop owner displaying one of Jacobs' lithographs a free ticket to the show—and indicates that these advertisements will be gathered up again for use in the next venue. Bills were also to be sent directly to the prominent citizens in town. In a postscript, Jacobs asks the printer to place an advertisement for the show in the local newspaper:

Dear Sir

I have forwarded a parcel containing posters and lithographs which I will thank you to get out immediately at the Bill Poster to promise a ticket to each person who exposes a lithograph which will be given on the day of performance—when they will be collected in again—print as many of the enclosed Bills as will do the town such— enclose same [?] in envelopes to all the principle families in the Place and send by Post to those [?] who are in the vicinity please to answer the Receipt of the parcel and thanking you for your kind attention

I am Dear Sir

Yours Respecfully

M Jacobs

Mr J Procter P—S put an advertisement in the paper

Temperance

Odd Fellows' Hall
~~HALIFAX.~~

FOR ONE NIGHT ONLY,
THURSDAY,
2 0th
March 6th, 1862.

PROFESSOR
JACOBS
THE RENOWNED
WIZARD OF WIZARDS,
VENTRILOQUIST AND IMPROVISATORE,

Whose unrivalled powers have attracted crowded, fashionable, and delighted audiences throughout Europe, Australia, America, Canada, New Zealand, Nova Scotia, Cape of Good Hope, California, &c., &c., has the honour of announcing he is making another Provincial Tour previous to retiring from his profession; the enthusiastic applause which nightly greets his

UNRIVALLED
ENTERTAINMENT!

Speaks for his popularity and the name his performances have acquired.   PROFESSOR JACOBS, on presenting his

SOIREES
FANTASTIQUES
TO HIS ADMIRING AND KIND PATRONS, BEGS TO STATE
The New Experiments

He has to introduce will retain him the fame he has so long enjoyed, that of being the principal Prestigiator of the 19th century.

THE MAGNIFICENT
APPARATUS

Used for the Experiments is of massive silver, and on a principle of Professor Jacobs's own invention.   The Entertainment is enlivened with the inimitable Comicalities, Drolleries, and Eccentricities of

GOBLIN SPRIGHTLY

Whose peculiar powers over the risible faculties of the audiences are inconceivable.   Juveniles and Adults are alike held by him in a continued round of laughter whenever he appears.—PROFESSOR JACOBS will introduce his pleasing powers as an

IMPROVISATORE

Receiving from the audience a number of subjects upon which he extemporises acting.   In this great gift of the Professor's the amusement afforded is only equalled by the astonishment of those present, at the facility with which he manages to make Rhymes and Reason of the most incongruous matter imaginable.   In this there is no deception or trickery, any person being allowed to propose a subject; and though the Italians are most famous for this kind of display, PROFESSOR JACOBS has, from great study and long practice, overcome the difficulties attending the English language.

THE PERFORMANCES WILL CONCLUDE, WITH A COMIC SCENE IN
VENTRILOQUISM!

In which he will imitate Twelve different Persons; varying, with strict resemblance to reality, the Characters supposed to be in conversation with him.   A few centuries back, there is no doubt this power was in the responses of the Oracles, for the purpose of imposing on the superstitious, it being confined to the knowledge of a certain few—then it added to the ignorance of the people; now it only affords them a hearty laugh and the means of passing away a pleasant hour.   Thus it will be observed that PROFESSOR JACOBS concentrates, in himself, the qualities of three distinct Entertainments.   Whether he is looked upon as an Ambidexterous Prestigiator, an Improvisatore, or a Ventriloquist, the result is the same, in each he is successful; and, above all, he is scrupulously careful, while carrying out these various interesting Performances, that nothing of an offensive nature is introduced.

DOORS OPEN AT HALF-PAST SEVEN.
The Wizard and his Goblin appear punctually at Eight o'clock.

Reserved Seats (numbered and secured), 2s.; *Second Seats,* 1s.; *Back Ditto,* 6d. *Children under 12 years and Schools, half price to Reserved and Second Seats.*

Tickets, Places, and every information may be obtained at Messrs. T. & W. Birtwhistle's, Booksellers, &c., where a Plan of the Reserved Seats may be seen.

CARRIAGES TO BE ORDERED AT TEN O'CLOCK.

T. & W. Birtwhistle, Machine Printers, Lithographers, &c., Northgate, Halifax.

9¼ x 28¹⁄₁₆

JOHANN NEPOMUK HOFZINSER

1863

IN THE MIDDLE OF THE nineteenth century Johann Nepomuk Hofzinser called playing cards the poetry of magic. His presentations with the pasteboards elevated the lowly card trick to the drawing rooms of Viennese society. Here is one of his original plots: a spectator chooses a card, notes its value, and places it on the table. The card changes to reveal the painted face of a clock. Someone is asked to name any hour. Hofzinser waves the card and displays the dial, which now shows the specified time. The card changes once again, transforming back to the original selection.

Interviewers have often asked me, "If you could go back in history, which performer would you like to see?" My time machine would have to travel to nineteenth-century Vienna to witness Hofzinser. He was clearly a brilliant magical thinker, far reaching in his technical accomplishments, and an innovator of artistic patter and presentation. He was so ahead of his time that he seems to have baffled contemporary witnesses. While the performing styles of other nineteenth-century entertainers have been vividly captured in the written accounts of observers, Hofzinser's stage persona remains elusive.

The course of his career is obscured by other circumstances as well. For most of his life he performed, as shown on this broadside, in salons under his wife's surname. As an employee of the Austrian Ministry of Finance he was unable to advertise his extracurricular activities, but in spite of this limitation he achieved high praise and celebrity. Until recently, the standard biographical material on Hofzinser claimed that he earned a doctorate; that he never performed outside his native Austria; and that he was in financial jeopardy. Seeing no worthy successors to his remarkable talents, it is thought, he deputed his wife to destroy all his notes and props on his passing. Important new research by Magic Christian of Vienna has shown that this scenario is almost entirely untrue, and Hofzinser is now the subject of a two-volume biography, with a third in preparation.

This flood of new documentation makes Hofzinser, and his success as a conjurer, all the more intriguing.

Hofzinser was an unlikely figure to have received the plaudits of Viennese society. Never the recipient of advanced degrees, he did not even earn the equivalent of a high school diploma. He was called "Dr." Hofzinser, a café or coffee-house epithet. He was, however, a poet as well as an accomplished critic, reviewing performances by the dancer Fanny Elsler, Franz Liszt, Johann Strauss, and Paganini, as well as the most talented magicians of the day. He won a devoted audience by his turn of phrase, his aptness of plot, his originality of effect, his ingenuity of method, and the brilliance of his sleight-of-hand technique. In his entertainments his wife performed with him and occasionally assumed the role of clairvoyant. One newspaper related that "Frau Hofzinser knows everything, even what she does not know; sees everything, even what she does not see and hears everything, even what she does not hear."

Although much new material has surfaced, playbills of Hofsinzer are rare. This broadside advertises a performance of May 1863. Set in Fraktur types, it is a modest affair that announced his most frequent offering, an entertainment entitled "An Hour of Deception." Among the pieces presented was an effect called "The Library," with which he often ended his show. Hofzinser exhibited nine volumes of poetry by writers such as Heine, Schiller, and Goethe. He transcribed one line of verse out of 300,000 possible choices and sealed it in an envelope that was passed to an observer. Four spectators now chose at random an author, a page, a poem, and a specific line. The envelope was opened and shown to contain four additional envelopes. On the first was written the name of the selected author, on the second the page number, on the third the poem, and on the fourth the line of verse. Hofzinser then transformed the four envelopes into a single sheet, a printed broadside, on which was revealed, in bold type, all the choices made by the spectators.

den 1. Mai 863

Eine

Stunde der Täuschung

im

SALON

der Frau

Wilhelmine Hofzinser.

PROGRAMM:

1. Der Kartenkünstler.
2. Automate parisien.
3. Zeitdifferenz.
4. Die Magie in Form der Poesie.
5. Botanisches Impromptu.
6. Die Somnambule.
7. Variationen über ein beliebiges Thema.
8. Mathematisches Problem.
9. Physikalisches Impromptu.
10. Die Bibliothek.
11. Der Fotograf.
12. Schlußpiece.

Warnung vor dem Hasardspiele.

(Diese Piece, mit Anwendung der unsichtbaren Volte, wird nur auf vielseitiges Verlangen gezeigt).

Anfang um 7 — Ende ¼ 10 Uhr.

Fauteuil à 2 fl., Sitz 1 fl. 10 kr., Entrée 1 fl., sind zu haben im Salon: Stadt, Wallfischgasse Nr. 8, 1. Stock, und in der k. k. Hof-Kunst- und Musikalienhandlung des Carl Haslinger am Graben.

Vorstellung:

Dinstag, Donnerstag, Samstag, Sonntag.

Wien. Wallishausser's Druck.

ETHARDO
SPIRAL ASCENSIONIST

1867

THIS PLAYBILL FOR THE Star Music Hall in Liverpool in 1867 is the kind of weekly advertising sheet that was used for mixed variety bills well into the twentieth century. These bills were often printed in two colors, but this is a particularly attractive three-color panel with an array of elaborate shaded and display type. It was printed by the firm of James Upton in Birmingham, later known for producing handsome lithographs for variety performers, including the great conjurer Chung Ling Soo.

The five points of the "star" in the Star Music Hall represented ballet, opera, comedy, madrigals, and burlesques. This engagement featured an assortment of opera singers, comedians, and acrobats, with orchestral accompaniment, including Persivani, the contortionist clown, and Sailor Williams, "The Nautical Vocalist." The headliner was Steve Ethardo, "The Spiral Ascensionist," an Italian acrobat who the year before had achieved his breakthrough success at the Crystal Palace in London. There he stood balanced atop a ball constructed of wood and iron, two and a half feet in diameter and seven and a half feet in circumference. Ethardo moved his feet with precision to propel the rolling ball upward on a corkscrew track 180 feet long until he was 50 feet in the air. His descent was even more perilous. At one point the musicians stopped playing for fear that the vibrations they generated might cause him to fall. According to *Harper's Weekly*—so impressed by the London performance as to publish an account of it in America—the track was only twelve inches wide and had no grooves or protective railing, and the ball contained no "rubber gutta-percha, or other adhesive material to assist the Signor in his difficult task."

The act was a tremendous success and Ethardo (his real name, though it sounds like a *nom de théâtre*) performed steadily in Britain and on the Continent until he suffered an accident at Boswell's Circus in Manchester in 1885. He was especially proud of an engagement at the Dante Festival in Florence for the king, Victor Emmanuel. He spawned numerous imitators of both sexes, who either tried to duplicate his act or offered variations such as spiral ascensions on bicycles or even unicycles. Achille Philion, who performed a version in which he descended amid flames and fireworks, died on January 17, 1914, from injuries he suffered in a fall from the apparatus in Crestline, Ohio.

After Ethardo's retirement he lived in London and trained acrobats, including his own children, some of whom performed versions of his act. His progeny were involved in the circus well into the twentieth century. He died on June 24, 1911, at the age of seventy-six.

THE STAR NEW

MUSIC HALL,

WILLIAMSON SQUARE, LIVERPOOL.
PROPRIETORS - - - Messrs. AMBROSE, FINEBERG, & DAVID.

MONDAY, APRIL THE 1st, 1867, AND DURING THE WEEK,

CROWDED NIGHTLY WITH ENTHUSIASTIC AND DELIGHTED AUDIENCES.

LAST SIX NIGHTS OF THE GREAT ORIGINAL SPIRAL ASCENSIONIST,

ETHARDO

WHO NIGHTLY RECEIVES A PERFECT OVATION.

FIRST APPEARANCE OF MR. & MRS. MARK

JOHNSON

THE CELEBRATED COMIC DUETTISTS.

Miss Milnes, | **Mrs. D. Saunders**
The Favourite Soprano. | The Popular Mezzo-Soprano.

RAPTUROUS APPLAUSE AWARDED NIGHTLY TO MR. T.

MACLAGAN

IN HIS POPULAR ENTERTAINMENT ENTITLED ODDS AND ENDS.

FIRST APPEARANCE OF SAILOR

WILLIAMS

NAUTICAL VOCALIST.

Mr. J. Busfield, | *Mr. D. Saunders*
The Great English Tenor. | Basso Profundo.

CONTINUED SUCCESS OF THE WONDROUS ACROBATIC ARTISTES,

PERSIVANI & PRESKOU

Production, for the first time, of a Grand Selection from FLOTOW'S Favourite Opera,

MARTHA

Supported by Miss MILNES, Mrs. D. SAUNDERS, Mr. J. BUSFIELD, Mr. BROWNE, and
Mr. D. SAUNDERS, with FULL BAND AND CHORUS.

By particular desire, and for the convenience of Families residing at a distance, the Management have
made arrangements for A GRAND

MORNING PERFORMANCE

ON SATURDAY NEXT, APRIL 6.

The Programme (in addition to the vast resources of the Establishment) will include

THE GREAT   THE VERSATILE

ETHARDO   MACLAGAN

And a Grand Selection from FLOTOW'S Favourite Opera,

MARTHA

Doors open at 2 o'clock, commencing at Half-past.

On this special occasion the Refreshment Bars will be closed and Smoking strictly prohibited.

Pianist and Musical Director   SIGNOR G. OPERTI | Chorus Mistress   Mrs. M. JOHNSON
Leader of the Orchestra   MISS ROSANNECK | Stage Director   MR. R. BARRETT

Reserved Front Stalls, 1s.6d.   Side Stalls and Promenade, 1s.   Body of the Hall, 6d.

Doors open at Half-Past Six o'clock, Performance to commence at Seven.

GENERAL MANAGERS   Messrs. SAUNDERS & SIMMONS

JAMES UPTON, Baskerville Steam-Printing Offices, Great Charles Street, Birmingham.

9¹⁵⁄₁₆ x 30⁵⁄₁₆

CHANG & ENG AND MILLIE-CHRISTINE
A PERPLEXING PAIR OF PAIRS

1869

NORTH CAROLINA WAS THE unlikely home of the most exotic pair of pairs in the history of show business. Chang and Eng, born in 1811 outside Bangkok, became the eponymous Siamese Twins and selected North Carolina as their base; Millie-Christine, the most famous conjoined Americans, were born there in 1851. Both of these sets of twins were super-star attractions of the nineteenth-century exhibition circuit.

In combing though my substantial cache of broadsides, pamphlets, and prints of Chang and Eng, and recalling the scores of images of them I have seen in other collections, I am struck anew by their enormous popularity. Their unprecedented ubiquity is conveyed in verses penned by Bulwer Lytton:

> In each engraver's shop one sees,
> Neat portraits of "the Siamese";
> And every wandering Tuscan carries,
> Their statues cast in clay of Paris.

They were not only endlessly displayed but also immortalized in the literature of the day, mentioned by Melville, Twain, and a host of lesser luminaries.

Chang and Eng were first shown in America and then in England in 1829. Early in their career the title page of an autobiographical pamphlet sold at their exhibition featured a cut of an American bald eagle with the motto, "E Pluribus Unum," united we stand. But stories of their impending separation dogged their career. By the 1860s the increasingly inebriated Chang and his teetotaling brother so disliked each other that they spoke of little else. Even this playbill mentions their imminent division, perhaps reflecting both genuine desire and a ploy designed to attract customers.

This decorative broadside heralds their return to London's Egyptian Hall forty years after their debut at that venue. No longer depicted as exotics, with queues and Asian blouses, they have embarked upon a more domestic phase of their performing career. Once touted as different from the rest of us they are now presented as surprisingly similar: they are accompanied by some of their children, and vignettes depict them fishing and hunting contentedly.

The same year, Millie-Christine are exhibiting at Tremont Temple in Boston. The woodcut on their showbill pictures a posture that they would have found quite unattainable: they had four arms, not two, and they were joined from the sacrum to the coccyx, so that they faced outward, unable to regard each other as the illustration poses them. They were advertised as if they were a single person, a technique also used by Chang and Eng, but only early in their career. Millie-Christine evolved from "The African Twins" or "The Carolina Twins" to "The Two Headed Lady" or "The Two Headed Girl," but more frequently "The Two Headed Nightingale." Chrissy was a coloratura and Millie a contralto. They accompanied themselves, admirably it was said, on guitars. Their temperament was thought cheerful and their conversation accomplished, in as many as five languages. One variable aspect of their printed publicity indicates the volatile cultural climate in which they appeared: their natural dark complexion was represented in a range of hues, including white.

In the 1860s, while the bickering boys were reluctantly coming out of retirement for the financial security of their formidable brood, the girls were enjoying the first bloom of what was to be a very successful career. Remarkably, in the autumn of 1866, double-billed as the "Combination Troupe," these two sets of twins appeared on the same program. To me nothing could be more curious, more compelling, more provocative, than this arranged encounter. In an essay on conjoined twins Stephen Jay Gould writes, "The aesthetic and ethical foundation of modern Western culture rests firmly on our belief in the distinctiveness of each individual." Linked even more closely than genetically cloned sheep, such twins pose questions to science, philosophy, and theology. How did these pairs of twins, already coping with profound challenges to the boundaries of identity — raised as, and exhibited as, paired but unique — respond to each other? How I would love to have been privy to their conversation. The girls adored each other's company; the fellows, especially in later years, spoke only of the prospect of separation. The girls were unmarried, with no progeny, the boys fathered twenty-two children. Did they find common ground in their audiences with Queen Victoria, or did each set feel diminished by having to share this distinction?

The Siamese pair, who came up from an oppressive childhood, owned slaves. Millie-Christine were slaves, and the children of slaves, who won their freedom. Did the girls dare utter the accusation, "How can you, in your personal, incontrovertible, bondage, have possibly chosen to secure in bondage, other human beings?" What did they speak of? Sadly, we shall never know.

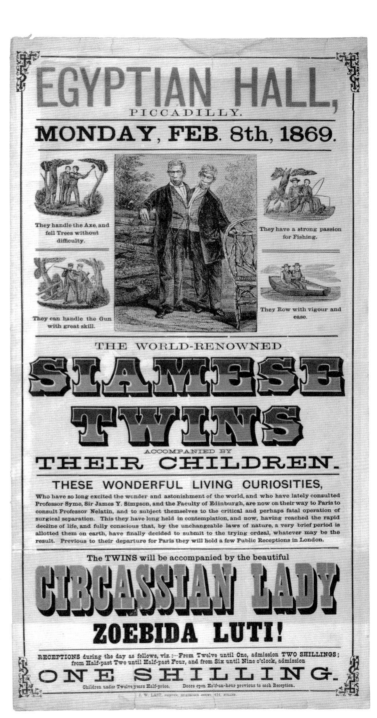

RUBINI "BEHEADING A LADY!"

1869

THE CONJURER RUBINI'S FAME, what little of it seems justified, rests largely on engagements at London's Egyptian Hall and later at St. James' Small Hall in 1867. The signature effect of his program, featured in these two playbills, is "Beheading a Lady," by most accounts a rather crude version of the decapitation illusion (see p. 72). A counterpoint to Rubini's rodomontade, an account penned by Thomas Frost in 1876 gives a more restrained assessment of the illusion:

The young lady seated herself, very composedly, in a large easy chair, and leaned against the cushioned back with no other manifestation of emotion than she would have displayed if about to have her hair dressed. Rubini, hovering about the chair more like a hairdresser than an executioner, covered the young lady's head with a shawl, to spare, as he explained, the feelings of the spectators and then went through the semblance of separating the head from the body. The shawl was removed, and what appeared to be a headless trunk remained on the chair. But the young lady had disappeared, for she showed herself a moment afterwards, with her head on her shoulders, though the headless double still occupied the chair.

On some of his advertising material Rubini chose to depict his decapitation with a lurid woodcut in which he holds a severed head dripping with bright red blood. On the two showbills displayed here, however, he uses verbiage rather than image to present his case. These broadsides are accompanied by Rubini's letter to the printer Procter requesting an additional thousand bills and outlining the modifications required for his engagement in York. The two broadsides and the letter provide insight into the complex relationship between printer and performer (see also no 140).

Rubini was an early exponent of the "gift show," a distinct theatrical genre in which patrons were induced to attend by the ploy of presents. On his American tour in 1870 Rubini had the misfortune to advertise the distribution of such premiums in Wilmington, North Carolina, just after an anti-lottery statute had been enacted. The performer was arrested and convicted, although not fined, under the new ordinance, but the case left ill feeling in the community. Some folks were offended that Rubini escaped financial penalty, implying an untoward agreement with the mayor. Others wondered why Rubini had been prosecuted at all, when the more famous American conjurer "Wyman the Wizard" had similarly given gifts but was not detained.

Rubini, it has been established, was the illegitimate son of the famous magician and publicist John Henry Anderson, "The Wizard of the North" (see p. 126). His given name was Philip Prentice Anderson. Perhaps one clue to his paternity is the Anderson-like phrase he sometimes used to characterize his theater, "Rubini's Resplendent Wizardian Cagliostomantheum of Prestidigitation."

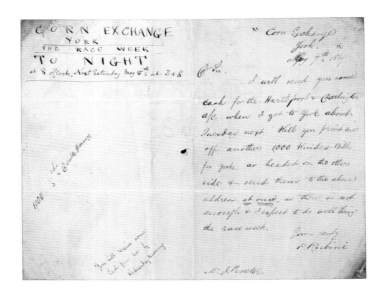

THE GIANT HUNGARIAN SCHOOLBOY

C. 1870

I MUST DECLARE AN INORDINATE fondness for this playbill, probably the most modestly produced of all the examples here exhibited. It is a typical example of mid-nineteenth-century show printing, set in pleasant but ordinary serif and sans serif type and printed on an undistinguished small sheet of paper, heralding an attraction that simply does not live up to his billing as "The Most Colossal Human Being on Earth." The text is equally unexciting. In a straightforward fashion it gives the dimensions of its corpulent subject, an eighteen-year-old who measures 38 inches around his calves, 103 inches around his waist, and weighs in at 420 pounds.

I am, I must admit, tickled with the phrase that heads the bill, "Always on View—Alive." But what makes me smile whenever I see this piece (and I have been its proud possessor for some two decades now) is the child's billing as "The Giant Hungarian Schoolboy." None of these words is in itself unusual, remarkable, or arresting, but in combination I find them endlessly appealing. I love the way they look on the page. I love the way they roll off the tongue. No matter how much one is mired in the complexities of life, no matter how seriously one is inclined to take oneself, no matter how depressing are the day's events—these vicissitudes are all assuaged by the presence of "The Giant Hungarian Schoolboy."

In the interests of continuing research I shall mention briefly a number of prodigious prodigies whose playbills I have chosen not to include, in deference to—say it with me now—"The Giant Hungarian Schoolboy."

—Master Wybrants, billed as "Mr. Lambert in Miniature," and Master T. R. Read, billed as "The Modern Day Daniel Lambert": both named after the legendary fat man who was one of the most famous characters in eighteenth-century England. Read tipped in at 265 as an eleven-year-old.

—A "Gigantic Child" born in 1779 and exhibited in a confectioner's shop, "To All Admirers of Uncommon Productions of Nature." Even after reaching the height of three feet three inches as a toddler, he was reared entirely on his mother's milk

—Master Daniel Hartley, later known as "The Great Golia[t]h of the Day," who weighed thirty-three pounds when only three days old. The "Giant Baby," shown at the Albert Palace in the 1880s, surpassed fifty-eight pounds before his first birthday.

—Master Pierce, "The Gigantic Shropshire Youth," weighed 420 pounds at age sixteen but was bested by Master Smith, "The Yorkshire Giant," who at seventeen outweighed Pierce by seventy pounds.

—In 1853 Mary Ann Adams, age three and one-half years, and her brother Thomas, age five and one-half years, weighed 85 and 115 pounds, respectively. They were heralded as "The Suffolk Prodigies."

None of them, however, no matter how exceptional, can eclipse in the pleasure of their billing the eighteen-year-old known as…

4⅛ x 3⁵⁄₁₆

THE PHANTASCOPE
"HUNDRED SURPRISING THINGS"

1872

THIS FIVE-COLOR SHOWBILL FROM 1872, a lovely example of the printer's art, was produced by the firm of James Upton (for another example see p. 144), striking lithographs of magicians. The magic featured on this show was part of the marvelous pre-cinema world of ghostly projections and materializations. Poole and Young presented an odd and appealing combination of scientific marvels and theatrical vignettes of literary luminaries. The Poole family was responsible for producing a variety of optical amusements from the 1840s well into the twentieth century, eventually converting their variety theaters into film houses.

Because of the popularity of these ghostly illusions there was a vogue for revamping literary classics that could accommodate such stage trickery. On this bill the all-star group includes Goethe, Schiller, Dante, Milton, and Dickens, who would preside over "The Carnival of Spirits: Introducing the most bewildering, and at the same time amusing and laughable Illusions it is possible for the mind to conceive." The vignettes were often engaging and ingenious, but they unfortunately relied on thinly veiled variants of a few magical effects that soon became over-familiar to spectators.

Although it is difficult to discern from this playbill, the effects presented in the performance owe much to the cunning of John Henry Pepper, a scientist-cum-lecturer-cum-inventor who in 1884 became the director of the Royal Polytechnic Institute in London. The major theatrical illusion of the nineteenth century was his "Pepper's Ghost," a device that allowed for a transparent image to appear on stage, walk though walls, and interact with live thespians. It was originally devised by Henry Dircks, a Liverpool civil engineer who called his invention the Dircksian Phantasmagoria. Its importance was quickly recognized by Pepper, who significantly refined and then debuted the illusion in a performance of Charles Dickens' Christmas story *The Haunted Man* in December 1862. As a student sat at a desk an ethereal presence gradually materialized. The strangely transparent skeletal form tormented the actor, who confronted his intruder by attacking it with his sword. The illusion created a sensation. It was imitated, varied, and shamelessly ripped off, exhibited in numerous venues and in many countries.

Although there were earlier precursors, the projections of Pepper were clearly linked to late-eighteenth-century phenomena known as Phantasmagoria. These were magic lantern shows with frightening themes and demonic projections that became very popular in Europe and America. For years this technique was believed to be the invention of a Belgian optician turned flamboyant showman, Gaspard Etienne Robert, who took the stage name Robertson. He applied for a patent for his ghost-projecting lantern, which he called a Fantascop, in Paris in 1799. But this apparently revolutionary show was taken largely from Paul Philidor, who had debuted in Berlin ten years earlier, and who confused historians by filing for patents and billing his shows under the name Paul de Philipstahl in London in 1802. The Phantascope listed on this bill of Poole and Young was just a variation of Pepper's Ghost. Yet another Phantascope was presented by Belzoni the Italian Giant, who displayed both formidable strength and conjuring illusions before gaining renown as the father of Egyptology.

Poole and Young also featured an effect called "Proteus" with the wonderful subtitle, "Or, We Are Here But Not Here." This was an important nineteenth-century magician's illusion that made use of certain properties of Pepper's Ghost. Figures would appear, vanish, or transform within an apparently empty cabinet. "Proteus" was originated by an architect named Thomas Tobin, who was employed with Pepper at the Royal Polytechnic. When it debuted in 1865 it was billed as the joint invention of Pepper and Tobin. Alas, Tobin is largely forgotten and his contribution is nowhere listed on this bill.

As later generations of ball-park hawkers were wont to cry, "You can't tell the players without a program."

PUBLIC HALL

IPSWICH.

POOLE AND YOUNG'S RETURN VISIT WITH SOMETHING NEW!

FOR SIX NIGHTS ONLY,

COMMENCING MONDAY, NOV. 4

ENDING SATURDAY, NOVEMBER 9th, 1872.

Tickets may be had, Plan seen, and Seats secured at the Hall, on and after Thursday, October 31st, from Eleven till Four.

Messrs. POOLE & YOUNG have the honour to announce to the Nobility, Clergy, Gentry, and general Public of this Town and its vicinity, the above Exhibitions of the New, Scientific, Musical, Literary, and PHANTOSCOPIC ENTERTAINMENT, which combines all the astounding effects of the

PHANTOSCOPE

AND SPECTRESCOPE.

And, in fact, all the Optical Appliances which have of late repeatedly astonished and delighted the civilized world. By means of this astounding combination, ABODIES ARE SEEN TO FLOAT IN THE AIR, and gliding imperceptibly through the ... HUMAN BEINGS LANISH IN AIR AT WILL, DEMONS ROLL IN MID-AIR, FIENDS DANCE ON WALLS AND CEILINGS. SPECTRES CREEP UP WALLS and appear in space: LADIES DANCE AMIDST FLAMES OF REAL FIRE, ARE BEING DEMOLISHED INTO ANOTHER, In fact, it would be utterly impossible to convey in language any adequate idea of this extraordinary and amusingly astonishing Exhibition, which TRANSCENDS EVERYTHING hitherto attempted, As exhibited in London, Edinburgh, Glasgow, Dublin, Birmingham, Manchester, Liverpool, Bristol, and, in fact, every city and town of importance in the United Kingdom, during the past eight years, and over 4000 CONSECUTIVE TIMES, to the elite of those Britain, being everywhere inspired with the most rapturous expressions of delight by crowded audiences. The present Programme is ENTIRELY NEW, and the Company, Scientific, Musical, and Dramatic, during the past years, and ... judgment, every endeavour will be the ceaseless consideration of the managers.

FIRST TIME IN THIS TOWN OF PROFESSOR PEPPER'S

PROTEUS

OR, WE ARE HERE BUT NOT HERE,

The same Entertainment which has recently created such a sensation in the ROYAL POLYTECHNIC INSTITUTION, LONDON, and is one of the most extraordinary illusions ever witnessed. "Nothing so perfect of its kind has ever been produced."—TIMES.

The Weird Marvels of the Newly-Invented and Wondrous

PHANTOSCOPE

Displayed in Readings from Goethe, Schiller, Dante, Milton, Dickens, &c.

PART 1.—An Adaptation of Schiller's Beautiful Poem, the

STORM OF THOUGHTS

Illustrated by the Phantoscope in 30 Tableaux. Dresses from those of the period, by German authorities. Scenery by first-class Artistes.

THE ARGUMENT!

PART 2.—An adaptation from Charles Dickens's well-known Christmas Work "The Christmas Carol"—A

HAUNTED MAN

The Illusions produced by the Newly-invented Phantoscope. Scene:—The Chemist's Chamber. Dramatis Personæ:—The Chemist—The Second Self—The Sister—The Betrayer. The Chemist Seated in his Laboratory.

Concluding with the Astounding Sensation,—MAN'S

METAMORPHOSIS!

THE COMIC FESTIVAL & A DREAM IN DREAMLAND,—A COMBINATION OF MYSTERY, MUSIC, & MIRTH!

THE SPECTRE SEEKER IN DREAMLAND

THE CARNIVAL OF SPIRITS

Introducing the most bewildering, at the same time amusing and laughable Illusions it is possible for the mind to conceive.

The Company—Vocal, Instrumental, and Histrionic—comprises the following distinguished Artistes, who have been permanently engaged with Messrs. POOLE AND YOUNG during the past eight years, and are eminently qualified to sustain the characters they represent:—

MISS A. SESTINA WILSON

PRINCIPAL SOPRANO.

| Miss A. VINCENT. | Miss L. CARPENTER, | Mr. J. M. ST. LEGER, |
| Miss H. Le FAVRE, | Mr. E. TYRRELL, | Mr. G. D. VINING, |

Choristers, Messrs. F. GOODMAN, H. POOLE, C. JAMES, & HENRY FALCONER

The New and Astounding Effects will be developed by an ingenious application of the

MAGNESIUM OXY-HYDROGEN!

Which, with the other Lights, will be produced under the superintendence of Mr. CHARLES POOLE.

Each Evening at 8; Doors open at Half-past 7.

RESERVED SEATS, 2s.   SECOND SEATS, 1s.   BACK SEATS, 6d.

Juveniles Half-price to 1st & 2nd Seats only.   Special Arrangements for Academies & Schools by application (Letters only) to the Manager.

Proprietors ... Messrs. POOLE & YOUNG.   General Business Manager ... Mr. J. C. MORETON.

JAMES UPTON, Baskerville Steam Printing Offices, Great Charles Street, Birmingham.

11¼ x 35

HERRMANN THE GREAT

1876

THE REPEATED MOTIF OF Alexander Herrmann on the left side of this playbill is the face of magic. More than any other performer, he defined the look of the modern magician: he was a figure tall and slim, sporting a mustache and goatee, decked out in white tie and tails. Minus the marceled hair, this remains even today the stereotypical Madison Avenue image of the conjurer.

This broadside announces Herrmann's "Grand Testimonial" or "Benefit Night" in Boston, with many well-known artists lending their support. Herrmann himself opened and closed the show. His featured stunt that evening was an entertaining rendition of the chicanery found in a typical séance of the period. Midway down the bill is the name of M'lle. Addie Scarsey, the "Parisian Velocipedist." Born in Belgium and raised in England, this intriguing red-haired dancer and cyclist had fifteen months earlier become Herrmann's wife.

Herrmann was born in Paris on February 10, 1844, the youngest of sixteen children of an itinerant Jewish conjurer named Samuel Herrmann. Alexander's eldest brother was the renowned magician Carl Herrmann (see p. 120). The youngster first came to America with his brother and was part of Carl's show at the New York Academy of Music and before President Lincoln in 1861. Alexander achieved triumphs in France, Portugal, Spain, Belgium, Poland, Russia, Germany, and The Netherlands, and he enjoyed a legendary three-year run at London's Egyptian Hall before adopting the United States as his homeland.

Like his brother, he was not known for originality as a conjurer but for his superb showmanship. His trademark humor became a featured part of his performance. He was a notorious practical joker. A friend named McConnell was once approached by Alexander to fill in for an assistant who suddenly took ill. Herrmann asked his friend to place a number of eggs, a pair of guinea pigs, and a rabbit in his pocket. McConnell agreed, "with all the innocent enthusiasm of childhood," and was ushered to an aisle seat. An hour into the show his services were still unsolicited, by which time the "guinea pigs commenced to squeal and the rabbit tried to gnaw his way out via my breastbone," and the eggs had turned to omelets in his pockets. Only then did McConnell realize that his help had already been tendered.

Herrmann returned to Boston many times. By 1894 Adelaide was re-creating Loie Fuller's famous "Serpentine and Butterfly Dances" at the Boston Museum, and Alexander himself was venerated by the press: "In a word," one paper enthused, "he gave an amazingly illusive, delicately droll, and vastly amusing exhibition of powers that two centuries ago would have given Herrmann a very warm berth indeed."

Herrmann achieved stardom even by today's standards, with a splendid mansion on Long Island, a personal yacht, and a private railroad car, with two additional cars to transport his equipment. He commanded exceptional salaries and his exploits were cited in the papers on a regular basis. His obituary made headlines across the country in December 1896.

Adelaide continued to perform his illusion show both in theaters and in vaudeville, and enjoyed a longer career before the public than either her husband or his brother Carl. She performed into her seventies, and by the time she died in 1932 was heralded as one of the most accomplished of all women magicians.

BOSTON THEATRE

TOMPKINS & HILL   PROPRIETORS

GRAND TESTIMONIAL

TO THE

GREAT HERMANN

THE

CELEBRATED PRESTIDIGITATEUR,

ON

WEDNESDAY EVENING, June 28th, 1876.

THE FOLLOWING TALENTED ARTISTS HAVE KINDLY VOLUNTEERED.

BEING THE EVENT OF THE SEASON

MISS LAURA JOYCE,

The Charming Vocalist and Comedienne.

HARRY MURDOCH,

Boston's Favorite Comedian.

MRS. DAUNCY MASKELL

England's Star Reader.

MR. JAS. S. MAFFITT,

The celebrated Pantomimist and Comedian; assisted by MR.

W. H. BARTHOLOMEW.

MISS GEORGIE DEAN SPAULDING

The Wonderful Harpist and Staff-Bell Soloist; accompanied by

W. P. SPAULDING.

THE ALMONTE BROTHERS,

In Eccentric and Startling Acrobatic Tumbling.

M'LLE ADDIE SCARSEY,

Parisian Velocipedist.

THOS. CHAPMAN

Pantomimist and Comedian.

MISS LILLIE ROBERTSON,

The Favorite Comedienne.

MR. N. D. JONES,

Comedian and Character Actor, will appear in MAFFITT's Comic Specialty, entitled

THE HAUNTED INN!

Mr JOHN BRAHAM

Conductor of Orchestra for the occasion.

AND THE

GREAT HERMANN

Who in addition to his wonderful Feats of

LEGERDEMAIN,

Will give his Astonishing and Mysterious

SPIRITUAL CABINET SEANCE.

THE CELEBRATED PANTOMIME,

LES DEUX FUGITIFS

Or, ROBERT MACAIRE.

Jacques Strop.....	The Fugitives	Mr. Jas. S. Maffitt
Robert Macaire......		Mr. W. H. Bartholomew
Dumont, an Innkeeper.....		Mr. Thos. Chapman
Pierre, a Waiter.....		Mr. James Almonte
Charles, a Lover.....		Mr. Charles Almonte
Loupy, a Gendarme.....		Mr. George Almonte
Clementine, Dumont's Daughter.....		Miss Addie
Marie, Macaire's Wife.....		Miss Almonte

Soldiers, Villagers, &c.

For further particulars see Day Bills.

PRICES AS USUAL,

F. A. SEARLE, PRINTER, JOURNAL BUILDING, 252 (OLD NO. 128) WASHINGTON STREET, BOSTON.

10⅛ x 29¹⁄₁₆

BERTOLOTTO'S INDUSTRIOUS FLEAS

C. 1876

TINY FLEAS, PERFORMING A VARIETY of astounding stunts while harnessed in fine wire, have been exhibited for centuries. It was apparently the harnessing itself that first elicited the most praise and attention. Mark Scaliot was celebrated for fashioning a forty-three-link gold flea chain, with miniature lock and key, in 1578. But even earlier, in the 1540s, the Italian writer Pietro Aretino referred to harnessed fleas in a way that suggested they were already long familiar.

Of all the categories of unusual entertainment that I have studied and celebrated, none is more likely to be greeted by derision and incredulity than the flea circus— a skepticism that is belied by the enduring success of these displays. One testament to the perpetual popularity of these demonstrations is the sheer number of surviving broadsides describing the diverse itineraries of flea troupes. I have obtained an average of one flea-circus bill per anum over the last twenty-five years. Distributed in western Europe as well as America, they date as far back as the middle of the eighteenth century.

The piece selected for this volume is quite attractive, given its humble and miniscule subject. Well laid out on yellow paper, it was printed in New York on Ann Street, the former site of P. T. Barnum's American Museum (Barnum, known for his acuity in sussing out wildly popular attractions, presented industrious fleas at his establishment). Although flea shows could, indeed, be deceptive (relying on mechanical apparatus rather than live fleas as the motive power), this one, and those presented by Barnum, were legitimate.

This performance took place in the Armory Hall on Washington Street in the 1870s, and is said to have been headlined by Signor Bertolotto himself. As this would have been some forty years after his Broadway debut, I am skeptical. Bertolotto was an Italian known as the inventor of the modern flea circus. He authored *The History of the Flea; Containing a Programme of the Extraordinary Fleas* *Witnessed by the Crown Heads of Europe,* reprinted in numerous editions. Like many of the performers depicted in these pages, he spawned imitators using similar names who tried to usurp his fame and fortune. This troupe consisted of a hundred tiny actors, "who, after the most unwearied perseverance, have been taught to go through a variety of feats truly wonderful."

In contrast, the show I saw as a kid, presented by Professor Roy Heckler at Hubert's Museum in Times Square, offered only fourteen, "that's four principals and ten understudies, and they perform four different acts." The featured act was presented with this bally: "But the act, ladies and gentleman, that most people talk about, the one they pay to see, three tiny fleas will be put in costumes and placed upon the ballroom floor and when the music is turned on those fleas will dance. I know that sounds hard to believe, but may I remind you that seeing is believing, and you'll see it all on the inside in Professor Roy Heckler's trained flea circus."

The broadside here illustrated presents a similar act as "The Ball Room, in which two ladies and a gentleman dance a polka. The orchestra is composed of 15 musicians playing on different instruments of proportionate size. Four having a game of whist. A little brunette on a sofa is flirting with a fashionable beau, while her mama's mind is engaged in the politics of a newspaper. The saloon is lighted by three elegant chandeliers. The performers in this, as well as in all the following pieces, are Fleas." Of course, all of these accoutrements showcased the verbal virtuosity of the outside talker and the publicist.

In deference to current events, one could witness "The Prince of Wales in India, on his highly caparisoned Elephant drawn by a Flea, six hundred times its own weight." A highlight of the exhibition was a tiny fortune-teller, "Mademoiselle Le Normand or the Sybil." In a lovely bit of anthropomorphism she is described as "a most weird-looking old flea."

SIGNOR BERTOLOTTO'S
ORIGINAL EXHIBITION
OF THE
EDUCATED

FLEAS

Whose extraordinary performance has received the distinguished patronage of the EUROPEAN SOVEREIGNS.   Now open at

No. 503 WASHINGTON STREET
AMORY HALL BUILDING,

Exhibited by SIGNOR BERTOLOTTO, the Inventor.

These surprising little creatures consist of a Troupe of **100**, who, after the most unwearied perseverance, have been taught to go through a variety of feats truly wonderful, of which the following is the

PROGRAMME:

THE BALL ROOM, in which two ladies and gentlemen dance a polka.   The orchestra is composed of 15 musicians, playing on different instruments of proportionate size.   Four having a game of whist.   A little brunette on a sofa is flirting with a fashionable beau, while her mama's mind is engaged in the politics of a newspaper.   The saloon is lighted by three elegant chandeliers.   The performers in this, as well as in all the following pieces, are Fleas, dressed, harnessed and instructed according to their respective tasks.

AN ELEGANT CARRIAGE, drawn by two Fleas ; the occupants and coachman are also Fleas, well dressed, with parasols, &c.

TWO MERRY-GO-ROUNDS, A Dutch windmill, are each set in motion by a Flea.   **ANOTHER AS GARDENER**, pushes a wheelbarrow full of flowers.   Another dressed in frock, shawl and collar, draws a bucket of water from a well.   Two Fleas decide an Affair of Honor, sword in hand , the arms are of steel, with golden guards.

DON QUIXOTE AND SANCHO PANZA, riding on well-caparisoned Fleas

THE AMERICAN STEAMER, carried by a Flea.

THE WILD FLEA, chained by a 400-link chain, by the ankle, showing the difference between wild and civilized.

A STREET CAR, drawn by a single Flea, and twelve hundred times the weight of the Flea.

MADEMOISELLE LE NORMAND, or the Sybil, will tell the visitor's fortune, a most weird-looking old Flea.   And a variety of other artistes too long to enumerate.   The beauty of the workmanship of the objects accessory to the Exhibition have excited the admiration of every beholder.

THE PRINCE OF WALES IN INDIA, on his highly caparisoned Elephant, drawn by a Flea, six hundred times its own weight.

Open from 10 A M. to 9 P. M.   Admission 25 Cents.

New York Printorium, 29 Ann Street, N. Y.

1876

SPIDERMAN

1877

LIKE SO MANY OF THE PLAYBILLS in this exhibition, this piece features the skills of an unusual and multitalented entertainer. Billed as Spiderman Koto, and also known as Yoro Yousen, this performer featured singing, dancing, and parlor tricks (perhaps a combination of juggling and sleight of hand). More surprising, however, were his physical characteristics: he could bend his arm in four places and his head was larger than all the rest of his body. He was born in Yonezawa in Uzen Province and became a disciple of Yoro Takigoro, who is here seen on his left. Misemono showmen in Japan have their counterparts in the Western fairground or carnival tradition, and Takigoro seems to be presenting his attraction like the "outside talker" of a classic American ten-in-one show.

This placard is a Ukiyo-e woodblock, with the characteristic chemical dyes of the Meiji period. As a contrast to this colorful print, I recall a broadside featuring Clarence Dale in a performance at the Wonderland Musee and Family Theatre (formerly Mechanic's Hall) in Utica, New York. According to the playbill for January 16, 1893: Master Dale is intelligent—sings, dances, and plays different instruments—is a polite entertainer, and will puzzle the scientific men and women of this generation. His head is 48 inches in circumference. Patient reader, just measure your own head and you will find that Master Dale's head is more than twice as large as yours, and it is full of brain matter. He is a handsome, curly-headed boy. Don't fail to call and be surprised and delighted with the Big-Headed Boy.

The accompanying illustration shows Clarence playing with a toy, and a small drum and a ball are visible at his feet. He sports what at first appears to be a headband but is actually a tape measure denoting his forty-eight-inch skull.

It is clear that Spiderman Koto, like Master Dale, was hydrocephalic, a condition that results from an accumulation of fluid in the cranium. It is life-shortening, and it usually diminishes the mental faculties, including memory. Spiderman's accomplishments are all the more remarkable as this playbill, printed in the tenth year of the Meiji period (1877), gives his age as fifty-two. Spiderman is especially commended for his personality: "his face radiates such friendliness that all the people cannot help loving him."

In his right hand Spiderman holds a fan, which he wields almost like a magician's wand. In front of him is a box of Daruma dolls representing the Bodhidharma, the first Zen patriarch. He holds a Daruma in his left hand. A lovely touch is the depiction of spectators, in various states of awe and wonder, who look up to enjoy the show from the bottom of the sheet.

LADY AND GENERAL MITE

1889

THE EXHIBITION OF LITTLE PEOPLE is an enduring attraction in the world of entertainment. We have elsewhere in this volume extolled the popularity of Charles Stratton (Tom Thumb), who may have been the most famous midget in history (see p. 118), but who later in life was considerably larger than the subject of this tiny playbill. General Mite was born Francis Joseph Flynn in Chenango County, New York, probably in 1863. Mite performed for Frank Uffner and his "Royal American Midgets." Just as Stratton's father tried to contest P. T. Barnum's management contract, Edward Flynn, Francis' father, tried to renege on a contract with Uffner, who brought suit against him in New York in 1877.

The men must have settled their differences, as young Flynn and Uffner sailed for Europe on October 30, 1880, accompanied by Lucia Zarate, one of the smallest women who ever lived. Like Tom Thumb, General Mite and his tiny compatriot were especially fascinating to Queen Victoria. Francis and Lucia were presented to her at Buckingham Palace on February 26, 1881. According to a souvenir program of the occasion, Mite was now 21 inches tall and 9 pounds; and Zarate, even smaller, only 4¾ pounds, although 18 years old. Needless to say, the showman's license for exaggeration was almost certainly invoked. The pamphlet took every opportunity to picture Mite as dwarfed by Tom Thumb. Taking the opposite tack, Uffner later exhibited General Mite in tandem with the Chinese giant, Chang (see p. 146).

Uffner next featured the General in the company of another midget, Millie Edwards, at Piccadilly Hall. The London *Daily News* announced their marriage, which took place on May 19, 1884, in Manchester. Accord-ing to this account, the General had grown an inch in height but retained his improbable weight of 9 pounds. Miss Edwards' vital statistics were given as 17 years of age, 19 ½ inches, and 7 pounds. It was said that the couple had fallen in love sometime before but had been compelled to postpone their vows over religious differences: the General was a Catholic and his bride a Presbyterian. Miss Edwards' religious predilections prevailed and the ceremony took place. "The little people," said the paper, "were quite self-possessed and showed no embarrassment. They answered questions and repeated the declarations in a thin piping voice." They announced a honeymoon on the Continent.

According to a hand-dated annotation on this broadside, Lady and General Mite appeared together in England in March 1889 with a new billing, "The Smallest Pugilists in the World," a challenge they backed with four hundred dollars. (If this seems a safe wager I should mention that little people have a long history as boxers and wrestlers.) In spite of their sparring in the gym, however, they had ballooned in weight. The General now tipped in at 25 pounds, and his wife at a hefty 30. Even with this additional ballast, they were billed as "The Smallest Married People in the World," and it does seem unquestionable that they were the tiniest married pugilists.

March 1889

CHALLENGE TO THE WORLD FOR

400 DOLLARS

The Smallest Pugilists in the World !

LADY & GENERAL

Mite

General, 2-Stone 1lb. Champion, is open to Spar all comers, his own height and weight ; the Lady the same, at 2-Stone 6lbs.

The Smallest Married People in the World !

Willson & Son, Printers, Leicester.

CINQUEVALLI
"KING OF THE JUGGLERS"
1898

ON JULY I, 1912, King George and Queen Mary, in the company of a noble entourage and a packed house with thousands of enthusiastic spectators, settled into their seats for the first ever royal command variety show at the Palace Music Hall in London. Chosen to appear on the bill were the greats of the vaudeville era, and prominent among them was the juggler Paul Cinquevalli.

Born in Poland and raised in Berlin, Cinquevalli took his Italianate name from the head of an acrobatic troupe that he ran away with as a child. When a serious injury, sustained in a fall during a performance in St. Petersburg, thwarted his career as an aerialist, he concentrated on juggling. He eventually became the most celebrated man in his profession.

His diversity was impressive. Unlike other specialists in his arena, he was comfortable balancing and manipulating

small objects. The sleight-of-hand artist Dai Vernon told me that he once saw him at a dinner table flip a fountain pen in the air for three revolutions, neatly catching it back in its own cap without moving his hand. Cinquevalli was equally at home with the drawing room props of the gentlemen or salon jugglers and the very heavy objects favored by the strongmen or "kraft" performers.

On this playbill he is dubbed "King of the Cannon Ball." Acts with guns and ammunition were both popular and plentiful in the nineteenth century. We have seen the playbills of Bosco and Anderson (see nos. 82 and 126), who caught bullets fired at them in feats of invulnerability. Men such as Holtum and Patrizio secured their fame by catching balls fired out of cannons in their bare hands, but this was performed as a demonstration of strength rather than conjuring skill.

Cinquevalli was lauded for the grace with which he controlled these heavy objects. Charles Waller, the Australian historian of variety acts, recalled, "I shiver still as I think of his efforts with the 48 lb. cannon ball....with the ball on top of a long pole, and the pole balanced on his chin, he stood for a time with arms outstretched. Then with a lightning movement, he knocked away the pole. Down came the ball to be caught and held on the nape of his neck. It remained there until he permitted it to fall with a mighty thud."

Cinquevalli was even more renowned for manipulating pool balls. With pockets sewn on his tight fitting jacket, fashioned from green baize, he performed as "The Human Billiard Table," twitching, rolling, and cajoling balls across his back, chest, and shoulders to their specific destinations. But his most riveting feat was this: between his teeth he held a wine glass in which were placed two billiard balls—on which was placed a cue, on which he balanced not one but two additional balls. Even now jugglers speculate about whether this feat was accomplishable by natural means, as it seems to defy the laws of science.

This playbill is novel in both its bold and uncommon use of diagonal design and its affirmation of Cinquevalli's celebrity. The supporting cast is not even listed, only Cinquevalli, "Whose Name and Fame as a Juggler is a Household Word throughout the Universe."

ARGYLE
THEATRE OF VARIETIES,
BIRKENHEAD.

Manager - - - - - - - - - Mr. D. J. CLARKE.

MONDAY, MARCH 28, 1898,
AND EVERY EVENING DURING THE WEEK.

Tremendous Success!

The greatest artistic triumph ever achieved by any Artiste.
The audience held spellbound. Every trick greeted with
thunders of applause.

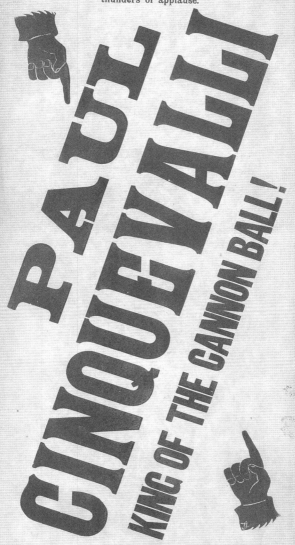

PAUL
CINQUEVALLI
KING OF THE CANNON BALL!

Whose Name and Fame as a Juggler is a Household Word
throughout the Universe.

BRILLIANT COMPANY
NEW AND NOVEL PROGRAMME.

MONDAY NEXT,
R. G. KNOWLES

R. GRIFFITH, PRINTER, 18, HOWSON LANE, LIVERPOOL.

11⅛ x 35⅛

BIBLIOGRAPHY

The following list of references and sources is intended to be thorough but not comprehensive. Numbers given at the end of many works listed refer to pages in this volume. These page numbers indicate that a source is of general relevance, and are often not supplied if a source has already been explicitly cited in the text.

Many entries quote scrapbooks, unattributed newspaper cuttings, and other ephemera in the author's collection.

An Account of the Life, Personal Appearance, Character, and Manners of Charles Stratton, The Remarkable Dwarf, known as General Tom Thumb, Junior. New York, 1843. 118

An Account of that Most Extraordinary and Interesting Phenomenon, Claude Seurat called the Living Skeleton. London, [1825]. 138

Alderson, William T., editor. *Mermaids, Mummies, and Mastodons: The Emergence of the American Museum.* Baltimore, 1992. 52

Altick, Richard D. *The Shows of London.* Cambridge, Mass., and London, 1978. 30, 58, 68, 88, 92, 98, 106, 107, 114, 118, 124, 128 138, 146

——— . *The Presence of the Present: Topics of the Day in the Victorian Novel.* Columbus, Ohio, 1991. 66

Anderson, George. *My Life and Travels.* n.p., n.d.

The Astonishing Birth and History of...Millie Christine. London, 1871. 146

Barnum, P. T. *Struggles and Triumphs; or, the Life of P. T. Barnum.* New York, 1927.

Bayer, Constance Pole. *The Great Wizard of the North: John Henry Anderson.* Watertown, Mass., 1990.

Berlinski, Allen. *Purvis: The Newcastle Conjuror.* Northville, Mich., 1981.

Bogdan, Robert. *Freak Show: Presenting Human Oddities for Amusement and Profit.* Chicago and London, 1988. 146

Bonnet, Jacques. *Histoire générale de la danse sacrée et profane.* Paris, 1723.

Braun, John. *Of Legierdemaine and Diverse Juggling Knacks: Columns from "The Linking Ring," 1949–1966.* Loveland, Ohio, 1999.

Burlingame, H. J. *Herrmann the Magician.* Chicago, Ill., 1898. 154

Chapuis, Alfred, and Edmond Droz. *Automata: A Historical and Technological Study.* Neuchâtel, Switzerland, 1958. 36

Chase-Riboud, Barbara. *Hottentot Venus: A Novel.* New York, 2003. 68

Christian, Magic. *Non Plus Ultra: Johann Nepomuk Hofzinser, 1806–1875.* Offenbach am Main, 1998. 120

Christopher, Milbourne. *Panorama of Magic.* New York, 1962. 38, 46, 120, 140

——— . *The Illustrated History of Magic.* New York, 1973. 72, 120, 126, 154

Clarke, W. Sidney. *The Annals of Conjuring.* Limited edition. Seattle, 2001. 38, 46, 140

Connor, Steven. *Dumbstruck: A Cultural History of Ventriloquism.* Oxford, U.K., 2000. 74

Cook, James W. *The Arts of Deception: Playing with Fraud in the Age of Barnum.* Cambridge, Mass., and London, 2001. 96, 102

Coxe, Antony Hippisley. *A Seat at the Circus.* London, 1951. 88

Daston, Lorraine, and Katharine Park. *Wonders and the Order of Nature, 1150–1750.* New York, 1998. 20

Davie, Kevin. "The Stomach Speakers: A History of Ventriloquism." Unpublished manuscript. 74

Davis, Grania, and Henry Wessells, editors. *The Other Nineteenth Century: A Story Collection by Avram Davidson.* New York, 2001. 56

Dawes, Edwin A. *The Great Illusionists.* Secaucus, N.J., 1979. 141

A Description of Mr. Haddock's Exhibition of Androides. Dublin, 1813.

Disher, M. Willson. *Greatest Show on Earth.* London and Southampton, U.K. 1937. 40, 60

——— . *Pleasures of London.* Letchworth, U.K., 1950. 34

Fechner, Christian. *La Magie de Robert-Houdin: Une Vie d'artiste.* Vol. 1. Boulogne, France [2002]. 83, 120, 126, 134, 136

Feng, Jieai. *The Three-Inch Golden Lotus,* trans. David Wakefield. Honolulu, 1994. 128

Findley, J. W. *Juggling through Four Reigns: Being a Short Memoir of "Old Malabar."* Glasgow, 1945.

Fiedler, Leslie. *Freaks: Myths and Images of the Secret Self.* New York, 1978. 146

Fitzsimons, Raymund. *Barnum in London.* New York, 1970. 118

Flint, Richard. "American Showmen and European Dealers: Commerce in Wild Animals in Nineteenth-Century America." In R. J. Hoage and William A. Deiss, editors. *New Worlds, New Animals: From Menagerie to Zoological Park in the Nineteenth-Century, with a Foreword by Michael H. Robinson.* Baltimore and London, 1996.

Forbes, Derek. *Illustrated Playbills: A Study Together with a Reprint of a Descriptive Catalogue of Theatrical Wood Engravings (1865).* N.p, 2002. 88

Freeman, Arthur. *Elizabeth's Misfits: Brief Lives of English Eccentrics, Exploiters, Rogues, and Failures, 1580–1660.* New York and London, 1978. 18

Freeman, Arthur, and Janet Ing Freeman. *John Payne Collier: Scholarship and Forgery in the Nineteenth Century.* New Haven, Conn., 2003. 22

Frost, Thomas. *The Lives of the Conjurers.* London, 1876. 46, 64, 140

——— . *The Old Showman and the Old London Fairs.* London, 1874. 84

General Chronicle and Literary Magazine. London, 1812. 52

George, Dorothy M. *Catalogue of Political and Personal Satires Preserved in the Department of Prints and Drawings in the British Museum, 1784–1819* (vols. 6–9); *1820–1827* (vol. 10). London, 1952–78. 49

Golby, J. M., and A. W. Purdue. *The Civilization of the Crowd: Popular Culture in England, 1750–1900.* New York, 1985. 138

Goodall, Jane R. *Performance and Evolution in the Age of Darwin: Out of the Natural Order.* London and New York, 2002. 84

Gould, George Milbry, and Walter Lytle Pyle. *Anomalies and Curiosities of Medicine.* Philadelphia, 1897. 138

Gould, Stephen Jay, and Rosamond Wolff Purcell. Crossing Over: *Where Art and Science Meet.* New York, 2000. 146

Gould, Stephen Jay. *The Flamingo's Smile: Reflections in Natural History.* New York and London, 1985. 68

Gowen, David Robert. "Studies in the History and Function of the British Theatre Playbill and Programme, 1564–1914." Ph.D. dissertation, University of Oxford, 1998. 10

H[ingston], E. P. *Biography of John Henry Anderson.* Birmingham, U.K., 1858.

Hagy, James. *Early English Conjuring Collectors: James Savren and Henry Evanion.* Shaker Heights, Ohio, [1985]. 134

Hamilton, James. *A Short Biography of Alexander Herrmann, Herrmann the Great, & Adelaide Herrmann, The Queen of Magic.* San Francisco, 1994. 154

Hampe, Theodor. *Die fahrenden Leute.* Leipzig, 1902. 10

Harris, Neil. *Humbug: The Art of P. T. Barnum.* Boston and Toronto, 1973. 52, 102, 118

Hatch, Richard, trans. *The Magic of J. N. Hofzinser.* Omaha, Neb., 1985. 82, 142

Heard, Mervyn. *"The Lantern of Fear: The True Origins of Screen Horror."* Grand Illusions Web site. URL: http://www.grandillusions.com/phntsmg.htm.

Hecht, Hermann. *Pre-Cinema History: An Encyclopaedia and Annotated Bibliography of the Moving Image before 1896.* London, 1993.

Herrmann, Carl. *First Prestidigitateur for the Grand European Theatres...* New York, 1861. 120

Highfill, Philip H., Jr., Kalman A. Burnim, and Edward A. Langhans, editors. *A Biographical Dictionary of Actors, Actresses, Musicans, Dancers, Managers, and Other Stage Personnel in London, 1660–1880.* 16 vols. Carbondale and Edwardsville, Ill., 1973. 22, 40, 42, 44, 82

An Historical Account of the Siamese Twin Brothers from Actual Observations. New York, 1831. 146

Hollander, Eugen. *Wunder Wundergeburt und Wundergestalt: In Einblattdrucken des Funfzehnten bis Achtzehnten Jahrhunderts.* Stuttgart, Germany, 1921.

Hone, William. *The Every-Day Book.* London, 1827. 98

Houdini, Harry. *The Unmasking of Robert-Houdin.* New York, 1908. 108. 80

Hudson, John Powell. *Poole's Myriorama.* Bradford-on-Avon, U.K., 2002.

Hunt, Gary. "Win a Few and Lose a Few: Rubini and His Giftshow." *Magical Past-Times,* Illusionata web Site. URL: http://www.illusionata.com/mpt/view.php?id=7&type=articles.

The Illustrated Exhibitor and Magazine of Art. n.d., n.p.

Jackson, Beverly. *Splendid Slippers: A Thousand Years of an Erotic Tradition.* Berkeley, Calif., 1997. 128

Jay, Ricky. "America's Prince of Humbug." *Los Angeles Times Book Review,* Sept. 17, 1989. 102

———. *Cards As Weapons.* New York, 1977. 120

———. *Jay's Journal of Anomalies.* New York, 2001. 26, 32, 96, 103 116, 120, 126, 142, 156

———. *Learned Pigs & Fireproof Women.* New York, 1986. 18, 24, 28 42, 66, 70, 76, 82, 114

———. *Many Mysteries Unravelled: Conjuring Literature in America, 1786–1874.* Worcester, Mass, 1990. 62

Joys, Joanne Carol. *The Wild Animal Trainer in America.* Boulder, Co., 1983. 94

Keyser, Marja. *Komt dat Zien! De Amsterdamse Kermis in de negentiende eeuw.* Amsterdam and Rotterdam, 1976. 86

[Kingston, Richard.] *The History of Man; or, the Wonders of Human Nature.* London, 1704. 50

Levy, Howard S. *Chinese Footbinding: The History of a Curious Erotic Custom.* New York, 1957. 128

[Longdon, William.] *Ten Thousand Chinese Things: A Descriptive Catalogue of the Chinese Collection in Philadelphia, Penn.* 1839. 128

Lytton, Baron Edward Bulwer. *The Siamese Twins: A Satirical Tale of the Times.* London and New York, 1831. 146

Maroccus Extaticus. Or, Banks Bay Horse in a Trance. [London], 1595. 18

Mathews, Mrs. *Memoirs of Charles Mathews, Comedian.* 4 vols. London, 1839. 68, 74

Mayer, David, and Kenneth Richards, editors. *Western Popular Theatre.* London, 1977.

McNamara, Brooks. *Step Right Up: An Illustrated History of the American Medicine Show.* Garden City, N.Y., 1976. 78

[Millar, W. J. L.] *How an American Brought the Great Italian Wizard before H.M. Queen Victoria.* London, 1899. 132

Miller, David Prince. *The Life of a Showman and the Managerial Struggles of David Prince Miller.* London, 1851. 136

Montague, C. W. *Recollections of an Equestrian Manager.* London and Edinburgh, 1881. 136

Moreheid, J. N. *Lives, Adventures, Anecdotes, Amusements, and Domestic Habits of the Siamese Twins.* Raleigh, N.C., 1848. 146

Moulton, H. J. *Houdini's History of Magic in Boston, 1792–1915.* Glenwood, Ill., 1983. 96, 104, 154

Newman, Richard, editor. *Narrative of the Life of Henry Box Brown, Written by Himself,* with introduction by Henry Louis Gates, Jr. New York, 2002.

O'Connell, Sheila. *The Popular Print in England, 1550–1850.* London, 1999. 20

Odell, George C. D. *Annals of the New York Stage.* Vols. 1–15. New York, 1927. 105

Oettermann, Stephan. *Ankündigungs-Zettel.* Vols. 1–7. Gerolzhofen, Germany, 2003. 86

The Original, Complete, and Only Authentic Story of "Old Wild's." Edited by "Trim" [William Broadly Megson]. London, [1888]. 91

Ord-Hume, Arthur W. J. G. *Clockwork Music: An Illustrated History of Mechanical Musical Instruments.* New York, 1973. 36

Pecor, Charles C. *The Ten Year Tour of John Rannie: A Magician-Ventriloquist in Early America.* Glenwood, Ill., 1998. 62

Price, David. *Magic: A Pictorial History of Conjurers in the Theater.* London, New York, and Toronto, 1985. 105

Purcell, Rosamond. *Special Cases: Natural Anomalies and Historical Monsters.* San Francisco, 1997. 53

Quaritch, Bernard. Catalogue #1311, *Circus Broadsides.* London, 2003. 122

Reiss, Benjamin. *The Showman and the Slave: Race, Death and Memory in Barnum's America.* Cambridge, Mass., and London, 2001. 102

Rollins, Hyder E., editor. *A Pepysian Garland: Black-Letter Broadside Ballads of the Years, 1595–1639.* Cambridge, 1922.

Rosenfeld, Sybil. *The Theatre of the London Fairs in the Eighteenth Century.* Cambridge, 1960. 22

Rubens, Alfred. "Jews and the English Stage, 1667–1850," *Transactions of the Jewish Historical Society of England,* vol. 24 (1975). 140

Ruggles, Jeffrey. *The Unboxing of Henry Brown.* Richmond, Va., 2003. 130

Saxon, A. H. *P. T. Barnum: The Legend and the Man.* New York and Oxford, 1989. 54, 102, 118

———. *The Life and Art of Andrew Ducrow & the Romantic Age of the English Circus.* Hamden, Conn., 1978. 42

———. *Enter Foot and Horse: A History of Hippodrama in England and France.* New Haven, Conn., and London, 1968. 60

Scot, Reginald. *The Discouerie of Witchcraft.* London, 1584. 72, 118

Senelick, Laurence. "Monsieur Gouffe." *Theatre Notebook,* vol. 52 (1998), no. 3. 84

Sharpe, Sam H. *Salutations to Robert-Houdin.* Calgary, Alberta, Canada, 1983.

Slout, William L. *Olympians of the Sawdust Circle: A Biographical Dictionary of the Nineteenth Century American Circus.* San Bernardino, Calif., 1998. 94

Smith, Pamela H., and Paula Findlen, editors. *Merchants and Marvels:*

Commerce, Science, and Art in Early Modern Europe. New York and London, 2002. 52

Spaeight, George. *A History of the Circus*. London, San Diego, New York, 1980. 40

Steinmetz, Andrew. *Japan and Her People*. London, 1859. 52

Steinmeyer, Jim. *Hiding the Elephant: How Magicians Invented the Impossible and Learned to Disappear*. New York, 2003.

————. *Two Lectures on Theatrical Illusion*. Burbank, Calif., 2001.

Stott, R. Toole. *Circus and Allied Arts: A World Bibliography 1500–1957*. Vols. 1–3, 1958; vol. 4, 1971. Derby, U.K. 22, 44

Strauss, Linda Marlene. "Automata: A Study in the Interface of Science, Technology, and Popular Culture, 1730–1885." Ph.D. dissertation, University of California, San Diego, 1987. 36

Thayer, Stuart. *Annals of the American Circus, 1793–1860*. Seattle, 2000. 94 100 112

Thompson, C. J. S. *The Mystery and Lore of Monsters with Accounts of Some Giants, Dwarfs, and Prodigies*. Reprint edition, with introduction by Leslie Shepard. London, 1968. 20

Timbs, John. *Curiosities of London*. London, 1868. 128

Turner, John M. *Victorian Arena, the Performers: A Dictionary of British Circus Biography*, vols. 1–2. Liverpool, 1995–2000. 84, 90

Uffner's Royal American Midgets. n.p., [1881].

Vail, R. W. G. *Random Notes on the History of the Early American Circus*. Worcester, Mass., 1934. 56

Van Hare, G. *Fifty Years of a Showman's Life, or, the Life and Travels of Van Hare. By Himself*. London, 1888. 136

Vaucanson, [Jacques de] M. *Le Mécanisme du Fluteur Automate*. Paris, 1738; trans. J.T. Desaguliers, London, 1742. 36

Waller, Charles. *Magical Nights at the Theatre*. Melbourne, Australia, 1980. 160

Warwick. *The London Pleasure Gardens of the Eighteenth Century*. London, 1896. 42, 98

Weeks Sale Catalog. N.p., 1834. 58

Wheeler, Joseph Towne. *The Maryland Press, 1777–1790*. Baltimore, 1938. 54

Winter, Marian Hannah. *The Theatre of Marvels*. New York, 1964. 84

Wood, Edward J. *Giants and Dwarfs*. London, 1868. 70, 78, 118

Wood, Gaby. *Edison's Eve: A Magical History of the Quest for Mechanical Life*. New York, 2002. 36

Wood, Robert. *Entertainment, 1800–1900: History at the Source*. London, 1971.

————. *Victorian Delights: Designed by Brian Denyer*. London, 1967. 108

Wright, Richardson. *Revels in Jamaica, 1682–1838*. New York, 1937. 32, 54

In another context I once described Ricky Jay's decidedly nineteenth-century persona as "half Holmes, half Moriarty." In the current context I'd invoke another problematic duality, that the visual arts make progress through the passions of brilliant amateurs—in the original sense of *lovers*—bringing materials previously outside the canon to the attention of professionals. My eternal gratitude goes to Mr. Jay for his passion and energy, his generosity and his friendship, in making this project possible.

Jay's breakthrough insight with regard to his collection has been that despite their humble origins as mass produced advertising pieces, these works stand up to serious scrutiny as both historically worthy art *and* as little time bombs of insight into the culture of their day. The broadsides and playbills in *Extraordinary Exhibitions* stand as proof that the art of juxtaposing splendid graphic design, handsome typography, and clever, hilarious, and often beautifully rendered images has been with us for centuries, and not solely in the domain of the fine arts. This book and exhibition are part of the opening of the field of museums to considering what people do with their time that is not overtly determined by corporate culture but rather bubbles up from working-class sources, youth and ethnic subcultures, and, as Jay puts it, fringe entertainments.

I first worked with an American original when as executive director of New Langton Arts I curated, with the artist Randy Hussong, a 1989 retrospective exhibition of the work of Ed "Big Daddy" Roth. Roth, who died recently, virtually invented the custom-car culture of Southern California in the 60s, and through his addled drawings, plastic models and Rat Fink teeshirts opened the eyes of thousands of kids to the visual styles of those living outside the world of decorum. Many of these people, I learned, grew up to become New Langton's core constituents. A few years later I curated a retrospective of the work of Syd Mead, who started as a Detroit auto industry designer and ended up as a vastly influential science fiction illustrator and futurist, the man who gave *Blade Runner* its convincing and original *look*. So pervasive is his influence that for most of us, when we picture the future in our minds, it is Mead's vision that we see. More recently I had the opportunity to organize an exhibition of the work of Don Ed Hardy, one of the world's great tattoo artists, noted painter, and curator and publisher of many exhibitions and books about the history of tattooing and artists influenced by that culture. If you or your niece or your granddaughter has a lower-back tattoo, it is probably because of Don Ed Hardy. Ricky Jay's *Extraordinary Exhibitions* is the culmination and apotheosis of this series of material culture exhibitions that I brought to Yerba Buena during my twelve-year tenure there. It was a wonderful ride.

Renny Pritikin
San Francisco
August 2004

ACKNOWLEDGEMENTS

As I have written and assembled this volume I have enlisted the aid of a slew of kindred spirits: friends, librarians, curators, editors, designers, publishers, collectors, and purveyors of ephemera. I am extremely grateful to them all. Frazzled as I am in the final throes of assembling this volume, I apologize for any I may have inadvertently omitted. It was Renny Pritikin, who as Chief Curator of the Yerba Buena Center for the Arts in San Francisco suggested presenting these broadsides as a show at his museum. I thank him, and Art for Art's Sake for providing a grant that helped us achieve this goal.

Heartfelt thanks to my indispensable and indefatigable editor Susan Green, my publisher Jim Mairs whose genuine love of books makes him a pleasure to work with, Larry Vigon of Vigon/Ellis, Paul Wang and Michael Kim who worked so diligently on the design of this volume. Thanks to Hugh Milstein of Digital Fusion, and to the printing firm of Mondadori in Verona for their swell efforts. I am especially grateful for the help and expertise of Michael Weber, Stan Coleman, Dan Chariton, Michael Zinman, John Solt, Bill Kalush, and Volker Huber, who seemed always available in spite of their own heavy schedules.

Steve Weissman, Arthur & Jane Ing Freeman, Bill Reese, Donald Heald, Bennett Gilbert, and Jonathan & Lisa Reynolds, were all most generous with their time and knowledge. I have a great fondness for the antiquarian book and print trade, as it is often peopled with characters as eccentric, quirky, and as marvelous as the subjects the these playbills advertise. I thank all those purveyors who have supplied me with the wonderful pieces represented in this volume. Thanks to Jim Cummins, Henry Wessell, Rusty Mott, Andrew Edmunds, Chris Mendez, Robert Harding, Ed Maggs, Jim Burmester, Jonathan Gestetner, Christopher Lennox-Boyd, Stuart Bennett, Russell Johanson, William Dailey, Victoria Dailey, Steve Turner, Robert Harding, Ed Maggs, Tony Heath, Martin Hamlyn, Joe Felcone, Clarence Wolf, Justin Schiller, Mark Selvaggio, Donnis DeCamp, Bruce McKittrick, Ian Smith, Alison Balfour Lynn, Valerie Harris, George Daily, Gianni Pasqua, and Paul Grinke. For their help with translations I thank Isotta Poggi, Lisa Melandri, Alan Swyer, and, Cecilia Gallena, Bill Kouwenhoven, Linda Lucero, and Haruko Iwasaki of University of California, Santa Barbara.

I greatly appreciate the input and assistance of Lori Matsumoto, Emily Halpern, Annette Fern of the Harvard Theatre Collection, Vanni Bossi, Nelson Franklin, Dick Flint, Peter Brauning, Dick Balzer, John Gaughan, Jim Steinmeyer, Mike Caveney, Steven Zax, John & Robin Bavis, Bob Read, Christian Fechner, Alan Jutzi of the Huntington Library, Laurence Senelick, Thea Klapwald, Mervyn Heard, Winston Simone, Mike Nilon, Andrew Solt, Eric Baker, David Wilson, Ren Weschler, Allen Berlinski, and Rosamond Purcell.

And finally, for a million kindnesses, profound thanks to my wife, Chrisann.

INDEX

Ricky Jay is considered one of the world's great sleight-of-hand artists. The former curator of the Mulholland Library of Conjuring and the Allied Arts, he is the author of two lauded histories of unusual entertainment: *Learned Pigs & Fireproof Women* and *Jay's Journal of Anomalies*, both *New York Times* "Notable Books." He has also written *The Magic Magic Book* for the Whitney Museum and *Dice: Deception, Fate & Rotten Luck with photographs by Rosamond Purcell*. He has defined the terms of his profession for the *Encyclopaedia Britannica* and the *Cambridge Guide to American Theater*. His consulting firm "Deceptive Practices" provides expertise on projects for film, theater, and televison. His heralded one-man theater shows *Ricky Jay & His 52 Assistants*, which won the Obie and Lucille Lortell awards, and *Ricky Jay: On the Stem*, which recently enjoyed a six-month run in New York. Both were directed by David Mamet, in whose films *House of Games, Things Change, The Spanish Prisoner, State and Main,* and *Heist* he has appeared. Mr. Jay can also be seen in many other films including *Tomorrow Never Dies, Magnolia,* and *Boogie Nights* and in the television series *Deadwood.* He has written and hosted his own specials for CBS, HBO, A&E, and the BBC. More information is available on the web site: www.rickyjay.com

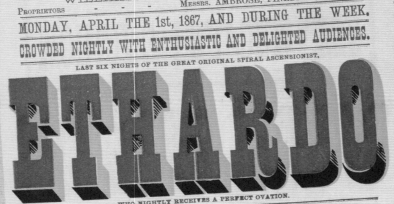